WITHDRAWN NDSU

MINORITIES OF SOUTHWEST CHINA

AN INTRODUCTION TO THE YI (LOLO)
AND RELATED PEOPLES AND
AN ANNOTATED BIBLIOGRAPHY

by
Alain Y. Dessaint

HRAF PRESS
New Haven
1980

INTERNATIONAL STANDARD BOOK NUMBER: 0-87536-250-8
LIBRARY OF CONGRESS NUMBER: 80-80017
© 1980
HUMAN RELATIONS AREA FILES, INC.
ALL RIGHTS RESERVED
PRINTED IN THE UNITED STATES OF AMERICA

TABLE OF CONTENTS

	Page
Acknowledgments	iv
Introduction	v
Minorities in China	1
Linguistics	8
History	12
Ethnography	27
Problems for Future Research	33
Bibliography	35
Index by Ethnic Group	319
Index by Periodical	338
Index by Subject Matter	353

TABLES

1.	Population of the Yi Peoples	4
2.	Ethnic Group Designations	6
3.	Autonomous Areas of Yi Peoples in China	24

FIGURES

1.	Benedict's (1972) Classification [of Sino-Tibetan]	9
2.	Chao's (1943) and Tung's (1953) Classification [of Sino-Tibetan]	9
3.	Shafer's (1955) Classification [of Sino-Tibetan]	11

Acknowledgments

I wish to take this opportunity to thank the many persons who have aided me in the preparation of this bibliography, and especially Drs. Chin Tsung, James Matisoff, A. Kohar Rony, Frank Joseph Shulman, Anthony Walker, Mrs. Chen K.-c., William Dessaint and Yvette Dessaint, and the staff of the Inter-Library Loan section of the University of Maryland Libraries. My thanks to Elizabeth Swift, editor at HRAF Press, for her patience and thoroughness. I also wish to express my gratitude for financial support received from the Reference Aids Subcommittee of the Committee on Research Materials on Southeast Asia of the Association for Asian Studies. Finally, my thanks to my many Lisu friends and hosts, who stimulated my interest in their culture.

A. Y. D.

Introduction

The aim of this work is to provide a review of the literature available on a number of Yi peoples, namely: the Yi (Lolo, Nosu), Lisu, Lahu, Akha, Woni (Hani), Lutzu, Achang, Tulung, Hpon, and Kadu. Although extremely important in the anthropology of South China and Southeast Asia, they have been neglected by scholars for a number of reasons:
  (1) these peoples are remote and widely scattered;
  (2) the literature is in many different languages, seldom read by a single scholar;
  (3) the literature is widely scattered in what are often obscure journals or publications that are difficult to obtain;
  (4) the literature is of uneven quality;
  (5) the lack of bibliographic aids or syntheses discourages the neophyte.

It is to remedy the last of these shortcomings in Yi studies that this work has been undertaken. It provides a brief introduction to the Yi peoples and a bibliography, which is:
  (1) multidisciplinary in scope and indexed by subject matter, so that scholars of any one discipline can quickly find relevant materials;
  (2) multilinguistic in scope, including not only the most important European languages but also Chinese, Japanese, Thai, and the languages of the Yi peoples;

(3) annotated, so that a researcher can quickly determine the value of consulting or translating a particular entry;
(4) interpretive, in that it is preceded by an evaluative summary of the literature, it points out errors or hypotheses for further study, and it incorporates cross-references between entries.

The bibliography, therefore, is not merely a list of titles but a medium for an introduction to the field of Yi studies. The annotations evaluate and inventory the available literature.

Annotations attempt to abstract the entry, instead of simply giving a list of topics discussed. It should be noted that the length of an annotation bears no necessary correlation to the importance of the entry. In fact, the most complete, detailed works cannot adequately be summarized. No attempt has been made to standardize the transliteration of Asian languages or the names by which the ethnic groups are referred to; the annotations follow the usage of the author. Confusion as to the names used to refer to particular ethnic groups may be partly remedied by consulting the Index by Ethnic Group.

There are three indexes: the first, by Ethnic Group, also contains some of the alternate names by which these ethnic groups are known; the second, by Periodical, may be useful to the library researcher who wishes to consult all the articles appearing in one periodical at the same time or to recall an imperfectly remembered reference; the third, by Subject Matter, follows the categories devised by George P. Murdock et al. in <u>Outline</u> <u>of</u> <u>Cultural</u> <u>Materials</u> (4th rev. ed., New Haven, Human Relations Area Files, 1971).

The references in this bibliography have been accumulated over some ten years of interest in Yi studies. Almost every one of the over 1,000 sources was personally checked and read. It would be impossible to provide a comprehensive list of all the sources and bibliographies that have been utilized during the course of this work. Many periodicals which publish articles about the anthropology, history, linguistics, sociology, and current affairs of minority peoples were consulted in English, French, German, Russian, Spanish, Portuguese, Chinese, Japanese, and Thai.

The following bibliographies, which are cited in this volume, were especially useful: Bernath 1964; Boon-Itt 196; Cramer 1970; Embree and Thomas 1950a, 1950b; Jacobs 1970; LeBar, Hickey, and Musgrave 1964; Liu 1940-41; Shafer 1957, 1963; Tribal Research Centre (Chiang Mai) 1967, 1973. Especially useful for works in Chinese is Takemura 1957-58.

In addition, several well-known reference works may be cited: Henri Cordier, Bibliotheca Sinica: Dictionnaire bibliographique des ouvrages relatifs à l'Empire Chinois (2d ed., 4 vols., Paris, E. Guilmoto, 1904-08), and Bibliotheca Indosinica: Dictionnaire bibliographique des ouvrages relatifs à la peninsule Indochinoise (4 vols. and index, Paris, École Française d'Extrême-Orient, 1912-15); the annual Bibliography of Asian Studies, published by the Association for Asian studies (prior to 1957 it was entitled Far Eastern Bibliography); Leonard H. D. Gordon and Frank J. Shulman, eds., Doctoral dissertations on China, A bibliography of studies in Western languages, 1945-1970 (Seattle and London, University of Washington Press, 1972); Pierre Bernard Lafont, Bibliographie du Laos (Paris, École Française d'Extrême-Orient, Publication L); Jane Godfrey Keyes, A bibliography of Western-language publications concerning North Vietnam in the Cornell University Library (Ithaca, Southeast Asia

Program Data Paper 63, 1966); Frank N. Trager, ed., *Japanese and Chinese language sources on Burma: An annotated bibliography* (New Haven, HRAF Press, 1957); Frank N. Trager, *Burma: A selected and annotated bibliography* (New Haven, HRAF Press, 1973); *Books and articles on oriental subjects published in Japan* (Tokyo, Toho Gakkai [The Institute of Eastern Culture], published annually); James Irikura, *Southeast Asia: A selected annotated bibliography of Japanese publications* (New Haven, Southeast Asian Studies, Yale University, in association with HRAF Press, 1956); Kenjiro Ichikawa, *Southeast Asia viewed from Japan: A bibliography of Japanese works on Southeast Asian societies, 1940-1963* (Ithaca, Southeast Asia Program Data Paper 56, 1965); Ruth Thomas McVey, *Bibliography of Soviet publications on Southeast Asia: As listed in the Library of Congress monthly index of Russian acquisitions* (Ithaca, Southeast Asia Program Data Paper 34, 1959).

Minorities in China

Although China's non-Chinese peoples (or, as the Chinese refer to them, "national minorities") comprise only about 6 percent of her total population, they are of considerable importance. First, they are spread over almost half of China's land area, including strategically important border regions. Second, they have contributed an important physical and cultural element to the present Han population, as they have historically become assimilated into Chinese civilization. Third, many of the minorities live both within and outside of China's borders. The relations between Han and non-Han is thus one aspect of China's attitudes toward her sovereign neighbors. (Since 1949, for example, national minority autonomous areas have served as models for China's neighbors, and are an important factor in China's appeal in East Asia.) Lastly, 6 percent of 800 million is 48 million, not an inconsiderable number of people.

China's national minorities may be classified in a number of ways, so that when someone states that there are 5 or 50 or 500 minorities, this is not very enlightening. The flag of China (both the old Republican five-bar flag and the present five-star flag) is said to symbolize the five major ethnic groups in its stars: Han Chinese, Manchu, Mongol, Muslim, and Tibetan. A more accurate grouping of linguistic, cultural, and racial differences would include:
(1) the Altaic group, including Turkic (Kazhak, Kirghiz, and Uighur), Tungu, Mongol, and Korean, strung out along the northern borders (the Indo-European Tadzhik might also be

included here);
(2) the Tibetans, who occupy China's southwestern quadrant;
(3) the Muslims, or Hui, who resemble the Han in most ways except in their religion, which has sufficed to keep them a separate group, often in conflict with their Han neighbors (the Hui are scattered throughout China);
(4) the Southern Group, mostly Sino-Tibetan speakers and a few Mon-Khmer, who originally occupied much of the southeastern quadrant, but who have now been assimilated, destroyed, or displaced (mostly vertically into the mountain regions).

Included in this last group are the Chuang and other Tai-speaking peoples, the Miao (Meo) and Yao (Man), and the Tibeto-Burmans. The Tibeto-Burman language family extends from the western Himalayas to southeastern China. In this work, we shall be concerned with what may be called the eastern upland Tibeto-Burmans: highlanders of Yunnan, Szechwan, and Kweichow, as well as neighboring North Vietnam, Laos, Thailand, Burma, and India. The largest of these groups, and the fourth largest minority in China, is the Yi (or Lolo), and we shall also consider the Lisu, Lahu, Akha, Woni (Hani), Lutzu, Achang, Tulung, Hpon, and Kadu.

Population statistics are notoriously unreliable for these highlanders, who live away from administrative centers and who constitute little-known minorities in states dominated by lowland peoples. In Burma, for example, no attempt has been made to count them for almost half a century. Our best estimates are given in Table 1.

One of the most frustrating factors in studying the Yi peoples is the multitude of names applied to the various ethnic groups: names differ according to the user, the time, the area; the same name may by applied to several quite different groups. Table 2 presents some of the names by which the groups are known; reference should also be made to the Index by Ethnic Group.

Many of the names used in pre-Communist China to refer to minorities had derogatory meanings, such as "tzu" ("egg, child"), "barbarians," or "dog." Thus terms such as Lolo or Lohei are no longer used. The etymology of such terms has been the subject of much discussion, but remains unclear (Feng and Shryock 1938: 103-05). "Lolo" has been said to mean: the basket that contains the spirit of the deceased (Clarke 1911); someone who does not speak the proper language (Reclus 1902); a derivative of "La," an ancient prefix meaning people (Bonifacy 1906a); a derivative of "lou" meaning ravish or take prisoner (Vissière 1914); a pejorative (Baber 1882); or a term with no meaning (Vial 1890a). This by no means exhausts the list of suggestions, but even after considering these, one is inclined to agree with Liétard (1913: 26), who asks what terms such as "Lolo" and "Lisu" mean, and answers himself: "Bien malin qui me le dira!" The Lolo were also called Man-tse (barbarians or southerners) and I or Yi (remote or foreigner), alone or in various combinations (I-chia, I-jen, I-pien). Some Lolo used that term to designate themselves and used "Lisu" as a prejorative (good-for-nothing) as do the Chinese (Liétard 1913). But most Lolo seem to prefer Nosu (there are various spellings), from "no" (black) and "su" (people). In Lolo, the adjective usually follows the noun (unlike Chinese), therefore it has been suggested that even this self-designation is the translation of a Chinese term (Yang 1935). The present Chinese designation is Yi, a term which the Yi are increasingly using for themselves, and the one that we will use here.

The Yi are divided into two castes: aristocratic landowners, called Black Yi or Black Bones (Hei-I, Hei Ku T'ou), and serfs, called

Table 1. Population of the Yi Peoples (in Thousands)

	China	Vietnam	Laos	Thailand	Burma	India	Total
Yi	3,254.3	29	5		0.8		3,284.1
Woni	553	5.3					558.3
Lisu	317.5		(a)	11	40	0.2	368.7
Lahu	183.1		2	16.4	66		267.5
Akha			4.5	9.9	40		54.4
Kadu					40		40
Achang	18						18
Lutzu	14						14
Tulung	3						3
Hpon					1		1
Total	4,342.9	34.3	6.5	37.3	187.8	0.2	4,608.2

Sources: China--1953 census; Vietnam--1960 census; Laos--LeBar et al. 1964, Leroi-Gourhan and Poirier 1953; Thailand--Dessaint 1972b, Tribal Data Project 1971-72; Burma--Dessaint 1972b, Grierson 1903-28, 1931 census; India--Dessaint 1972b. The Kutsung are included with the Woni. The Nakhi (Moso), Minchia, and Kachin are not included. (a) Teston and Percheron (1932) mention a few families of Lisu in Laos.

White Yi or White Bones (Pe-I, Pei Ku T'ou). Since they are widely scattered, various local groups are known by distinct names (Liétard 1913, Eberhard 1942, Gaide 1903).

The confusion that exists for the Yi names also exists for the other ethnic groups. The Woni are now called Hani by the Chinese, but are known as Akha in Thailand, Burma, and Laos. They also have named subgroups, seven or nine, according to some sources (Telford 1937, Scott and Hardiman 1900, Gaide 1903, Henry 1903). Walker (1970b) has collected the names of twenty-three Lahu subgroups.

Table 2. Ethnic Group Designations

English name	Chinese name (pre-1949)	Lisu	Lahu	Akha	Lutzu	Woni, Houni
	Yi, Lolo, Nosu	Li, Liso, Lihsaw, Lishu, Lisu, Lip'a, Lutzu, Yeh-jen	Lohei, Mussuh	Hani, Woni, Aka, Houni	Lutzu, Lutze, Noutzu, Nusu, Nutzu, Kiutse	Ha-Nhi, Uni, Houo-ni, Ho-Nhi, Ouo-ni
	Lolo, Hei-I, I, I-chia, Lo-kuei, Manchia, Pei-I Man-tzu, Wu-man					
(post-1949)	I, Yi	Lisu	Laku	Hani	Nu	Woni
Akha name		Lisu				
Kachin name		Yawyin, Yaoyen				
Karen name		Lisu				
Lahu name		Lisu	Lahu			
Lashi name		Lasi				
Lisu name	Lolo	Lisu	Lahɔ	Akha		
Lutzu name		Lisu			Anu, Nu, Nusu	
Maru name		Lasi, Lashi				
Miao name		Lisu				

-6-

Table 2. Ethnic Group Designations (cont'd)

English name	Yi, Lolo, Nosu	Lisu	Lahu	Akha	Lutzu	Woni, Houni
Nakhi name		Lisu, Lusu				
Nung name		Anung, Lashi				
Thai name		Khae Lisaw	Muhso, Mussuh	Ekwa, Ko, Ikho, Kha Ko		Woni, Houni, Kha Ko
Tho name	Mia					
Tulung name		Lisu				
Shan name		Che-nung	Mussur		Khanung, Nung	
Vietnamese name	Hac Lala, Man Khoanh, K'an-t'eou Lolo					Ha-Nhi
Yao name		Lisu				
Yi name	Nosu, Mosu, No, Ngosu, Nesu, Neisu, Leisu, Dji, Gni Mung Za, Manzi	Lip'o				

Linguistics

Most linguists would recognize all the ethnic groups with which we are dealing as belonging to a Lolo subgroup of the Burman-Lolo group of Tibeto-Burman. Early travelers and linguists have recognized the close relationships of Lolo, Lisu, Lahu, and Woni (including Akha) (Orléans 1898, Monbeig in Madrolle 1908 and Liétard 1909b, Davies 1909, Rose and Brown 1911, Fraser 1922, Goré 1939). Terrien de Lacouperie (1894a) also noted the close relationship of Lisu to Mosso (Nakhi) and Lutzu. Anderson (1876) and Colquhoun (1883) pointed out the similarity of Lisu and Burmese. Eales (cited in Rose and Brown 1911), George (1915), and Fraser (1922) noted the closeness of Lisu to Atsi Kachin.

Pater Wilhelm Schmidt, in Die Sprachfamilien und Sprachenkriese der Erde (Heidelberg, Carl Winter, 1926), recognized Aka, Lisu, and Lahu as forming a single subgroup within the Burmese group of Arakan-Burmese, itself part of Tibeto-Burman. However, he classed Lolo with Mosso (Nakhi) in a separate Sino-Tai family. Other linguists have not accepted this division: Sir George Grierson (1903-28), working with Sten Konow, recognized a Lolo-Moso group of Assam-Burmese; Benedict (1972) recognized a Lolo-Burmese group (see Figure 1); Chao Y.-r. (1943) and Tung T'ung-ho (1953) recognized a Lolo-Moso group (see Figure 2); and Shafer (1955) recognized a Lolo branch of his Burmish section of the Burmic division of Sino-Tibetan (see Figure 3).

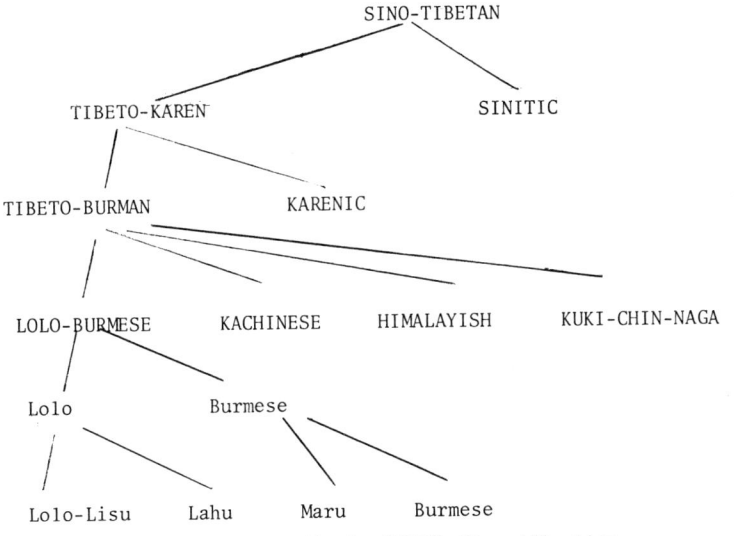

Figure 1. Benedict's (1972) Classification

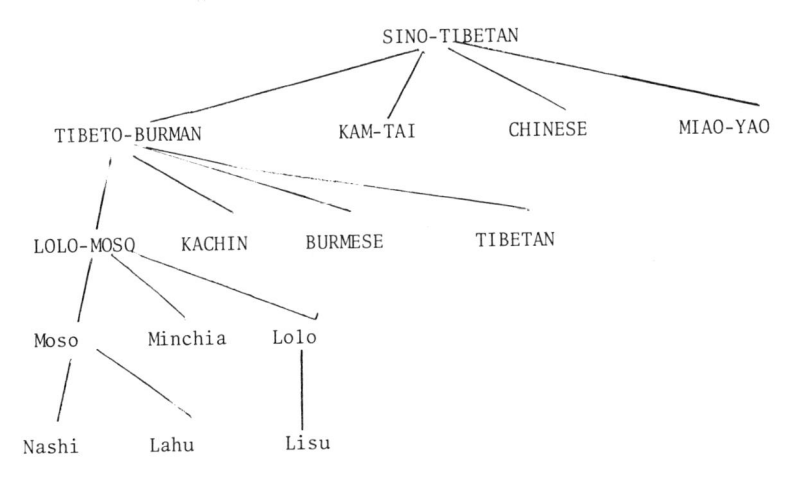

Figure 2. Chao's (1943) and Tung's (1953) Classification

Hpon (Phun), Achang, and Kadu are linguistically closer to Kachin; Shafer (1955) classifies the first two with Maru and Atsi (see Figure 3), and Leach (1954) notes the similarity between Kadu and Jinghpaw. No adequate studies exist of Achang, Hpon, Kadu, Lutzu, or Tulung languages. Good descriptive studies exist of the major Lolo languages, however:

Yi:	A-si (A-hi) of Yunnan	Yüan 1953; Liétard 1909a, 1911-12
	I of Szechwan	Fu 1944a, 1944b
	Lo-I of Szechwan	Lo 1950
	Lü Ch'üan	Ma 1948a
	Nasu	Kao 1958
	Sani (Gni) of Yunnan	Ma 1951; Vial 1890a, 1898, 1909
Lisu:	Lisu of Yunnan	Ruey 1948a; Zui et al. 1959
	Lisu of Burma	Fraser 1922
	Lisu of Thailand	Hope 1968, 1972; Nishida 1967a, 1968a; Roop 1970
Lahu:	Lahuna of Burma	Telford 1938
	Lahuna of Thailand	Katsura 1968b; Matisoff 1967, 1973b
	Lahushi of Thailand	Nishida 1969
Bisu:	Bisu of Thailand	Nishida 1966a, 1966-67
Woni:	Hani of Yunnan	Hu and Dai 1964; Kao 1955
	Woni of Yunnan	Yüan 1947
Akha:	Akha of Burma	Lewis 1969-70
	Akha of Thailand	Dellinger 1967; Katsura 1966b, 1968c, 1970; Nishida 1965-66

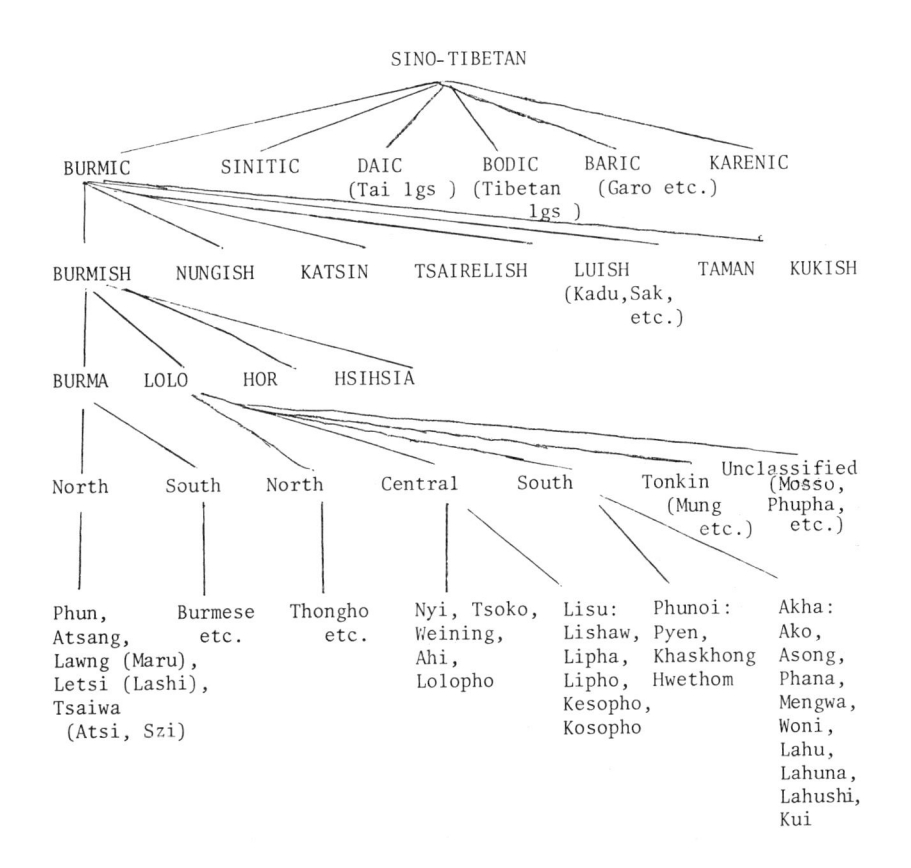

```
                              SINO-TIBETAN
        ┌──────────┬──────────┼──────────┬──────────┬──────────┐
     BURMIC     SINITIC     DAIC       BODIC      BARIC      KARENIC
                          (Tai lgs)  (Tibetan   (Garo etc.)
                                       lgs)

  BURMISH    NUNGISH    KATSIN   TSAIRELISH   LUISH        TAMAN   KUKISH
                                             (Kadu, Sak,
                                                etc.)

  BURMA    LOLO    HOR    HSIHSIA
```

						Unclassified
North	South	North	Central	South	Tonkin	(Mosso,
					(Mung	Phupha,
					etc.)	etc.)

Phun,	Burmese	Thongho	Nyi, Tsoko,	Lisu:	Phunoi:	Akha:
Atsang,	etc.	etc.	Weining,	Lishaw,	Pyen,	Ako,
Lawng (Maru),			Ahi,	Lipha,	Khaskhong	Asong,
Letsi (Lashi),			Lolopho	Lipho,	Hwethom	Phana,
Tsaiwa				Kesopho,		Mengwa,
(Atsi, Szi)				Kosopho		Woni,
						Lahu,
						Lahuna,
						Lahushi,
						Kui

Figure 3. Shafer's (1955) Classification

History

The Yi and related peoples are mentioned in the oldest Chinese records, usually in connection with banditry, rebellion, and Chinese suppression. Because of the confusion over the names given to these ethnic groups, it is not always possible to be certain which group is being referred to. However, the Yi seem to be mentioned in Se-Ma Cen's Biographie des étrangers du sud-ouest, the Three Hymns Celebrating the Virtue of Han (ca. first century A.D.), the Yuan Annals, and Fan Chuo's Man Shu ("Book of the Southern Barbarians," ca. 685 A.D.). The first known ruler of the Yi was Zhuang Kao, probably a Chinese who "became" a Yi, ca. 223 B.C. Li (in Siguret 1937: 153) cites a history of Yunnan according to which the Lisu lived in Yunnan prior to the coming of Zhuang Kao during the Chou dynasty. In 594 A.D., another ruler of Chinese origin, Cuan Wan-si, who had declared independence of an area in the Szechwan-Kweichow-Yunnan border area, was attacked by Chinese forces. In 712, the Yi of Yao zhou were involved in a revolt. By 738, eastern Yunnan is said to have been primarily a Yi area, but under Chinese governors. The Yi have probably inhabited Liang Shan since the early years of our era, and certainly since the tenth century. It has served as a region of refuge from Chinese "pacification" on several occasions: for example after 1730, when a Yi chief "Yang" was captured in Yunnan, numerous "raw" Yi (independent Yi) escaped there (Hsü 1944). The area east of Huang Mao is called Xiao Liang Shan, "Lesser Cool Mountains," and the area to the west is called Da Liang Shan, "Greater Cool Mountains." (Until 1955, Da Liang Shan was part of Sikang Province; both Xiao and Da Liang Shan are now in Szechwan.) Between 1796 and 1821, the Chinese extended their influence into Xiao Liang Shan. At times when the Chinese were weak, the Yi expanded out of Da Liang Shan: for example in 1802, 1814, 1838-39, and from 1875 to 1892. By 1907, the Yi controlled most of Xiao Liang Shan, with Chinese fortified in the towns. During the troubled times of the early Republic, the number of Chinese troops was reduced in the area, and the Yi consequently became more troublesome: in 1919, the Lolo invaded Zhaojue, in 1920 they burned Xining, and in 1937 they killed the magistrate of Leibo. During the late 1930s and early 1940s, the Sikang Border Pacification Army (which included both Chinese and Yi regiments) built roads and suppressed Yi rebellions; its Chinese soldiers were encouraged to marry White Yi (Zeng 1947, Sun 1942, China at War 1941). Some Black Yi were even recruited for the Central Military Academy at Chengdu. Even so, most of the Chinese population had fled: Sun (1942) estimates that there were one-and-a-half million Han in the Anning River Valley two centuries ago, but only half that number by 1942. Even the largest towns, such as Sichang, kept their gates closed at night. When Lín (1947) was in Leibo in 1943, bands of Yi plunderers would swoop down upon a Han house, kidnap its inhabitants, and burn what was left--this happened nightly. (See Feng and Shryock 1938, Rock 1947, Táo 1948, and Yang 1935, 1936b.)

Prior to 1949, the Yi people were regarded by the Chinese as lesser branches of the Han to be assimilated or as barbarians to be pacified (China at War 1941, Sun 1942). These attitudes were reflected in the derogatory names given to them.

Two historical trends may be found among the Yi proper: co-existence between White Yi and Han Chinese, and constant warfare between Black Yi and Han. In fact, the Black Yi kidnapped great numbers of Han Chinese for ransom or for slavery. Lín (1947) reports that in 1940, 200 Han of a "reclamation" village in Leibo were abducted and enslaved. He also tells the story of a Han kidnapped when he was seven years old and ransomed twenty years later (Lín 1947: 109-10). Zeng (1947) disagrees that large numbers of Chinese were enslaved, considering these stories exaggerated, and thinks that Black and White Yi were originally two different cultures. Most observers (e.g. Winnington 1959, Hsú 1944), however, state that these Han slaves ("Han Wa Tse") or their children would eventually become White Yi. The assimilation process included both physical and cultural coercion: for example chaining them at night, prohibiting them to speak Chinese, and finding them spouses.

Yi social structure consisted of two endogamous castes in Da Liang Shan (in other areas, which were more sinicized, the structure was different): Black Yi aristocratic landowners and White Yi tenants, serfs, and slaves. Winnington (1959) provides an estimate of the composition of the population of the Norsu (Yi) of Da Liang Shan, the major concentration of Independent Yi (in southwestern Szechwan):

Black Yi	10+ slaves	2.5%
	1 to 9 slaves	2.5
White Yi commoners	10+ slaves	3.0
	1 to 9 slaves	25.0
	no slaves	20.0
White Yi slaves	separate slaves	33.0
	house slaves and slaves of slaves	14.0

Winnington may have underestimated the percentage of Black Yi, since Lín (1947) claims they comprise 10 to 20 percent of the population, Zeng (1947) cites one estimate of 20 percent, Fei and Lín (1956) claim that they make up 15 percent of the population, and Ko (1949) estimates 23,850 Black Yi (about 9 percent), 45,000 slaves, and 190,200 White Yi commoners. Hsú (1944) provides the following estimates for an area near Leibo in Xiao Liang Shan: Black Yi 1.67 percent, White Yi commoners 89 percent, White Yi slaves 9.33 percent. Liang Shan Autonomous Zhou, which today includes both Da and Xiao Liang Shan, now has an estimated Yi population of 700,000.

Within each caste, considerable mobility was possible. In addition to the intake of Han captives as slaves, White Yi could also become slaves if they were taken captive in war, if they were heavily in debt, or if there was some advantage (access to land, for example) to be gained. On the other hand, a slave could buy his or her freedom. Slaves usually began as house slaves (domestic servants). When a son of the master married, he was given some male slaves as part of his inheritance; when a daughter of the master married, she received some female slaves. These slaves would then be paired off with the slaves of the other marriage partner, and they would set up house as separate slaves, working land or tending livestock for their new masters. When these separate slaves had children, the children would be sent to the master's house as house slaves. (This system is an interesting contrast to that which existed in the antebellum American South, where domestic slaves had a higher status than field slaves.)

The Black Yi of Da Liang Shan owned an estimated 80 percent of the agricultural land (Winnington 1959). They were owed certain feudal rights and respectful behavior, which served to emphasize their superior status. White Yi commoners were either serfs who worked their lord's land or freemen who leased or owned their own land. Most Black Yi did no agricultural work at all, but hunted, carried out raids and feuds, and looked after their houses. This has led some writers (e.g. Lín 1947) to suggest that they may have originally been a pastoral people. The shamans--even those who could read and write Yi characters--the blacksmiths, and the carpenters were all White Yi. White Yi contributed several days' labor to their lords and also provided contributions and services in times of war, births, marriages, and funerals. These were not inconsiderable, since a Yi bride-price is said to have been 300 or 500 tael for a Black Yi, 600 to 1,000 for a Black Yi chief, and 100 to 300 for a White Yi (Hsu 1944, Ko 1949); or 500 to 800 ounces of silver for a Black Yi, and 100 to 200 for a White Yi (Lín 1947); or a race horse (which might be valued at several hundred tael of silver), ten ingots of silver, ten cattle, and a hundred sheep, plus various gifts to middlemen and to the bride and her parents (Winnington 1959). This bride-price was largely made up of contributions from the master's serfs and slaves.

Outside Da Liang Shan, the power of the Black Yi was not as great, and some White Yi were actually wealthier and more influential than Black aristocrats (Hsú 1944). In Weican, Yunnan Province, Han Chinese absentee landlords held feudal rights over Yi tenants, although these were considerably curtailed after a series of rebellions between 1847 and 1872 (Fei 1951-52; Li, Fei, and Chang 1943). In southwestern Lancang, in the same province, the Lahu were under Tai headmen, and a "primitive class system" prevailed (Chen 1964).

In addition to the contact between Yi and Han resulting from raids, kidnappings, banditry, rebellion, and suppression, there was also some contact between the Yi and Han traders, who sought wax insects, coffin planks, hides, herbs, and other local products.

To travel in Da Liang Shan, an outsider had to buy or otherwise retain the protection of a Black Yi; since the area suffered from endemic feuds between the various local groups and families, this personal protection was only good in some parts of the area. In Da Liang Shan, Han Chinese migrant laborers were employed to tap opium poppies (Hsú 1944, Lín 1947), but the cultivation of opium poppies as a cash crop probably did not begin until the nineteenth century (and ended in the early 1950s).

The Han also appointed Yi and other minority individuals as "tussu" ("headmen or officals") and "tumu" ("officers"), but this system seems seldom to have worked well: some officials were sinicized and lost contact with the people they were supposed to administer; others had no real power (Fang 1945b). The system began in some areas as early as the Han dynasty, but many officals were sacked during the Ming, and those reinstated during the Ch'ing were without real power. (The system among the Hani is discussed by Súo 1962.) The Han were therefore forced to resort to fortifications, militias, the holding of hostages in towns, and forbidding Yi to spend the night in towns (Clarke 1911, Lín 1947, Zeng 1947, Wang 1951, Winnington 1959). These measures only further added to the mutual distrust and dislike.

The first contact between the Yi and the Communist Chinese was during the Long March in 1935 (Wilson 1971, Winnington 1959). The Red Army was apparently greeted with the usual antagonism displayed toward any Chinese soldiers, but some Yi were won over, especially through a Communist officer of Yi origin (Rén-mín rì-bào 1972a). After the Liberation, People's Liberation Army units and Communist Party cadres arrived to administer the Yi areas (some Yi helped to finish off Kuomintang army units in Da Liang Shan). Small teams of two to five cadres (officials), some trained in the Yi language at the Central Academy for National Minorities, began to create the desire for change in the traditional social structure, now so much at odds with China's new ideology (Jì 1958, China Reconstructs 1953, Fei 1952, Rén-mín rì-bao 1962). It was also deemed necessary to alter the social structure for economic reasons: traditional social structure offered little motivation to increase production, since all the work was done by one group (serfs and slaves), but almost everything that was produced went to a much smaller group (Black Yi lords).

Through propaganda and discussion meetings, the abolition of slavery, land reform, and the cancellation of debts was decreed in 1956 (Chang 1959, Jì 1958, New China News Agency (NCNA), Kunming 1956c, 1959b, NCNA, Peking 1958b, Pu 1958, Tie 1959, Winnington 1959). Black Yi former aristocrats caused some problems by slaughtering their cattle, spreading false rumors about Han intentions, or taking to guerrilla tactics. In fact, Fei (1951-52: 57) claims that most of the "Tu-Mu" (Yi headmen) became bandits (cf. Pu 1958, Winnington 1959). But most of the problems resulting from the abolition of slavery seem to have involved helping the exslaves think and plan for themselves: for example they would eat all the relief supplies provided them by the Han, and then refrain from work in the hope of getting more. Some of the problems were solved by grouping exslaves in cooperative units of various sizes from ten households up (NCNA, Chaochueh 1956b, NCNA, Chengtu 1965c, Winnington 1959).

The change from a slave society to a socialist society is certainly one of the most intriguing aspects of Yi studies: if the changes reported in the Chinese press are true, they would represent social changes of even greater magnitude than those undergone by the Han themselves in the past three decades. The same changes have occurred on a lesser scale among the Hani (NCNA, Kunming 1959b),

Lahu (Huang 1958a), Lisu (Zhang 1958; Huang 1958a, 1965; Ma 1958), and Nu (Huang 1959a).

In agriculture, which remains the basis of the economy, opium is no longer grown (Chang 1952, Winnington 1959), but Yi minorities are said to produce a surplus of grain crops (Chang 1959, Ji 1958, <u>China Reconstructs</u> 1953, Gūang-míng ri-bào 1959, NCNA, Chengtu 1958a, 1959b, 1965e, 1965g, 1966; NCNA, Kunming 1958c, 1964b; Tian 1959, Wang, W., 1959; Lisu-Zhang 1964, Huang 1959b, Gūang-míng ri-bào 1971, NCNA, Kunming 1958b, 1958g, 1958h, 1964f, 1964h; NCNA, Peking 1958a; Lahu-NCNA, Kunming 1959d). This was accomplished by a wide variety of innovations: new tools (many locally made), manuring (both animal and human), doublecropping, irrigation, and terracing (NCNA, Chengtu 1963c, 1965d; NCNA, Kunming 1960b; Wang, H., 1959; Yi and Hani--Huang 1958b; Lisu--Zhang 1958, Zhang 1964, Hsu 1965, NCNA, Kunming 1955b, 1964c; Rén-mín ri-bào 1959a, Yang, T., 1955, Huang 1958a; Lahu--Huang 1958a; NCNA, Kunming 1963a, 1963b; Gūang-míng ri-bào 1957). Perhaps of greater importance than these technical innovations have been the social innovations: the agricultural population was organized into mutual aid teams, cooperatives, and, later, communes. By 1959, about 87 percent of the Yi in Liang Shan were in cooperatives (NCNA, Chengtu 1959a, 1964a, 1965e, 1965g; NCNA, Peking 1959b; Wang, W., 1959). By 1958, about 86 percent of the Lisu and other minorities living in Nujiang Autonomous Zhou were in cooperatives (NCNA, Kunming 1958a, 1958g, 1964h; Zhang 1958, Chang 1959, Yang, T., 1955; Lisu and Nu--Huang 1959a). As in other parts of China, the very rapidity of cooperative and commune formation (the bulk of the population was brought into these organizations within a matter of weeks) raises some question as to the deepness of the changes. Yet there is no question that today's commune organization is continuing to change away from traditional norms (Ji-niu-bu 1971; Gūang-míng ri-bào 1972b; Yaoshan

Commune Party Committee 1972; Lisu--NCNA, Kunming 1969b, 1970b, 1972d).

Communization has gone hand in hand with diversification of the economies to include a greater variety of crops (some minorities did not plant rice before 1950) and livestock, lumbering, paper-making, metallurgy, tool-making, electricity, vehicle repair and operation (Ji-niu-bu 1971; NCNA, Chengtu 1958b, 1965b; NCNA, Kunming 1965b, 1971; NCNA, Peking 1959b, 1972; Rén-mín rì-bào 1959b; Wang W., 1959; Yi and Hani--NCNA Kunming, 1970a, 1972b; Lisu--Zhang 1958; Chang 1959; Zhang 1964; Huang 1959b; NCNA, Kunming 1958f, 1964d; Dong and Xue 1959).

In modernization, self-sufficiency, socialism, and other ways, the Yi now "learn from Dazhai" (Rén-mín rì-bào 1972a; Guāng-míng rì-bào 1972a). "In the past we only knew that by getting nearer to the stove we could warm ourselves. Now we know that the Communist Party is warmer than the stove" (NCNA, Kunming 1957, 16 Aug.). In the Nujiang Lisu Autonomous Zhou, once known as "poor hills, bad waters," the Lisu now sing:

Everyone can eat his fill without paying,
Our forefathers never heard of such a thing.
Is it a dream?
No, it is the truth.
Where is it?
Right here in our commune.
The east is red,
Long live Chairman Mao! (NCNA, Kunming 1958e)

Schools were established, so that the majority of the population now has some literacy in Chinese, and some minority individuals have gone on to technical schools and colleges (Chang 1952, Chang 1959,

Jì 1958, NCNA, Chengtu 1956a, 1963a, 1971; NCNA, Kunming 1958d; Yi and Lisu--NCNA Kunming 1972a, Wang, L., 1959; Lisu--Chou 1963; Gūang-mǐng rì-bào 1973b; NCNA, Kunming 1955c; Rén-mín rì-bào 1963; Dǒng and Xúe 1959; Lahu-Gao 1960). There are now Yi and other minority newspapers and publications (Gjessing 1957; NCNA, Kunming 1960a, 1961, Tsung 1954, Yang, G., 1955a, 1955b; Lisu--NCNA, Kunming 1973).

Medical centers were established and doctors trained (Chang 1952, Chnag 1959, NCNA, Chengtu 1965f; Yi, Lisu, Tulung, and Nu-NCNA, Kunming 1972e; Lisu-Chou 1963, China Pictorial 1963, NCNA, Kunming 1969a; Dǒng and Xúe 1959; Lahu-Yang 1963a), leading to population increase (Gūang-mǐng rì-bào 1973c, NCNA, Kweiyang 1959; Lahu-Chen 1964) and new towns (Rén-mín rì-bào 1959c; Lahu--Gūang-mǐng rì-bào 1957, NCNA, Kunming 1963b; Yang 1963a, 1963b). Cooperative banks and trading organizations were opened (NCNA, Chengtu 1963b; NCNA, Kweiyang 1973; Lisu--Chou 1963, NCNA, Kunming 1964g; Lahu--Yang 1963b). Transport and communications were greatly improved (Chang 1952, NCNA, Chengtu 1959d; Lisu--NCNA, Kunming 1955a, 1964a, 1964g; Hani--Jiang 1958).

Yi and other minority members have become responsible cadres (officials) and Communist Party members (Ji-niu-bu 1971, Rén-mín rì-bào 1972a, Wa-cha-mu-chi and Wang 1959; Yi, Hani, and Lisu--Wang 1956; Yi, Hani, and Nakhi--Yúnnán rì-bào 1956a; Yi, Lahu, Hani, Pulang, and Kutsung--Rén-mín rì-bào 1973; Yi, Lisu, Nu, Tulung, Nakhi and Pumi--Lichiang Regional 1973; Lisu--Gūang-mǐng rì-bào 1971), Youth League members (Hani and Lahu--Zhōng-gúo Qīng-nían-bào 1956a), and soldiers in the People's Liberation Army, which also has separate minority regiments (China Reconstructs 1973).

Amicable interminority relations have also increased, with various minorities sharing autonomous administrative regions and communes, working together, and joining in each other's celebrations (Gūang-mǐng rì-bào 1972a, Hsin 1973, Huang 1965, NCNA, Kunming 1956a, 1958e, 1959e, 1964e, 1972c, 1972d; NCNA, Peking 1959c, 1972; Rén-mín rì-bào 1959b).

Han-Yi relations since 1949 have reflected national political directions: during times of radical change, such as the period of socialist transformation and the Great Leap Forward (1956-62), as well as the Great Proletarian Cultural Revolution (1966-69), the emphasis has been on rapid movement toward socialism and criticism of "local nationalism." The Communists have attempted to make these periods as shattering to the minorities' social structures as it was to the Han's, as this statement by Zhnag (1958: 34) concerning the Lisu makes clear:

> The Great Leap Forward has not proceeded smoothly at all times. Apart from the struggle of the two lines mentioned above, there was the acute struggle of the two roads, which was manifested principally in the struggle against counterrevolutionaries both in the country and abroad, the landlords, rich peasants, rightists, and nationalists. In the past, it was thought by some that since class distinctions among the Lisu were not quite clear-cut, since the landlord class had not yet been formed, and since a rich peasant economy was not yet developed in certain areas, class struggle would not be acute. The opposite, however, was true. It is true that class distinctions have never been quite clear, but that does not mean that classes do not exist. Moreover, the class struggle is still quite complicated and acute. We have dealt resolute blows to a group of reactionary landlords, rich peasants and counterrevolutionaries. Meanwhile, class education has been carried out in the rural areas. The masses were urged to make recollections and comparisons between the past and the present, to air their grievances and trace their origins, and to expose the crimes of the reactionary upper strata and headmen of the nationality, so as to increase the ideological consciousness of the masses.

Traditional customs were criticized as wasteful superstitions: "There is blasting day and night, and after sunset there are thousands of torches. The spirits are frightened away, and there are no more gods" (Zhang 1958; cf. Yi and Hani--Huang 1958b; Hani--Li 1958; Lisu--Ma 1958). The habit of buying off the old aristocrats ("upper-circle personages") by giving them official positions and allowances was reversed: old aristocrats were "reeducated," and class origin was emphasized in appointing new officials and Party members (Ji-niu-bu 1971, Gūang-míng rì-bào 1972a, 1972b; NCNA, Kunming 1956b, Rén-mín rì-bào 1972a, 1972b; Wen 1970). During the Cultural Revolution, Mao thought-study classes were initiated, and the Yi were able to quote Mao as well as the Han (Investigation Group 1971, Rén-mín rì-bào 1972a; Lisu--China Reconstructs, 1969, NCNA, Kunming 1968, 1969b; Rén-mín rì-bào 1970; Tulung--NCNA, Peking 1968).

During the lulls between these periods of rapid change (1950-56, 1962-66, 1969-75), more stress has been placed upon regional (political) and minority (cultural) autonomy (see Table 3). Great Hanism (excessive centralization and ethnocentricity) was criticized (Fei 1952, Moseley 1973, Winnington 1959). Each nationality was to be guided into socialism at its own pace, peaceful transformation was achieved through discussion and demonstration and the granting of special treatment to the exaristocrats (NCNA, Chengtu 1956c). As in the rest of China, not only was there a slowing down of reforms but there was also some backstepping: in 1962, for example, 70 percent of the cooperatives in Nujiang Lisu Autonomous Zhou were slashed back, and the number of schoolchildren was reduced (NCNA, Kunming 1968). During such lulls in revolutionary fervor, the continuity with the past can be discerned: the Lisu are still scattered in small groups of households (NCNA, Kunming 1969a), bandits still harass remote areas (NCNA, Kunming 1969 [Aug. 11] and 1970 [Feb. 7]).

The Yi peoples have therefore learned to dance to the same tune as their Han neighbors: two steps forward, one step back. A detailed study of recent history would probably show that this pattern also holds within the larger periods of time considered here. Despite temporary emphasis on rapid or slow reform, on centralization or local autonomy, on class antagonism or the attempt to smooth over class differences, the goal is still socialism. Paradoxically, what the Chinese before 1949 could not accomplish by force, they are now accomplishing as a by-product of a quite different goal, all the while encouraging respect for minority differences: the Yi minorities are becoming ever more assimilated into national political, economic, social, and cultural institutions. The Yi, formerly known as "iron peas" because they could not be assimilated, are joining the stew.

Ethnography

Chinese interest in the southern "tribes" is ancient. For example in the second century A.D., Yang Fu wrote Nan I I Wu Chih ("Strange Things from the Southern Borders"). Wan Zhen's Nan Chou I Wu Chih ("Strange Things of the South") dates from the fourth century. Man Shu ("Book of the Barbarians"), by Fan Chuo, dates from about 685, and Wen Hsien Thung Khao ("Historical Investigation of Public Affairs"), by Ma Duan-lin, was published in 1319.

It was not until the second half of the nineteenth century, when Britain and France were seeking a back door to China, that Southwest China attracted attention from Western scholars. The earliest useful information on the Yi people was written by missionaries. For the Yi proper, we have excellent accounts by Paul Vial (1893-94, 1898, 1909), who lived among the Gni from 1886 on; Samuel Clarke (1911), who spent over twenty years in Kweichow; and Alfred Liétard (1913), who spent some eight years with the Ahi (A-si) of Chaotung in northeastern Yunnan. Missionaries among the Lisu who left important publications include l'Abbé Dubernard (1873, 1875), Auguste Desgodins (1872, 1873), Alexandre Biet (in Biet and de Croizier 1877), Théodore Monbeig (in Liétard 1909b and Madrolle 1908), and James Fraser (1922) of the China Inland Mission, who devised a writing system still in use among Christian Lisu.

A great number of travelers have also left accounts of ethnographic value. Edward Baber (1882) was one of the first English travelers to write enthusiastically of Southwest China, and of its Lisu and Yi inhabitants. Henri d'Orléans (1898) and Emile Roux (1897) visited the Yi, Lisu, and Akha peoples in Yunnan in 1895. Henry Davies (1909), who was trying to promote a rail link between India and China via Yunnan, made some observations on its inhabitants. Henri d'Ollone (1911) passed through Liang Shan and other areas of Yi and Lisu occupation in 1907, as did Jacques Bacot (1912, 1913). Archibald Rose and J. Coggin Brown (1911), the former a British consul at Dengyue and the latter a geologist, wrote the first extensive description of Lisu customs, based on their familiarity with Yunnan and the Shan States.

Modern Chinese ethnographic studies began in the 1930s. In 1934, Hsiang Ling-ching and other researchers of the West China Science College spent two months in Liang Shan. In 1939, Mǎ Cháng-shoû (1942-44) and other scholars of the Szechwan-Sikang Scientific Research Group traveled through Da Liang Shan. In 1940, Hsú Î-táng (1944) and members of the Szechwan Education Department spent several weeks in Xiao Liang Shan, near Leibo. Zeng Zhao-lun (1947) traveled through Da and Xiao Liang Shan in August and September 1941. Lin Yâo-húa (1947) studied in Da and Xiao Liang Shan from July to September 1943; his monograph follows closely Hsu's (1944) report on many points. After 1949, Jí Xí-chén (1958) and Alan Winnington (1959), an Australian adviser in Da Liang Shan between 1957 and 1958, wrote reports of the changes taking place among the Yi.

Taó (1945, 1948) spent some weeks in 1935 with the Lisu of the Biluoxue Mountains, between the Salween and the Mekong, in Yunnan. His brief reports include some interesting observations and several legends. Chén (1947) visited Dechang in Szechwan in 1946, and reported that Lisu clans were organized in a dual fashion, an observation that has yet to be confirmed.

Only sketchy ethnographic information exists for the Achang, Akha, Woni (Hani), Lutzu, Tulung, Lahu, and Kadu in China.

Those Yi peoples who inhabit areas outside China have also been the subject of ethnographic enquiries. The Lisu of Thailand have been described by Bunchuai Srisawat (1952, 1963), Alain Dessaint (1972a), E. Paul Durrenberger (1971), and others. The Lahu of Thailand have been the subject of an exhaustive study by Anthony Walker (1970b, 1972c), Harold Young (n.d.), and Oliver Young (1961). The Akha of Thailand are the subject of an excellent study by Hugo Bernatzik (1947); Paul Lewis (1969-70) has written about the Akha of Burma.

The caste system dividing the Yi into Black and White has already been described above. Marriage (or sexual relations) across caste lines was severely forbidden. Marriage might be within the clan, "so as to strengthen the ties between two families" (Hsü 1944). The preferred mate is a cross-cousin; Lin (1947: 40-56) states that marriage with a parallel cousin is forbidden, but Hsü (1944) asserts that marriage with the mother's sister's daughter sometimes occurs. The Yi are not as strict as the Chinese about marrying within one's generation, so that one may marry someone standing in an "aunt" or "niece" or even "stepmother" relation (Hsü 1944, cf. Ko 1949).

The marriage ceremony (Liétard 1913: 156-59, Hsü 1944: 44-50) takes place preferably when the couple are thirteen, fifteen, or seventeen years old, on a day chosen in consultation with a shaman for its auspiciousness as determined by its conjunction with the couple's birthdates and those of their parents. The men of the groom's party are greeted by the women of the bride's family, first with witty remarks, then with buckets of water; their faces may be smeared with pepper and soot, and some girls even physically attack them. Once the ice has been broken, the pig and other ingredients for the marriage feast are prepared. After the feast, the bride is taken to the groom's home, with much weeping and protestation. For three to five days the bride remains at the groom's parents' home, during which time the groom and bride are separated. The bride then returns to her parents' home for a "waiting-at-home-period" that may last for one or two years or until she is pregnant. During this time, the bride takes lovers--often cousins--and the groom (who is living with his parents) must not only bring presents if he wishes to have sexual intercourse with her but must usually use force to do so. This is a probationary period, which allows both parties to reconsider the match and allows the woman to prove her childbearing abilities. Polygamy, the sororate and levirate, are also practiced, particularly among high-status Black Yi.

The relative status of men and women among the Yi is quite equal, although the women do more work. Most activities are not restricted to one sex: women even do the heavy work in the fields, chop wood, and make musical instruments (Hsú 1944). Only the tending and shearing of sheep is masculine work (Hsú 1944). Normally, men and women eat together, but when there are important guests, they will eat separately, or the men will eat first.

Women could inherit land and even chiefly offices. Women were important in stopping feuds or wars, but they could also cause them by claiming mistreatment, by committing suicide, by arguments over bride-price, and by discovery of sexual liaisons between members of different clans. One girl is said to have committed suicide because a member of her husband's family let out gas in her presence (Hsú 1944).

Since the Black Yi refrained from most manual work, an important part of their lives consisted in enforcing rules of etiquette within and between clans. Hsü (1944) writes that there are 485 Yi clans, with each clan or group of clans occupying a distinct territory. Clan feuds seem to have been endemic in Da Liang Shan. They were caused by arguments over women, insults to Black Bone men or women, murder, theft (especially of slaves or horses), and defaulting on a debt; but, as elsewhere, the reasons for most feuds were long forgotten, and each clan had traditional enemies. Battles or war could be averted if the offenders paid an indemnity in silver or horses, or, if the offending clan were poor and no loss of life were involved, the wrong-doer might go on horseback (wearing a silk dress with a mirror in his hair and raw beef in his mouth) to apologize and to offer wine and beef to the offended party. Preparations for war included sending out a wooden tablet calling on all members of the clan, its tenants, serfs, and slaves to assemble; each family would assent by making a mark on the tablet; tallying the marks would indicate how large a fighting force might be expected. War costumes were extremely colorful: some wore hats of woven bamboo covered with white cloth, thin woolen felt and yellow satin, with animal hair that would wave in the wind; they would carefully prepare their hair, interweaving it with a strip of cloth and tying it into a horn just above the forehead; some would cap this with a sheep horn wrapped in colorful silk and red pompons; squares of silk would be sewn on their clothing. They reminded Hsü (1944) of the warriors in Chinese operas. Like these warriors, the Yi would run forward, shout out their names, and challenge their enemies to fight.

The War songs were equally awe-inspiring:
>
> We are the famous Black Nosu!
> We are the tigers who eat up human flesh!
> We are the butchers who skin people alive!
> We are the supermen, the nonpareil! (Hsü 1944: 61)

War tactics were more mundane: ambushes and surprise attacks were favored; because of lack of ammunition, battles were often hand to hand; the goal was not so much to kill the enemy as to capture him. A Black Yi would be held for ransom or allowed to commit suicide; White Yi or slaves were held for ransom or enslaved. Witchcraft and amulets were used extensively.

Battles and wars were often ended or averted by the mediation of a third clan, or by a "waiting-at-home" bride related to both parties (if her pleas were unsuccessful, she would commit suicide). Peace negotiations were long and required expert debaters: compensation had to be decided upon for each life lost. Finally, the hide of a bull was spread over a wooden frame, under which representatives of both sides would drink wine with chicken blood, and take a peace oath. If either party broke this oath, its members would meet the same fate as the slaughtered chicken.

Ji (1958) states that in 1949, one feud between two clans resulted in the mobilization of 20,000 men. Another feud between two of the largest clans had lasted a century, and resulted in the deaths of over 300 persons.

Problems for Future Research

The gaps that exist in our knowledge of the Yi peoples are obvious: the greatest need is still for reliable descriptive studies--ethnographic, archeological, linguistic, sociological, psychological, and historical. This is especially true of the smaller ethnic groups, such as the Achang, Hpon, Kadu, Lutzu, and Tulung. Much of the written data on the Yi peoples, however, remain undigested. Among some of the more urgent problems are the following:

(1) Further investigations of the historical phonology, morphology, and syntax and of the comparative lexicon and the internal relationships of the Yi languages (not to mention their external relationships to other Tibeto-Burman groups). As Matisoff (1972a, 1973c) has pointed out, such studies will also make a contribution to broader theoretical issues, such as the mechanism of tonogenesis, grammatical effects on sound change, protovariation, and the notion of "cognacy."

(2) The identification and delimitation of Yi ethnic groups and subgroups, both in terms of self-identification and in terms of social processes; the nature of their relationships and the problems of changing ethnic identity, either at a group or at an individual level (Hanks, Hanks, and Sharp 1965; Leach 1954); in other words, the nature of "ethnicity" in highland Southeast Asia.

(3) Historical study of local gazetteers and Yi texts, with the goal of correcting histories written solely from a Han (or lowland) point of view.

(4) Documentation of the recent changes undergone by Yi peoples

in China, and comparisons with changes undergone by Yi peoples in Southeast Asia; the change from swidden to irrigation agriculture taking place in both areas will be especially significant.

(5) Comparative studies of shamanism and curing methods, to explore the sexual division of labor in shamanism, methods of inducing trance states, relationship of shamanism to value systems, and the changes brought about after the acceptance of external medical systems.

(6) Comparative studies of social structure and value systems, to determine whether a core common to all Yi peoples exists, and to find out which variations may be traced to ecological or historical causes.

BIBLIOGRAPHY

Each citation is alphabetized under the author's last name (the author's own transliteration is used; where this is not provided, the Pinyin System is used for Chinese, and the Mary Haas system is used for Thai). The citation continues with the date of publication, followed by the title of the work, place of publication, publisher, and number of pages. In the case of periodicals, the title of the article is indicated in quotes, followed by the serial title, volume number, issue number (if appropriate), and page numbers. In some cases, important re-editions, reprints, and translations have been indicated in parentheses following the main citation. If the item is available in the Human Relations Area Files, the notation HRAF is followed by the file number.

Each annotation begins a new paragraph, which usually starts off with the name(s) of the ethnic group(s) discussed. The abstract is followed by a note on ethnographic maps and photographs, but only if they refer to the ethnic groups mentioned. Cross-references and book reviews are then noted, if appropriate. The author's spelling of proper nouns is retained in each case, and where several spellings are used these are indicated. The more common spelling in use today is indicated only where identification might be difficult.

As in any such bibliography, there are bound to be accidental omissions. The following categories of works are usually omitted: missionary tracts, Chinese district gazetteers, works in Lolo languages, and unpublished manuscripts. Works published through 1975 are included.

Anonymous
1955 Bon ma ve aw lawn 24 ceu (24 sermon outlines), Rangoon, n.p.
Lahu sermon outlines.
1959 Lahu k'a mui li (Lahu hymn book), Pangwai, Kengtung, n.p. (Second edition, 1970, Bangkok.)
1970a Ca Law cu yi hen ve (Ca Law the wise man), 2 vols., Bangkok, n.p. (First edition, Rangoon.)
Lahu reader.
1970b Lahu li-Aw hkui pui hen tu ve (Lahu primer), Bangkok, n.p. (First edition, Rangoon.)

Aàdsǎalii, Sěerii
1963 Sìbhâa phàw nai Thai (Fifteen peoples of Thailand), Bangkok, Sǎmnákphim Phidjaakaan. 216 pp.
Akha, Lisu: Descriptions of dress, housing, livelihood, marriage, divination, and spirits. Based mostly on Srisawat 1952.

Abadie, Maurice
1924 Les races du Haut-Tonkin de Phong-Tho à Lang Son, Paris, Société d'Editions Géographiques, Maritimes et Coloniales. 194 pp.
Lolo: The only Lolo in Tonkin are located in Bao-lac, where they are called Heu-lolo (Black), Peu-lolo (White), Dji, Gni, or (by the Annamities) Man-khoanh. Although they are often immoderate in their use of alcohol, tobacco, and opium, they are more gentle than the northern Lolo. Description of dress: men adopt Thai dress except for burial. Houses of the rich are on piles, others on ground. Meo and Lolo often have the same chief

(of the more numerous group). Adoption and buying of children. After marriage, the wife lives with her parents until her first pregnancy. The Kan-t'eou-lolo ("head-cutting Lolo") exhume their dead, cut off the skulls, and place them in wooden boxes. They believe in spirits and worship ancestors at an altar with figurines made with the stem of the orchid, 7 knots long for the males and 9 for the females. Other groups which may be related to Lolo include the Fou-la (Peu-pa, P'ou-la), a few hundred of whom are scattered along the Chinese border; the Xa-pho (Lao-pha), 3,000-4,000 of whom live on the right bank of the Red River; and the Ho-nhi (Ouo-ni, Woni) who number 200-300. Descriptions of their dress and houses. The Xa-pho have mixed with Thai and Nhang; they do not have a deluge legend, but their origin legend says that the first human couple had four sons: Xa-pho, Thai, Man, and Meo; the mother made cloth for the Thai and Yao, but, running out of material, she had to make a shorter dress for the Meo and a very short one for the Lolo.

Adams, Marie Jeanne (or Monni)
1974 "Dress and design in highland Southeast Asia: The Hmong (Miao) and the Yao," Textile Museum Journal 4,1: 51-66.

    Akha grow cotton.
    Lahu and Lisu emphasize the upper arm of the jacket, wear plain shirts with elaborate sashes.
    Photos.

Ainscough, Thomas M.
1915   *Notes from a frontier*, Shanghai, Kelly and Walsh, Ltd.
(Reprint: 1971, Taipei, Ch'eng Wen Publishing Company.)
90 pp.

Lolo: Chinese military currently suppressing Lolo rebellions near Sanya and Yen T'ang (pp. 17, 36-38). According to d'Ollone, the Lolo originally inhabited southern Yunnan and Kuei Chou, but rebelled against the Chinese in 1727 and fled north to the Ta Liang Mountains. North of the T'ung River are Tributary Lolo, south of it are Independent Lolo, who raid and enslave local Chinese. The only Chinese who regularly enter the Ta Liang Shan are the collectors of white wax insects and those who slit opium poppies, the Lolo being inexperienced in this. The main road to Yunnan through Chien Chang Valley is defended by blockhouses every mile; subsidies are paid to nearby Lolo chiefs, and Lolo hostages are kept, but even so the road is unsafe. Even more so since the Revolution; scarcely a hamlet from Fulin to Huili Chou has not been pillaged (pp. 23-26).

Anderson, John
1871   *A report on the expedition to western Yunnan via Bhamô*, Calcutta, Office of the Superintendent of Government Printing. 458 pp.

Leesaws and Kakhyens inhabit Hotha and Sanda valleys and grow rice, tobacco, opium, and maize (p. 83). Leesaws and Myautze live east of Momien (p. 118). Kakhyen sometimes exact tribute from the Leesaw. Description of Leesaw dress, which resembles Chinese and Shan. Met

Leesaws in Sanda and Muangla markets carrying vegetables, firewood, and planks. Their language resembles Burmese (pp. 135-36). Visited a Leesaw village, where Chinese and Shan also live, overlooking Hotha; one enters through wooden gate and leaves through long, enclosed passage of climbing plants (pp. 163-64). Leesaw vocabulary (pp. 401-09). Map.

1876 Mandalay to Momien, A narrative of the two expeditions to Western China of 1868 and 1875 under Colonel Edward B. Sladen and Colonel Horace Browne, London, Macmillan and Co. (Reprint: 1972, Taipei, Ch'eng Wen Publishing Company.) 479 pp.

Leesaws: Anderson was the expeditions' medical and scientific officer. He claims that Leesaws in Hotha and Sanda valleys, between Tengyueh and the Burmese border, are the same people Cooper calls Leisu in northern Yunnan. They sell oil, bamboo, and firewood. Men and women shave a circle around the head, leaving only a large patch from which hair is gathered in a short pigtail. Description of dress. Language akin to Burmese (p. 257). Village with wooden gate and covered passage (pp. 276-77). Vocabulary (pp. 464-73). Maps, illustrations.

Anthony, K. R. M., and F. R. Moorman

1964 Agricultural problems and potentialities of a hill tribe area in Thailand, Bangkok, National Economic Development Board. 11 pp.

Lahu and Lisu of Tak nikhom (government reservation) included.

Antisdel, C. B.
1911a "Elementary studies in Lahoo, Akha (Kaw), and Wa languages," Burma Research Society, Journal 1,1: 41-64.
   Lahoo, Akha: Information from pupils in Kengtung. Words, simple phrases.
1911b "Lahoo narrative of creation," Burma Research Society, Journal 1,1: 65-69.
   Lahoo: Creator was Gusha, who planned (daw) and thought (ga), so that Adaw and Aga are interlocutors.
1911c "Lahoo traditions--continued," Burma Research Society, Journal 1,2: 32-35.
   Lahoo: Brother and sister rescued from flood. Dispersal of peoples from pagoda in Mung Miehn (Shan word for Lahoo). Myinchias of Tali are a branch of Lahoo. One party of Lahoo killed a stag and distributed it; another party killed a porcupine but did not eat it, since it was small; however, since the quills were longer than the hairs of the stag, the first party was vexed and separation of the two Lahoo groups resulted. (Karen and Chin are said to have same tradition.) According to one legend, both groups started south, but one group stopped to boil molluscs, hoping the shells would soften; the other group did not wait and went on. (Karen and Akha have same story.) There is a prophecy that this latter group will one day return and bring with them the precepts of God, which were written on rice cakes, and restore them to political supremacy. (Akha, Wa, and Karen have legends of writing on buffalo skin.)

Arritola, Marlene
1972   "Hilltribe silver jewelry," Sawaddi, Nov.-Dec.: 15-18.
                Akha, Lahu Na, and Lahu Nyi wear silver extensively as jewelry and dress ornamentation.
                Lisu wear silver chains attached to both ears.
                Photos.

Asian Analyst Supplements Agency
1969   National minorities in China. n.p. 42 pp.
                List of minority areas. Discussion of immigration of Han cadres, literacy drives, insistence on common culture during Cultural Revolution, religious persecution.

Audretch, C. C., and C. C. Chaffee
1969   The Lahu tribes of Thailand and Burma: Specific information, bibliographic references, and sources, Bangkok, Battelle Memorial Institute, Thailand Information Center. 16 pp.
                Lahu: Sources of authority and power, values, the legend of a "man-god" with warrior followers, qualities that might give rise to a Lahu army. See Hill Tribe Welfare Division 1970.

Ba Te
1912   "Lahoo Folklore. The hunt for the beeswax," Burma Research Society, Journal 2,1: 65-71.
                Lahoo: Translation of a folktale.

1926   "A marriage custom among the Ahkas and Myinchas," Burma Research Society, Journal 16: 43-45.
                Ahka: Young men and women meet at dances, after which a youth and his companions may "forcibly" abduct a girl. The first mouthful eaten by her in the youth's

house makes her his wife. An elderly man of the groom's village settles bride-price with girl's father.

Baber, Edward Colborne
1882   "Travels and researches in western China," Royal Geographical Society, London, Supplementary Papers 1: 1-152. (Reprint: 1971, Taipei, Ch'eng Wen Publishing Company.)

Lolos used to defeat Taipings (pp. 55-56). Road to Chien-Ch'ang subject to Lolo attacks; some border Lolos help guard it; these speak Chinese but retain Lolo dress. Tall, well-built, with prominent cheekbones and chin. Hair is gathered into a knot over forehead and twisted in a cotton cloth to resemble a horn. Sinicized Lolo wear both horn and pigtail or may shave entire head. Felt mantle and leggings, Chinese cotton trousers. Silver, copper, and iron mines near Yueh-hsi T'ing in Lolo country. A Lolo T'u-ssu (chief) at Yueh-hsi. Call themselves Lo-su, No-su, Ngo-su, Le-su. Black-bone nobles, white-bone retainers; Wa-tzu are captive Chinese slaves. Description of marriage ceremony. High position of women. Bad relations between Lolo tribes. Ultimogeniture in property and chieftainship. Communicate with spirits through shamans and omens. Le-su is a widely used term but may be the same people as Desgodins' Lissou, Andersons's Lee-saw, and Cooper's Lei-su (pp. 58-72). Lolo and Leesaw numerals, Lolo vocabulary from left bank of T'ung River (pp. 72-78). Fear of Lolo attack causes panic in Li-chou in 1850. Stones are stored in case of Lolo attack at a custom house, which had been looted and its officers stripped a few weeks previous to Baber's visit. Half the population of Yenyuan district are Moso tribes. Moso writings (pp. 79-89). Lolo Tu-ssu at Tu-ke. Lolos blamed for Chinese banditry, blamed for revenging themselves against Chinese who kidnapped Lolos (pp. 105-06). English translation of kidnapping of Fenouil in 1862 (pp. 118-24). Lolo writing (pp. 125-29, 9 plates). Stone statue said to be of Hsi-po, an ancient Lolo king; they still burn incense to him (pp. 139-40). Comment on Lolo writing by Terrien de Lacouperie (pp. 142-43): It is phonetic, and it resembles writing of Sumatra. Map.

Bacot, Jacques

1909 Dans les marches tibétaines autour du Dokerla, Novembre 1906-Janvier 1908, Paris, Plon-Nourrit. 215 pp.
Lissou mentioned. Map, photos.

1912 "Les populations du Tibet oriental," Revue d'Ethnographie et de Sociologie 3: 203-10.
Lissou: Bacot believes that the Lissou of Yunnan were forced into the mountains by Tibetan invaders.

1913 Les Mo-so, Leiden, E. J. Brill
Lissou: Bacot considers them indigenous to north western Yunnan.

Bangkok Post

1973a "Igor tribesmen prefer peace and solitude," Bangkok Post, Nov. 6: 5.
Igor (Akha) unresponsive to government's family planning program. Photo.

1973b "Visitors study Lisu," Bangkok Post, Aug. 14: 6.

Lisu will be target of literacy program by Jesse
Yangmi, Eugene and Robert Morse, and four of their
sons.
    See Boh 1967; Morse 1962, 1974.

Bangkok Technical College
1968 Report from Bangkok Technical College on a Volunteer
    Camp, Bangkok, Bangkok Technical College. 52 pp.
    Lahu provided with houses, playground, medicines,
and clothes In Thai.

Bangkok World
1967 "Getting to know the Red Lahu," Bangkok World Sunday
    Magazine, Mar. 12: 6-8.
    Lahu Nyi of Amphoe Phrao: Sketch of the study
being carried out by Anthony Walker. Photos.
1973 "First Lisor teacher trains tribesmen," Bangkok World,
    May 29: 6.
    Lisor (Lisu) teacher in Tak Province. Photo.

Bank of China: see Zhōng-guó yín-háng.

Barnard, J. T. O.
1925 "History of Putao," Burma Research Society, Journal 15:
    137-41.
    Lisu arrived in 'Nami and Alikyang valleys three
or four generations ago. They levied tribute from Daru
and Nung, some of whom left.
1930 "The frontiers of Burma," Central Asian Society, Journal
    17: 173-88.
    Lisu considered truculent. When casualties occur
in quarrels, women intervene. They wash for gold.
Suspension bridge. Maps.

Bastian, Adolf
1866-71 Die Voelker des Oestlichen Asien, Studien und Reisen, 6 vols., Leipzig, Verlag von Otto Wigand; London, Truebner & Co.
   Laulau or Lolo (Nui) mentioned (1: 177)

Baumann, William H.
1970 Integrating of mountain peoples (hill-tribes) in provincial police of Thailand, Bangkok, United States Operations Mission. 10 pp.
   Akha, Lahu, Lisu, and other highlanders could be recruited as police.

Beauclair, Inez de
1956a "Culture traits of non-Chinese tribes in Kweichow Province, Southwest China," Sinologica 5,1: 20-35. (Reprint: 1970, in Tribal Cultures of Southwest China, Taipei, The Orient Cultural Service, pp. 40-59.)
   Yi: Miao call Chung Chia "Yi" in Anshun, and Kweiyang Chinese call them "Yi Chia." Wiens (1954: 280) uses "Yi" for Chung Chia and includes the Tai, Tung Chia, and Shui Chia. Lolo stone defense towers serve as hiding place, storeroom, and lookout.

1956b "Ethnic groups," in Hellmut Wilhelm, ed., A General Handbook of China, New Haven, Human Relations Area Files, Subcontractor's Monograph No. 55. (Reprint: 1970, in Tribal Cultures of Southwest China, Taipei, The Orient Cultural Service, pp. 1-39.)
   Wu-man, 93 tribes of "Black Barbarians," including Lolo, Nu-tzu, Ku-tsung, Mo-so, Li-su, and Wo-ni, left original habitat in east Tibet. Vanguard, which may have

been Woni, reached south Yunnan by Han times. Lisu, Akha, and Lahu later drifted south and east from the upper Salween; the Lisu reaching south Yunnan by Ming. Lahu, between the lower Salween and Mekong, arrived several centuries ago. Lolo moved south and west in historic times, reaching Kweichow in Han, driven back west in Ming, and reaching Annam several centuries ago. Physical data and population figures. Kutsung and others frequent Tali medicinal market; Lolo frequent Tatsienlu market, where wool, felt, fox skins, yak tails, and rhubarb are exchanged for tea, cloth, tobacco, needles, and spices. White Lolo have assisted Chinese in fighting Black Lolo. Lolo landlords mistreat Miao tenants, confiscating their belongings when they are unable to pay. Miao refer to Lolos' overbearing attitudes in their myths, and when sending deceased's spirit to ancestors the Miao priest warns him to stay away from Lolo.

Beauvais, J. (See also Zaborowski-Moindron 1901, 1904, 1905.)

1907 "Notes sur les coutumes des indigènes de la région de Long-Tcheou," Ecole française d'Extrême-Orient, Bulletin 7, 3-4: 265-95.

T'ou-jen: Detailed notes on customs pertaining to childhood, marriage, death, and day of dead among t'ou-jen (土人). Translation of passage from Long Tcheou ki lio.

Bendict, Paul K.

1941 Kinship in southeastern Asia, doctoral dissertation, Harvard University. (Not available through University

      Microfilms.) 525 pp.
      Lolo kinship.

1947   "Languages and literatures of Indochina," Far Eastern Quarterly 6,4: 379-89.

      Akha (of northern Laos) and Lolo (of northwestern Tonkin) included in "immigrant" languages of Tibeto-Burman stock.

1948   "Tonal systems in Southeast Asia," American Oriental Society, Journal 68;4: 184-91.

      Burmese-Lolo tonal systems have common origin. A number of languages (including Lahu and Lisu) have 4, 5, or 6 tonemes with a simple high-low contrast in checked syllables. (See Matisoff 1972a, 1973a.)

1975   Austro-Thai: language and culture, with a glossary of roots, New Haven, HRAF Press. xxiv, 490 pp. (Pages 1-133 originally published in 1966-67, Behavior Science Notes 1: 227-61; 2: 203-44, 275-333.)

      Akha, Lisu, Lolo, Moso vocabulary items used for comparative purposes (pp. 88, 100, 109, 113, 116).

Benedict, Paul K. (and James A. Matisoff, contributing editor)

1972   Sino-Tibetan, A conspectus, Cambridge, Cambridge University Press. 230 pp.

      Comparative linguistics. Based on a manuscript of 12 volumes (at University of California) completed in 1943, with some revision, mostly by Matisoff.

      Review: Kun Chang, 1973, Journal of Asian Studies 32,2: 335-37.

Bernath, Frances A.

1964   Catalogue of Thai language holdings in the Cornell

University Libraries through 1964, Cornell University, Southeast Asia Program, Data Paper 54. 236 pp.

Bernatzik, Hugo Adolf

1938 Die Geister der gelben Blatter, Munchen, F. Bruckmann. (Various reprints, including English translation by E. W. Dickes, 1958, Spirits of the yellow leaves, London, R. Hale. French translation by A. Tournier, with notes by G. Condominas, 1955, Les esprits des feuilles jaunes, Paris.) 240 pp.

Lisu mentioned. Photos.

1940 "Die Lahu verweigern uns Gastfreundschaft," Atlantis 12,6: 214-19.

Lahu of Fang, Chiangrai, and Kengtung. Photos.

1947 Akha and Meau, 2 vols., Innsbruck, Kommissionsverlag Wagnerische Univ.-Buchdr. (English translation: 1970, Akha and Miao, New Haven, HRAF Press.) (HRAF AO 1-39, in German and English.) 568 pp.

Akha: Complete ethnography.

Lisu said to be most similar to Miao; much intermixture with Lahu and Chinese; economically dependent on latter. Lisu most distrustful of outsiders and resist missionaries. Kin terms. Maps, photos.

Reviews: Inez de Beauclair, 1950, Studia Serica 9,2: 108-16.

1954 Die Neue Grosse Völkerkunde, Frankfurt/Main, Herkul G.M.B.H., Verlagsanstalt. (Reprint: 1962, Einsiedeln, Bertelsmann Lesering.) xvi, 976 pp.

Achang, Akha, Lahu, Lisu, Lolo, Woni: Passing mentions (especially 2: 126-29). Maps, photos.

Bernot, Lucien
1971 "Les langues Tibéto-birmanes," Asie du Sud-est et Monde Insulindien 2,4: 11-24.
1972 "Presentation des feuilles de cartes de la famille Tibéto-birmane," Asie du Sud-est et Monde Insulindien 3, 4: 5-6.

Akha, Lisu, Lahu, Lahuhsi, Lahuna, Lishaw, Lisu, Lolo Blanc, Lolo Noir, Lolopho, Man-khoanh, Moso, Nosu: Words for "dog," "tooth," and "salt." Maps.

Bertreux, Henri
1922 Au pays du dragon, Paris, Maisonneuve et fils. 381 pp.

Lolo: Missionary in Kien-tchang. Lolo toll-collectors (p. 155). It is almost always the Chinese who break treaties with Lolo. For six centuries, Chinese have tried to colonize the Lolo. Witnessed cremation Houses. Chinese soldiers have married Lolo (pp. 307-28). Map, photos.

Bhruksasri, Wanat
1970 "Other points and guidelines for the solution of hill tribe problems," Journal of Sociology and Anthropology (Chiang Mai University) 3,2.

Akha, Lahu, Lisu: Cites contradictory ideas of Australian anthropologists on defense, development, and administration of Thai highlands. Notes that the solution to problems lies in the similarities between highlanders and Thai, also increased capabilitiy of Border Patrol Police, training of officials, and economic development.

Biet, Alexandre, and Marquis Edme Casimir de Croizier

1877 "Vocabulaire lyssou recueilli à Tsekou..." Société Académique Indochinoise, Mémoires 1: 22-41. (Reprint: 1879, St.-Quentin, Jules Moureau.)
    Lyssou pay tribute to the Chinese. Vocabulary.

Birnbaum, Norman
1970 Communist China's policy toward her minority nationalities: 1950-1965, doctoral dissertation, New York, St. John's University. (Dissertation Abstracts International 31,6: 2831-32A, University Microfilms order no. UM 70-25, 590.) 238 pp.

Bishop, Mrs. J. F. (Isabelle L. Bird)
1899 The Yangtze Valley and beyond, London, John Murray. 557 pp.
    Lolo bandits make the trade routes above Ping-chan insecure.

Blakiston, Thomas W.
1862 Five months on the Yang-tsze, London, John Murray 380 pp.
    Miau-tze (Huh-I, I-jin) sketch, with horns from Ta-lia-shan (pp. 271-72, 284). Maps.

Blanchard, Wendell: see Henderson 1971b.

Boell, Paul Victor
1899 Contribution à l'étude de la langue lolo, Paris, Ernest Leroux. 21 pp.
    Lolo: Linguistic material collected in 1892 from three dialects in Kiu-tsing-fou, Yunnan: A-hsi of Fong-hoang-chan village, Na-so-po met at I-liang-hsien, and Nyi of Lou-mei-i (Vial's village). Comparisons from Doudart de Lagrée, Baber, and Hosie. Two texts in Nyi-pa: A song and a geography.

Boh, Shwe
1967 "Nation-building in Far North," Forward 6,5: 12-17.

    Lisu trained at Central Frontier Areas Missionary Institute in Myitkyina. Morse, a missionary, induced some Lisu of Milashidi village near Putao to follow him into exile. They were later readmitted to Burma "shivering, hungry and helpless."

    See Bangkok Post 1973b; Morse 1962, 1974.

Boiteux, L.
1935 "Comment on frôle le martyre," Les Missions Catholiques 67,32З6: 624-28.

    Lolo: Visit. Photos.

Bonifacy, A. L. (See also Soulié and Tchang 1908.)
1905 "Etude sur les langues parlées par les populations de la Haute Rivière Claire," Ecole française d'Extrême-Orient, Bulletin 5: 306-27.

    Black Lolo of Bao-lac is compared to Tibetan, Burmese, Chin, and Kachin (by Huber) and shown to drop the final consonant (except nasals).

1906a "Les groupes ethniques du bassin de la Rivière Claire (Haut Tonkin et Chine Méridionale)," Société d'Anthropologie de Paris, Bulletin et Mémoires 5,7: 296-330.

    Lolo derives from "la," meaning people in many languages of Tonkin and South China. In the deluge and creation legends, bamboo plays an important part; it invited brother and sister to unite, protected their union with its shadow; newlyweds cannot cut bamboo; ancestor figures are placed on bamboo. Sky spirit is Mo nè, spirit who intercedes for man is Tchung nè. Fowl and pork are taboo for married women. Both husband and wife stay in house 15 days after a birth (pp. 321-22).

Five tribes: (1) Mung (Muong) near Bac Mè, speak and dress as Thô; similar to Lajonquière's Xapho, near Bao ha. (2) Black Lolo near Baolac. Men wear Thô costume. Grow wet and dry rice, but Meo encroaching on their land. Rebury bones of dead, using bamboo stick to determine end of odor; their neighbors maintain that the skulls of dead are kept in baskets in their houses. Physical type. Photos. (3) White Lolo at K'ai hoa fou are similar to Black, with whom they marry, but not subservient to them. Photo. (4) Pu-la at Hoang thu bi, near Xin man, are 12 families. More similar to Vial's Lolo. Photo. (5) Pu-la at Lang dan (north of Hà giang) are 2 families (pp. 300-25). Photo. La qua, called Pen-ti Lolo by Chinese and classed with Lolo by Devéria 1886 and Lunet de Lajonquière 1906 (but with Thai in his 1904), are not Lolo (p. 321).

1906b "Les populations montagnardes du Tonkin," Revue des Troupes Coloniales, série 2: 335-63, 431-59.

See his 1919.

1908 "Etude sur les coutumes et la langue des Lolos et des La-qua du Haut Tonkin," Ecole française d'Extrême Orient, Bulletin 8: 531-58.

Lolo located in Tu.o.ng.yên phu of Tuyên-quang Province: Mung, Black Lolo (including Man Khoanh, whose men have adopted Thai language and dress), White Lolo. La-qua are not Lolo, have Meo chief. For past 50 years, Meo have increasingly taken Lolo lands and assumed political dominance. Some Lolo villages have Thô priests; may conduct ordeal of putting hand in boiling oil in presence of Yao or Chinese priest. Pray to ancestors on 9th-10th day of 6th month. Different forms of ancestor tablets illustrated (p. 541). Village spirit sacrifices. Birth, marriage, and death customs; levirate, with exception that elder brother cannot marry younger brother's wife; bones reburied. Legend of brother and sister, survivors of a war, told by turtle and bamboo to marry; they have 3 sons and 3 daughters, who marry and have Man-zi, Mung and M'ti (Thai), from whom other tribes are born. 18 souls and 18 vital spirits. Houses on piles. Vocabularies.

1919   Cours d'ethnographie indochinoise, Professé aux élèves de l'Ecole Supérieure d'Agriculture et de Sylviculture, Hanoi-Haiphong, Imprimerie d'Extrême-Orient. 110 pp.

Lolo found in Third Military Territory, upper Black and Red rivers. Includes Houni, Pu-la (Xa-phô), Mosso, Kha reng, and other Kha and Kouy in Laos, Upper Cambodia, Siam, and the Shan States. Near Bac Mê are Mu-ng who refuse to admit it but speak a Lolo language. White better off than Black. They use stylized representations of human body as ancestor tablets, and three different types from less to more stylized may be distinguished (sketches).

1923   "Les habitants du Haut-Tonkin," L'Eveil Economique de l'Indochine No. 315-16.

See his 1919.

1924   "Conference sur les groupes ethniques du Haut Tonkin

au nord du fleuve Rouge," <u>Société</u> de <u>Géographie</u> de <u>Hanoi</u>,
<u>Cahiers 7:</u> 1-30. (Reprint: 1924, <u>Moniteur</u> d'<u>Indochine</u>,
<u>Nos. 298-300</u>, Nov. 1-15.)

        Lolo: Summary of his 1906 and 1908. Photos.

Bonin, Charles-Eudes

1899   "Lettre," <u>Société</u> de <u>Géographie</u>, <u>Compte Rendu 33-37</u>.

        Lolo: Crossing of Leang-shan. Map. See Cordier
1907: 77, Maitre and d'Ollone 1909.

1903   "Vocabulaires," <u>T'oung Pao, série 2,4:</u> 117-26.

        Mau-tse (Lolo) (pp. 124-26).

1907   "Lettre," <u>La Géographie 16,4:</u> 270-71.

        Lolo: Itinerary of 1898 crossing of Leang-shan.
See Cordier 1907: 78, Maitre and d'Ollone 1909.

1911   <u>Les royaumes des neiges</u> (<u>Etats himalayens</u>), Paris,
Librairie Armand Colin. 306 pp.

        Mosso: Translation and discussion of Mosso
manuscript from Li-kiang-fou; Marco Polo calls them
Mosso-man. In Sung, they descended from Tibet to Likiang,
where they were conquered by Nan-chao and by Mongols
(1255). In 1277, they joined the army of Mongol Nasser-
ed-din (along with Lolo and Pa-y) against the Burmese.
Chinese kept Mosso king in mandarinate. Mosso train as
lamas in Lhasa.

Bons d'Anty, Pierre

1904a   "Explorations dans le Seu-Tch'ouan par M. Bons d'Anty,"
<u>La Géographie 10,5:</u> 317-20.

        Lolo: Chinese have begun to come into Lolo country.

1904b   "Le sud du Yun-nan," <u>Guides Madrolle: Chine du Nord:</u>
pp. 85-104. (Reprint: n.d., Paris, <u>Comité de l'Asie</u>

française.)

T'a-lang-t'ing inhabited by Po-wo-mi (call themselves Pi-yo). Map showing general ethnic locations and routes of explorers.

Boon Chuey Srivasdi: see Srisawat, Bunchuai.

Bcon-Itt, Kultida

196-[?] Bibliography on the Lahu (Muzer), Bangkok, Battelle Memorial Institute, Thailand Information Center. 50 pp.

Lahu: About 90 entries.

Boucher, André

1935 "Mgr. de Guébriant, apôtre du clergé indigène," Les Missions Catholiques 67,3222: 178-82.

Lolo: Missionary among Lolo. Photo.

Bourne, Frederick Samuel Augustus

1888 China, No. 1, Report by Mr. F. S. A. Bourne of a journey in south-western China, London, His Majesty's Stationery Office. 92 pp.

Lolo: Finds Lolo in Kweichow cut up by Chinese Moslems. Lolo chief smokes opium. Bought Lolo manuscript. Vocabularies from Ta-Chê-ping, T'ang-t'ang, and Ma-hê Lolo. See Cordier 1907: 65-70; Nature 1888.

Boutmy

1889 "Mes premieres impressions dans le Yun-nan," Les Missions Catholiques 21,1055: 406-08; 1057: 430-31; 1058: 441-44; 1059: 453-56; 1060: 464-67; 1061: 478-79; 1062: 486-88; 1063: 505-06; 1064: 511-14; 1066: 540-41; 1068: 561-64.

Lolo religion. Oldest son of deceased takes a handful of grass from near the tomb to make a figurine (1060: 465-66).

Bradshaw, Angela
1952 World costumes, London, Adam and Charles Black. 101 pp.
Lahu and Lihsaw costumes (pp. 43-44).

Brandt, John H.
1965 Recommendations on a hill tribe health program, Bangkok, Memorandum to United States Operations Mission, Public Health Division. 6 pp.
Akha, Lahu, Lisu: USOM health activities, including nikhom (reservations) at Chiangdao, Mae Chan, and Tak, and at eastern Chiangrai and northern Nan in Thailand.

Bridgman, E. C.
1859 "Sketches of the Miau-tze," North China Branch of the Royal Asiatic Society, Journal 3: 257-86.
Translation of selections from a Chinese work (cf. Clarke in Colquhoun 1883, Cordier 1907: 4-6). Ko-lo (originally Lou-lou) in Ta-ting prefecture includes Black and White divided into 48 clans with chiefs of 9 ranks; women governors; A-ho of Pau-ting may be related to Pe (White) Ko-lo.

Brooke, J. W.: see Maitre and d'Ollone 1909; Meares 1909a, 1909b; Starr 1911.

Broomhall, A. J.
1947 Strong tower, London, China Inland Mission. 255 pp.
Nosu: Medical missionary in Ta Liang Shan, 1947-51. Chinese use mortars and planes against Nosu (pp. 18-

19). Chinese fear Nosu raids; soldiers stationed among them trade in opium; Nosu bandits (pp. 31, 36-37). The nearer to the Nosu, the less cared for were Chinese fields, though it had been 10 years since the last raid (p. 46). Stories of American pilots held as Nosu slaves probably refer to northern Chinese deserters (p. 75). Lepers are killed by Nosu (pp. 50-51, 75). Use of hen's lower jaw for divination (p. 77). Attack on Chinese post harboring escaped slaves, clan feuds, Chinese held for ransom, (pp. 116-17, 143-45). Nationalist guerrillas operate from Chaokioh, March-May 1950; dispute over tolls with Nosu (pp. 217-28). Map photos.

Broomhall, Marshall

1907 The Chinese Empire, A general and missionary survey, London, Morgan & Scott. 472 pp.

Lolo in northeastern Yunnan, by John M'Carthy (pp. 244-45) and northwestern Kweichow, by Samuel R. Clarke (pp. 251-52).

1917 "Some tribes of south-west China," International Review of Missions 6,22: 267-81.

Lolo includes Lisu, Laka, Kang-i (Kopu), Bapu. Nosu fled to Taliangshan before Manchus in 1727. Now Chinese must pay 75-150 taels to collect wax insects there. C. G. Gowman notes the similarity of Lisu demon rites and those in Leviticus XVI: 2 goats are 2 Lisu chickens, idea of blood pervades. Flowery Lisu near Tengyueh are being missionized. Caste hierarchy of Nosu; they worship Mü-p'ü-mö (spirit of heaven) and le-su (lord of life and happiness). Pollard invented script for Nosu.

Brown, John Coggin (See also Rose and Brown)
1910 "A Lisu Jew's harp from Yunnan," Asiatic Society of Bengal, Journal, n.s. 6: 589-92.

Hwa Lisu of Ku-yung-kai, Yunnan. Jew's harp previously noted by Orléans (1898).

Bruk, Solomon Il'ich
1958 "Distribution of national minorities in the People's Republic of China," Sovetskaia Ethnografiia 1. (Reprinted in English: Stephen P. Dunn and Ethel Dunn, eds., Introduction to Soviet Ethnography, Berkeley, Highgate Road Social Science Research Station, 2: 629-54.)

I-tsu include Hang-i (Woni), Li-su, Na-hsi (Moso), La-hu (Lo-hei), Pai (Buddhists), A-ch'ang, T'u-chia. A group of T'u-chia has recently been located in Hunan. Maps.

1959a Naselenie Indokitaia: Poyasnitel'naia zapiska k karte narodov, Moskva, Institut Etnografii imeni N. N. Mikluho-Maklaia, Akademii Nauk SSSR.

Ethnographic map and booklet on Indochina.

1959b Naselenie Kitaia, MNR i Korei: Poyasnitel'naia zapiska k kartė narodov, Moskva, Institut Etnografii imeni N.N. Mikluho-Maklaia, Akademii Nauk SSSR. (English translation 1960, Peoples of China, Mongolian People's Republic, and Korea, Washington, U.S. Joint Publications Research Service, No. 1710.)

1953 census of minority populations. Yi subdivisions include Nosu, Ache, Asi, Sani, Laloba, Menhua, and Yulo. Yi group includes Hani, Lisu, Nasi, Lahu,

Pai, Achang, Tuchia (of Hunan); Dulung have much in common with Lisu. Subdivisions and locations of each of these minorities. Ethnographic map.

Bruk, Solomon Il'ich, and V. S. Apenchenko, eds.
1964   Atlas narodov mira, Moskva, Institut Etnografii imeni N. N. Mikluho-Maklaia, Akademii Nauk SSSR.

Ethnographic atlas. Map omits the Lisu of Thailand and Kengtung. The large concentration of Lisu east of 96° E probably consists of Kachin and Kachinized Lisu. Greatly underestimates the number of Lisu in Thailand.

Brun, Viggo
1973   "An English-Akha vocabulary," Acta Orientalia 35: 139-59.

Akha of Saen Caj, Mae Chan district, Thailand. Contains 414 entries, including Swadesh's 200-word list.

Brunhuber, Robert
1912   An Hinterindiens Reisenstromen, Berlin-Friedenau, Franz Ledermann. 120 pp.

Liessou, or Lissu, are located along Salween River from Dagatse (25°18'N) to 27°N, north of which are Lutzu. Location and size of settlements. Brunhuber and Schmitz left Bhamo and Tengyueh in 1908, and were murdered at about 27°20'N, near the Salween, on January 5, 1909. Map, photos.

Buchanan, Keith
1970   The transformation of the Chinese earth, New York and Washington, Praeger Publishers; London, G. Bell & Sons, Ltd. 336 pp.

Yi: 1958 visit to Yi Commune in Yunnan, general description of agriculture, industry, health, and schooling (p. 168).

Bunchuai Sisawat: see Srisawat.

Bunnâag, Suraphong

1963 Chaaw khǎw (Hill peoples), Bangkok, Sǎmnákphim Kâaw Nâa. 253 pp.

  Lisu: Visit to Doi Laan, Mae Suaj district in Chiangrai Province. Descriptions of dress, names (which Bunnâag believes sound Japanese), origin, distribution, housing, spirits, New Year, courting. He notes that they often live in same villages as Lahu, and that Lisu women work harder than men (pp. 77-111).

  Lahu: Visits to Doi Jo Lo and Doi Paa Khaa, Fang district in Chiang Mai Province. Descriptions of dress, names, courting, marriage, New Year. Like the Akha, they seldom bathe, due to fear of water spirit (pp. 183-208).

  Akha: Visit to Seen Jai, Mae Chan district in Chiangrai Province. Dress, food, courting, marriage, dances, New Year, spirits. Women work harder than men. Spirit gate. Trade with Ho Chinese (pp. 15-46). Numerous photos.

Burling, Robbins

1966 "A problem in the phonology of Lahu," in Ba Shin, Jean Boisselier, and A. B. Griswold, eds., Essays Offered to G. H. Luce by His Colleagues and Friends on His Seventy-Fifth Birthday, Ascona, Artibus Asiae.

1967 "Proto Lolo-Burmese," International Journal of American Linguistics 33, no. 2, pt. 2, Indiana University, Research Center in Anthropology, Folklore, and

Linguistics, Publication 43.

    Proto-Loloish (Lisu, Lahu, Akha) and Proto-Burmish (Burmese, Atsi, Maru) derived from Proto-Lolo-Burmese. Lisu phonology apparently based mostly on Fraser (1922) (here sometimes misspelled Frazier). Read together with the review of James A. Matisoff, Language 44: 879-97 (1968).

Carey, Fred W.
1899   "A trip to the Chinese Shan States," Geographical Journal 14,4: 378-94.

    Akka are a Shan people who have lost their original language.

    Lolo (Tsuan-man) fast mixing with Chinese, to whom they pay taxes. Rent land from Shan. Trade and trade routes. Superior branch includes Pu la of Mengtse and A Mi-chu, Tu la of Kai Hua, Ta T'ou of Sumao, Lo Hei of Chen Pien. Inferior branch includes Pu Tu, Woni, and Kato (all three between Mekong and Red rivers) and Ma Hei of Pu Erh and Sumao.

Carrapiett, William James Sherlock
1929   The Kachin tribes of Burma, Rangoon, Superintendent, Government Printing and Stationery, Burma. viii, 119 pp.

    Lisu child-brides (p. 36). Atzi in Yunnan levy 3 squirrels per year per Lisu household for use as nat offering (p. 70).

Carriquiry, Ph.
1939   "Dans les montagnes du Kientchang," Les Missions Catholiques 71,3305: 65-66.

    Lolo missionary visit.

Central Census Steering Committee, Democratic Republic of Vietnam
1960   "Official government report on 1960 census in North Vietnam," Nhan Dan 2419: 3 (Nov. 2). (English translation: Joint Publications Research Service, No. 6570, 7 pp., Jan. 13, 1961.)

Lolo number 6,898 (3,331 males, 3,567 females), 0.04% of population. Xa (a Yi subgroup) 22,500 (11,121 and 11,379), 0.15%. Uni (Woni) 5,259 and 2,690), 0.03%.

Chaffee, Frederic: see Whitaker and Shinn et al. 1972.

Chang, Chi-jen (Pinyin: Zhang, Ji-ren)
1956   The minority groups of Yunnan and Chinese political expansion into Southeast Asia, doctoral dissertation, University of Michigan. (Dissertation Abstracts 17,6: 1308, University Microfilms order no. 21, 160.) 199 pp.

Three phases of Han expansion: cultural colonization or sinicization, Communist political conquest, implementation of regional autonomy. Table shows number of conflicts between Han and minorities (p. 4). Tibetans of Chiang group migrated east and mixed with aborigines (P'u), creating Wuman (Lolo), which itself gave birth to Lisu, Moso, Lutzu, etc. Central lake area of Yunnan: Lolo, Minchia, Nu-tzu, Lisu, Moso, etc. (pp. 39-40, 48-50). Vertical distribution of tribes. Maps of Akha, Lahu, Wo-ni, Nutzu, Moso, and Liso from Tao Yun Kwai. Lists of minorities, autonomous regions, populations, and maps (from Wiens 1954, Handbook of Current Events 1955, and other sources). Centralizing forces: assimilating to Han majority, Communist Party, structure and policies of government, mass organizations and movements, interlocking leadership, economic development, cultural institutions, military (this section based on Hinton 1955). This dissertation is based wholly on published and secondary materials; large portions are summaries of published data; lacks details or critical approach.

Chang, Jen-kai (Pinyin: Zhang, Ren-gai)
1952   "The minority races of South Szechuen," China Monthly Review 122,4: 361-64.

I: 300,000 I have representatives in governments of Obien, Mabien, and Leipo hsien. There are 400 I enrolled in 8 primary schools; 7,000 treated medically. Branches of State Trading Company and People's Bank. Conference of 13 tribes guaranteed to plant rice instead of opium. Addicts treated. Mutual aid teams organized.

Cháng, Lúng-chìng, Shī Huaí-rén, and Yú Dé-jùn
1935   "Sì chūan shěng léi mǎ e píng diao chá jì (A record of the investigation of the Lei-po, Ma-pien, O-pien, and Ping-shan districts of Szechuan)," Zhōng gúo xī bù kē xúe yuàn tè bíe dì yí hào (West China Union University Bulletin), Special Issue Number 1.

Chang, Sen (Pinyin: Zhang, Sen)
1959   "China's national minority areas prosper," Peking Review 26,21: 8-11.

Lisu established agricultural cooperatives in 1956, communes in 1958. They had 14 factories and mines in 1956, 612 in 1958.

Yi slaves freed 1957. Grain yield in Liangshan was 70 jin per mou before Liberation, 300 in 1958. By 1958, 8 middle schools with 2,566 students, 595 primary schools with 46,583 pupils, 65 hospitals and health centers.

Chao, Wei-pang (Pinyin: Zhao, Wei-bang)

1950 "A Lolo legend concerning the origin of the torch festival," <u>Studia Serica</u> 9,2: 95-104.

   Lolo legend says the festival held on the 24th day of the 6th moon is held to offer sacrifice as payment to heaven for the life of its rent-collector killed by Lolo. But it is primarily a buckwheat harvest festival. Also observed by P'o-jen, K'u-ts'ung (who observe it as New Year's), Chuang and Yao of Kwangsi, Chinese in Yunnan and southeastern Sikang, etc.

Chao, Y.-r. (Pinyin: Zhao, Y.-r.)

1943 "Languages and dialects in China," <u>Geographical Journal 102</u>: 63-71.

   Lolo-Moso group includes Lolo (and Lisu) and Moso (and Lahu and Nashi).

Chariwan, Suthep

1970 "Hill tribesmen and modern civilization," <u>Bangkok World</u>, July.

   Akha, Lahu, and Lisu population, difficulties of government administration because of nomadic habits, limited contacts with lowlands, limited knowledge of tribesmen about Thailand and its government. Visits of tribesmen to Bangkok.

Charria, Sylvain

1905 "Les inscriptions lolo de Lou-k'iuan," <u>Ecole française d'Extrême-Orient, Bulletin</u> 5: 195-97.

   Lolo: This inscription mentioned in <u>Siu yun nan t'ong tche kao</u>. Photo does not include Chinese inscription next to it. Inhabitants say it dates from reign of Hong-wou (1368-98). There is a second (possibly more) inscription nearby. See Chavannes 1906.

Charusathira, Prapas
1965 "Thailand's hill tribes," United Asia 17: 388-93. (Reprinted in Thai and English, 1966, Bangkok, Ministry of Interior, Department of Public Welfare, Hill Tribe Welfare Commission.)

Akha, Lahu, Lisu: Border Patrol Police has run schools for highlanders since 1960. Hill Tribe Division of Department of Public Welfare has four nikhom (land settlement projects) to develop permanency, improve livestock, marketing, health, education, tea planting (Lahu), wheat (Akha). Development and Welfare Centers with mobile teams. BPP courses for headmen. Problems: opium, granting of citizenship, land rights and obligations.

Chaturaphun, Preecha (also spelled Chaturaphand)
1970 "Introducing the dog-eaters," Standard Bangkok Magazine, May 3: 8-10, 22.

Akha: General description, Mae Chan nikhom, emphasizing different customs, such as dog-eating. Photos.

1971a "Into the domain of the kings of the dried chilis," Standard Bangkok Magazine, Feb. 21: 8-11, 23.

Lahu: General description. Photos.

1971b "Lisu- One big happy family including the horse," Standard Bangkok Magazine, Mar. 28: 12-15,23.

Lisu: General description. Photos.

Chauveau
1873 "Yun-nan (Chine). La prise de Ta-ly," Les Missions Catholiques 5,232: 542-45.

> Lyssou villages extend 10-12 days south of Tsekou. Six moukoua (chiefs) named. Ferocious brigands, who in the last few years have cultivated opium, mined gold, and so trade at Ouy-si. Chinese criminals find refuge among them.

Chavannes, Edouard
1906 "Trois inscriptions relevées par M. Sylvain Charria," T'oung Pao série 2,7: 671-701.

> Lolo: Chinese text found on the same rock as Lolo text copied by Charria (1905). Chinese inscription is dated 1533, therefore Lolo must be 1527-33. It gives the genealogy of Fong Tchao, a Lolo chief loyal to the Chinese, back to 1174. Translation of section of Ming history dealing with Wou-ting (Min che 314). Map from Tien hi, by Che Fan (1817), locates some of the localities mentioned.

1909a "Quatre inscriptions du Yun-nan (Mission du Commandant d'Ollone)," Journal Asiatique, série 10, 14,1: 5-46.

> Lolo: Chinese texts and French translations of inscriptions found at: (1) Lou-leang tcheou (458 A.D.) and (2) K'iu-tsing fou (405), both funerary inscriptions of Ts'ouan (Lolo) chiefs subject to Chinese; (3) Tchao-t'ong fou (25 B.C.?), funerary inscription of Mong Siuan; (4) K'iu-tsing fou (971) showing that Lolo had attempted to throw off Chinese domination. See 1909b, below. and Farjenel 1910.

1909b "Note additionnelle sur l'inscription de Che-tch'eng (971 p.C.),"Journal Asiatique, série 10,14,3: 511-14.

    Lolo: A corrected translation of the fourth inscription in his 1909a; the upper part of the inscription is read left to right, the lower right to left. See Farjenel 1910.

1912 "Documents historiques et géographiques relatifs à Li-kiang," T'oung Pao, série 2,13: 565.

    A chronicle of the aboriginal chiefs of Li-Kiang. Lolo chiefs adopted "Ts'ouan" as family names.

Chazarain-Wetzel, Paul

1910 "Les populations autochtones du Yunnan," A Travers le Monde, n.s. 16,19: 145-48.

    Lolo always at war. Taoists. Lin-ngan-jen have flowing pants, vests with buttons, and red turbans, and they chew betel.

    Tchong-kia (T'ou-jen, "men of the earth," or Lao-pan-kia, "habitants of the country") call themselves Pou-Dieï.

    Lissou are hunters.

    Houni, Min-chia, Mosso mentioned. Photos.

Che Fan: see Soulié and Tchang 1908.

Chen, Ding (or Ting) (transliterated Tch'en in French)

1905 "Le mariage chez une tribu aborigène du sud-est du Yunnan, d'après une relation de Tch'en Ting- traduite et annotée par T'ang Tsai-fou," T'oung Pao, série 2,6: 572-622.

    First-hand account of a Chinese (ca. 1651-) married to an aboriginal girl (possible Ho-ni) in 1667.

1934 "Account of the marriage customs of the chiefs of
Yunnan and Kweichow," American Anthropologist 36: 524-47.
A new translation by John K. Shryock of 1905, above.

Chen, Yin
1964 "La-hu zú (Lahu race)," Mínzú Túanjíe no. 4: 46-48.
Lahu: 170,000 Black, Yellow, and White Lahu in Sse
Mao and Lan Ts'ang, including Lan Ts'ang Lahu Autonomous
Xian and Mung Lien Thai-Lahu-Wa Autonomous Xian
established in 1953-54. Originally Chiang from Ching
Hai, they settled in Ehr-Hai (Yunnan) in the third to
fifth centuries A.D. After the tenth century, Lahu and
Lahu Hpu (White) moved south to Kengtung and east to Sse
Mao, while Lahu Na (Black) entered Lan Ts'ang and Shuang
Chiang. Constant uprisings against oppression by higher
classes (i.e. Han), including the eleven-year-long
rebellions at Shuang Chiang and Lan Ts'ang. Before the
liberation their development varied: some were exploited
by landlords through labor contributions and loans; in
southwest Lan Ts'ang they were under Tai headmen, and a
primitive class system prevailed. After Liberation,
depending on local conditions, peaceful negotiation or
direct transition was carried out; agricultural techniques improved, irrigation, small industry, electrifica-
tion, state trading agencies, better communications, educational and medical advances. Lan Ts'ang Xian had a
10% population increase 1949-59; its capital Meng Lang
Pa has 10,000 inhabitants.

Chen, Zhang-feng (or Chang-feng)
1972 On the long march with Chairman Mao, Peking, Foreign
Languages Press. (First edition, 1959.) 124 pp.

Yi welcomed Mao, despite their reputation for hating the Chinese, because they recognized that he was different (pp. 50-55). Map, drawing. See Wilson 1971.

Chén, Zōng-xiáng (or Tsūng-hsiáng)

1947 "The dual system and the clans of the Li-su and Shui-t'ien tribes," <u>Monumenta Serica</u> <u>12</u>: 252-59.

    Lisu of Szechuan divide patrilineal surname groups into She-tsu (twelve clans named after rats) and Mai-tsu (ten clans named after animals or plants), who cannot use the Chiang-tzu tree and the Yang-chiao tree, respectively, in accordance with a deluge legend. (This dual organization has not been reported or confirmed by others.)

1947-48 "Xī kāng lì-sù sǔi tiān míng zú zhī tǔ téng zhī dù (The tu-teng system of the Lisu of lowland Sikang)," <u>Bian-zhèng gōng-lùn</u> (Frontier Affairs) <u>6</u>,<u>4</u>, and <u>7</u>.<u>1</u>.

1948a "Liáng-shān lǔo zú xì pǔ bǔ (The genealogy of the Liang-shan Lolo)," <u>Bian-zhèng gōng-lùn</u> (Frontier Affairs), <u>7</u>,<u>2</u>.

    See Dīng 1936, Dǒng 1940, Fang 1945a and 1945b, Lo 1944a, 1944b, 1945a and 1945c, Ma 1942-44 and 1946, Shiratori 1957.

1948b "Lǔo-ló de zōng jìao (The religion of the Lolo)," <u>Bian-zhèng gōng-lùn</u> (Frontier Affairs) <u>7</u>,<u>2</u>.

Chêng, Chǎo-lúñ: see Zēng Zhāo-lún.

Chêng, Tê-k'un, and Liang Ch'ao-t'ao (Pinyin: Zhêng, Dê-kun, and Liang, Chao-tao)

1945 <u>An introduction to the southwestern peoples of China</u>, Chengtu, West China Union University Museum Guidebook,

Series no. 7. 16 pp.

Lolo during Chou known as Lu, and, according to the Shu-ching, helped Emperor Wu-wang against the Shangs. Chinese call them Yi-chia or Man-chia; they call themselves No Su, I-jia, or Hei-ku-t'ou; along the Red River, they are known as Wo-li; along the Salween, Li-so; between the Salween and the Mekong, Lo-hei; in south Yunnan, A-k'a. They use armor of untanned leather. Map.

Chevalier, Stanislas

1899   Le Haut Yang-tse de I-ichang fou à P'ing-chan hien en 1897-98, Voyage et description, Shanghai, Imprimerie de la Presse Orientale. 97 + 91 pp.

Lolo: Several Lolo hostages kept at P'ing-chan (p. 87). See Cordier 1907: 26-27.

Chiang, Yung: see Jiang, Yong.

Chieri, Virgilio

1943   "I Lolo Neri del Se-ciuan (Cina)," Reale Società Geografica Italiana, Bollettino, serie 7,8, no. 6: (80): 350-55.

Lolo, Black and White location, clans, and classes, tombs, marriage. Short trip near Opien.

China at War

1941   "The Lolos of Sikang," China at War 7,5: 11-23.

Lolo in southern Sikang outnumber Chinese 1,500,000 to 800,000. Policy of assimilation through political influence, education, and, as last resort, military force. About 100 have been sent to Central Military Academy at Chengtu. Lolo depend on Chinese for salt, cloth, and wine. General Teng Hsiu-ting suppressed Lolo uprisings for 20 years, when Lolo broke into Yuehsi, Mienning, and Sichang to free Lolo hostages. He uses old feuds and caste hatreds to divide and conquer, along with one Lolo and two Chinese regiments. Major Lin Kwang-tien, a Lolo, commanded several thousand Lolo who worked on Loshan-Sichang highway. He hopes to raise 100,000 Lolo soldiers for Nationalists and to help Lolo "catch up" with Chinese (Cf. Sun 1942).

China Journal

1931   "A Lolo charm," China Journal 14,2: 56.

A fossil seashell with dot design including 8 triangles (equivalent of 8 trigrams); a little in water is used as medicine. Drawing.

China News Agency

1943   "School for Yunnan aborigines," China at War 10,1: 47.

Kachin, Lisu, Lolo, Mosu, Lutze, Nama, Payi, and Chinese included among 200 normal school and 100 middle school pupils at Tali.

China Pictorial

1963   "Training national minority doctors," China Pictorial 7: 14-15.

Lisu in Kunming Medical College.

China Reconstructs

1953   "The Yis of Taliangshan," China Reconstructs 2,2: 37-39.

Yi pushed into mountains perhaps as early as Han times. Of 3.4 million Yi, 700,000 live in Taliangshan. 270 chiefs were called together to sign pact of unity. In Oct. 1952, 328 representatives elected a government

	council of 27 Yi, 8 Han, 1 Miao. Progress in agriculture literacy, education, medicine. Chaochueh, the capital, has a 700-seat auditorium, a bank, and a store; the daily market accomodates 1,000 buyers and sellers. A model peasant claims that before liberation he harvested 900 lbs. of grain a year, by 1951 2000 lbs., and his son earned money in town hauling stones. Photo of Wachamuchi, chairman, Yi Autonomous Government. Photos.
1960	"Communism will come flying to us," China Reconstructs 9, 12, Supplement: 36.
	Lisu: A modern song.
1969	Photograph, China Reconstructs 18, 11: cover.
	Lisu: Shows Lisu studying Mao's work.
1973	"Ex-slaves hold the gun," China Reconstructs 22, 6: 30-32.
	Yi People's Regiment of People's Liberation Army formed, 1956. Photos.
1975	"Motor highways for impossible mountains and valleys," China Reconstructs 24, 9: 44-45.
	Lisu, Nu, Tulung, and Yi of Nukiang Autonomous Chou have built a road from Pikiang to Fukung and Kungshan. All five counties of the chou are now connected by roads, and 63% of the communes can be reached by truck. Grain output in 1973 was double that of 1953, and industrial production rose fivefold (mostly since 1965). Local products include lacquer, animal skins, rhizoma coptis, and fritillaria verticillata (medicinal herbs). Photos.

Chou, Tse-yu (Pinyin: Zhou, Ze-you)

1963	"The Lisu people along the Nuchiang River," China Pictorial 5: 32-34.
	Lisu paid one or two antlers for a handful of salt

-72-

before the Liberation. Now, marketing cooperatives supply each town, and Pichiang, capital of the Nuchiang Lisu Autonomous Chou, has a hospital and secondary school staffed by Lisu. Photos.

Chung-kuo ch'ing-nien pao: see Zhong-guo Qing-nian-bao.

Chung-kuo tso chia hsieh hui: see Zhong-guo zuo jia xie hui.

Clarke, George W.: see Colquhoun 1883.

Clarke, Hyde

1882 "Lolo and Vei characters," Athenaeum 2: 370.
See 1883, below.

1883 "The Lolo character of western China. Abstract of a paper read Aug. 28, 1882," Report of the Fifty-second Meeting of the British Association for the Advancement of Science, London, John Murray: 607-08.

Lolo: Similarities between Baber's Lolo manuscript and Vy (of West Africa), with combinations like the Khita (Hittite, which resembles Moso manuscript of Gill) pointing to a common ancestry. See Terrien de Lacouperie 1882a. (Read for humor only.)

Clarke, Samuel R.

1911 Among the tribes in South-west China, London, China Inland Mission. (Reprint: 1970, Taipei, Ch'eng Wen Publishing Company.) (HRAF AE5-7) 315 pp.

Lo-lo or Nosu entered Kweichow from Tibet. In Chinese, "lo-lo" refers to the hamper which contains the spirit of deceased Lolo (photo). Also called by Chinese "I-chia" and "I-pien," where "I" means remote, foreign, and "pien" means boundary. Black landholders, White tenants (called Black- "bones" in Szechwan but not in

Kweichow). Often outnumbered by Miao tenants. Ancestors were two brothers, Wu-sa and Wu-meng, who struggled in the womb, hence their fondness for fighting. Coming to Chaotung Plain, they found the P'u (Yao-ren), who have left behind mounds with unhewn stones and burnt bricks. Branches of Lo-lo include Hsi-fan (north Yunnan); Li-su, Laka, and Kang-I (all north of Wuting); perhaps Man-tsi. In Chantung and Weining districts, Lairds have built up sizable estates by conquest or claims on land of extinct families. Land disputes frequent. Decadence: whiskey, opium, dirt. Brought under Chinese rule during Manchu, the lairds pay taxes and are continuously bringing disputes to courts. Lairds have Chinese and Miao concubines. Tenants pay nominal rents but also contribute to lairds' funerals, weddings, litigations, wars, and feuds, and also labor on lairds' land. Live on maize, buckwheat, oatmeal, never milk. Mud hovels with straw thatch. Each family has pony, 2-3 cows, few pigs, dozen sheep and goats, some fowl. Use aconite as arrow poison. Lairds have Chinese teachers and compete in civil examinations. After buckwheat harvest, thanks is given to Je-so-mo. Ancestor and hill worship: exorcist determines propitious day in the fourth month each year, an altar of rock and tree trunk is erected and a ceremony performed to keep evil spirits away. Creation. Flood story: man and three sons (Nosu, Han, Miao) saved in wood cupboard. Miao used straw boundary markers, Nosu stone; when fire came, Miao lost their land. Arranged marriage; bride capture. Bride does not revisit her parents for several years but then may stay 2-3 years. Diseases caused by demons. At death, a pig or sheep is sacrificed in doorway to maintain intercourse with spirit. Close relatives bring a strangled fowl, distant relatives have a sheep struck by a son of the deceased. Formerly cremated (Independent Lolo still do), now buried (pp. 112-36). Vocabularies: Nosu (pp. 307-12); Chaotung and Weining Nosu by Hicks; Laka, Kangi, and Wutingchow Lisu by Nicholls (pp. 314-15). Photos. See Hicks 1910.

Review: J. W. W., 1912, <u>North China Branch of the Royal Asiatic Society, Journal</u> 43: 94-95.

Cochrane, Wilbur Willis

1915   <u>The Shans</u>, Vol. 1, Rangoon, Superintendent, Government Printing, Burma.

       Lahu use gourd organ (p. 26).

       Akha and Lahu frequent Kengtung bazaar and speak Shan (p. 93).

Collis, Maurice Stewart

1938   <u>Lords of the sunset: A tour in the Shan States</u>, New York, Dodd, Mead (London, Faber and Faber).

       Lishaw in Tawng Peng (Loi Lung) state. Lishaw and other hill tribes will become Burmese; a Lishaw expresses desire for bicycle (pp. 322-23). Photo (facing p. 321).

Colquhoun, Archibald Ross

1883   <u>Across Chrysê, Being the narrative of a journey of exploration through the South China border lands from Canton to Mandalay</u>, 2 vols., London, Sampson Low, Marston, Searle and Rivington. (French translation by Charles Simond, 1884, <u>Autour du Tonkin, La Chine méridionale de Canton à Mandalay</u>, 2 vols., Paris et Poitiers, H. Oudin.) 420 + 408 pp.

Lolo: Translation of manuscript on Miao-tsen by George W. Clarke (c. 1730) (cf. Bridgman 1859, Cordier 1907: 7-8, Playfair 1876). Lolo wear hair in hornshape. Their habitat called "The Devil's Net." in 221 A.D., a Lolo named Chi-ho helped Marquis Wu defeat Mong-hwo and conquer Yunnan, for which he was made Prince of Lo-tien-kwoh (near Ta-ting-fu), which is now divided in 48 sections, each with a chief, and 9 head chiefs who live at Ta-ting-fu. If a chief dies, first wife may assume chieftaincy until a son is of age (2: 300-02). Colquhoun did not find the Lolo "horn" nor felt cloak, and White (Pei, Pe) were superior to Black (Hei, He). Hwa Lolo are probably a subdivision of White. "Man-tzu" probably refers to Lolo, but is loosely used (2: 302-03). Chinese are contemptful and coercive toward the Lolo, corrupting them with customs such as foot-binding. Near Meng-hua, White Lolo women are married to Chinese and very Chinese in appearance (1: 228, 341; 2: 168, 297). Lolo raid and kidnap Chinese. They cultivate opium but do not smoke it (2: 298, 307-08).

Li-ssu (Lissou, Le-su, Lo-su, Ngo-su) "are the wildest of the hill-people of Western Yunnan." They are of the same stock as the Lolo, and their language is close to Burmese. They hunt musk-deer with dogs and hunt vultures with decoys (2: 309-10). Lissu, Lolo, Hwa Lolo, Hei Woni, Po Woni: sketches.

1884 "On the aboriginal and other tribes of Yunnan and the Shan country," Anthropological Institute of Great Britain and Ireland, Journal 13,1: 3-4.

Li-ssu, Lolo, Si-fan, and Burmese languages similar. See also 1883.

1885   Amongst the Shans, London, Field & Tuer. New York, Scribner & Welford. 392 pp.

Lolo women have high status. In the third century, Lolo had prominent political dominion in eastern Setchuen and Kweitchou.

Cook, T.
1936   "The Independent Lolo of South-west Szechwan," West China Border Research Society, Journal 8: 70-81.

Lolo: Called Man Chia or I Chia by Chinese, call themselves Hei or Pai Ku T'ou (Black or White Bones). Black Bones are lairds. White Bones are Chinese subjects or serfs of the Black (three degrees of serfdom). Giles thinks their writing is of Chinese origin, some 2,000 years old. Lolo mentioned by Chou Kung in 1122 B.C. White Bones only go back to Ming, when General Cheng Ke Ching was exiled in 1368 to Yuehsi (ancient Szechwan), where his descendants still rule. New Year, foods, dress, marriage, divorce. Cremate dead, remains are covered with stone and brush and not revisited. Branches kept as idol in house. In September 1926, Black Bones attacked frontier. Photo of letter calling for rebellion. Chinese and White Bones drove them back and peace pledges were made over a sacrificed ox, whose hide is saved as a token.

Coolidge, Harold Jefferson, and Theodore Roosevelt
1933   Three kingdoms of Indo-China, New York, Thomas Y. Crowell Company. 331 pp.

Lolo number 10,000-20,000 in Laos and Tonkin. They have assimilated to the Thai (pp. 303-05, 320).

Kako (Akha?) women wear cloth caps with long silver earrings, near Paka village on the Chinese border (p. 125). Sketch.

Cooper, Thomas Thornville
1871   Travels of a pioneer of commerce in pigtail and petticoats, London, John Murray. (Reprint: 1967, New York, Arno Press.) 475 pp.

Leisu north of Weisi are Chinese Buddhists, have Chinese schools, and include some recent Christian converts. Some are subordinated to Mooquor and Ya-tsu chiefs. Near Weisi, Cooper saw many burnt houses due to rebellion, and was attacked by dogs and the Leisu.

Lu-tsu occupy a fifty-mile strip between the Lan-tsan and Nou-kiang rivers. They raise no crops, but depend on hunting and predation on neighbors. They pay no tribute to Chinese (pp. 310-11).

Moso are fast losing their identity and becoming merged with Ya-tsu, whose chief governs them. They use Chinese language. Dress (pp. 312-13).

Ya-tsu look Chinese, grow opium.

Cordier, G.
1915-16   "Le Yunnan," Revue Indochinoise, n.s. 24,11-12: 403-36; 25,1-2: 99-134; 25,5-6: 371-98. (Reprint: 1928, La province du Yunnan, Hanoi, Le-Van-Tan. 573 pp.)

Lolo (Ts'ouan): 21 divisions, locations listed (pp. 375-76). Li-so and Kou-tsong included under Tibetan. Lolo of Black River use chicken femurs for divination. Pai Lolo may live to 180, by which time they are abandoned. Liso will eat earth mixed with honey when hungry (pp.

378-83). Marriage and death customs. Dress. Wo-ni mentioned.

Cordier, Henri
1907 "Les Lolos 打猓 打猓. Etat actuel de la question," T'oung Pao, serie 2,8,5: 597-686. (Reprint: 1907, Leide, E. J. Brill. 90 pp. Abridgment: La Géographie, Jan. 15: 17-40).

 Lolo: A summary of published studies, Lolo origins, names, manuscripts, reprint of map of Ta Liang Shan obtained by Vicomte de Vaulserre in 1898. 21 family chiefs of Siao Liang Shan kept as hostages by yamen of Lei Po. Reprint of Fenouil (1862), who was a prisoner of Lolo bandits. Discussion of Lolo marriage from Rocher 1879-80; husband usually does not recognize first child as his, since wife lives with her parents until its birth.

 Reviews: Madrolle 1908, Comité d'Asie francaise, Bulletin: 396.

Crabouillet
1873 "Les Lolos," Les Missions Catholiques 5,192: 71-72; 194: 94-95; 195: 105-07.

 Lolo of Su-tchuen. First human was Ou-lang, hunter and inventor of cereals, who is represented by clothing on a stick. After death, soul goes to sky and becomes a star. The whole tribe will avenge a homicide, adultery, theft of a slave. Wood tablets used for messages, marriage agreements, or calls to war. Lolo are being sinicized; this is especially evident in their clothing, which is becoming less coarse, and in their hair style, in which the horn is being replaced by the pigtail. Dress.

                Shamans chase away evil spirits with chants, gestures, and drum; sacrifice cattle and sheep; the humerus of sheep is consulted by reading the number and disposition of fissures. The Lolo are divided into many independent tribes, which feud and raid Chinese and rob strangers. Women prevent large massacres. Captured Chinese are made slaves, forbidden to speak Chinese, and exchanged for livestock. Writing is probably only superstitious signs. Food. New Year. Marriage (bride-price, in some tribes fake capture). Funerals, burial with head and arms between knees, legs folded.

Cramer, Carol J.

    1970   Bibliography on the Lisu, Bangkok, Battelle Memorial Institute, Thailand Information Center. 25 pp.

                Lisu: About 50 entries.

Credner, Wilhelm

    1930   Yunnanreise des Geographischen Instituts der Sun Yat Sen Universität, Allgemeine Reisebericht 1.

                Lisu going to market; diversity of crops; freedom of Lisu women (pp. 24ff.).

    1935a   Cultural and geographical observations made in the Tali (Yunnan) region with special regard to the Nan-Chao problem, Bangkok, The Siam Society. (Translated by Erik Seidenfaden.) 20 pp.

                Lisu agriculture said to be adaptable to many soils, slope steepness, and exposition. Winter crops include barley, wheat, opium; summer crops are maize, buckwheat, kaoliang, millet, rice.

1935b   Siam: das Land der Tai, Stuttgart, J. Engelhorns
             Nachfolger. (Reprint: 1966, Osnabruck, Otto Zeller.)
             (HRAF A01-21.) 422 pp.

Crider, Donald M.

1963   "The work among Kachins, Lisus, and Nagas," in Maung Shwe
             Wa, Genevieve Sowards, and Erville Sowards, eds., Burma
             Baptist Chronicles, Book 2: 367-82, Board of Publications,
             Burma Baptist Convention.
                    Lisu first baptized in 1902 at Myitkyina by Geis
             (p. 372).
                    See Maung Shwe Wa 1963, Saw Aung Din and E. E.
             Sowards 1963.

Croizier, Marquis de: see Biet and Croizier 1877.

Cultural and Education Section, Mabien Xian, Szechwan

1958   "Liangshan's Yi nationality people learn to read the Han
             language," Guang-ming ri-bao, Dec. 15. (English trans-
             lation in Survey of China Mainland Press, 1931: 4-6.)
                    Yi formerly forbidden to learn Han by slavemasters
             and elders, who thought it would make Yi forget their
             ancestors and become Han. Through mass meetings and
             door-to-door campaigns, the advantages of learning Han
             were appreciated.

Cunningham, E. R., Leslie G. Kilborn, James L. Maxwell, W. R. Morse,
    Harrison J. Mullett, and F. Dickinson

1933   The Nosu tribes of western Szechwan: Notes on the
             country and its peoples and on the diseases of the region,
             Shanghai, Department of Field Research, Henry Lister
             Institute, Supplement to the Chinese Medical Journal.
             (Abstract, "Epidemiology of the Nosu, Western Szechwan,

China," Nature 134: 294-95.)

Nosu blood pressure low and falls with age. Nosu diseases contrast with Chinese in frequency; whereas smallpox and tuberculosis are rare, malaria absent, and syphilis less common, leprosy is most serious. Lepers may be burnt or buried alive. Roundworm most common among children, but infantile diarrhoea is most fatal. Chronic indigestion. Few scabies. Goiter near the Yunnan border. Caries almost absent, but gum diseases almost universal; much abrasion owing to the food. The Mongolian fold occurs in less than half the population.

Review: 1933-34, West China Branch of the Royal Asiatic Society, Journal 6: 270-72.

Dai, Qing-sha: see Hu, Tan, and Dai, Qing-sha 1964.

Dassé, Martial

1974 Le problème des minorités ethniques en Asie du sud-est continentale, Doctorat d'Etat, Montpellier I. ix, 360 pp.

Minorities in Southeast Asia and China: their cultural assimilation, political integration, and roles in revolutionary wars.

Dauffès, A. E.

1906 "Notes ethnographiques sur les Kos," Ecole française d'Extrême-Orient, Bulletin 6: 327-34.

Akha of Muong Sing give birth in special house. Bride-price of 4-5 piastres. Deceased wrapped in white cloth, money and rice placed in mouth, chicken and rice on a plate, shaman asks spirits to allow the soul to attain "Hima-lasa," the land of the ancestors. Ceremonial calendar.

Davies, Henry Rodolph
1909　　Yün-nan: The link between India and the Yangtze, Cambridge, Cambridge University Press. (Reprint: 1970, Taipei, Ch-en Wen Publishing Company.) (HRAF AF16-5.) 431 pp.

　　　　Lahu: Chinese establish forts to subdue Lahu, soldiers marry Lahu and grow opium. Ch'uan-lo was capital of Lahu state to 1891; they had driven Shan out 4 or 5 generations ago. Many Lahu have now adopted Chinese customs (pp. 89-93). Mixed Chinese-Lahu villages (p. 104). Locations (pp. 192-93 and passim). Vocabulary.

　　　　Lolo have adopted Chinese language and customs (pp. 64, 73, 79, 107). Some Lolo have adopted Shan Buddhism and Lahu dress (p. 89). Christian Lolo (p. 217). Miao driven back north by Lolo (p. 232). Lolo first learn Chinese language and adopt Chinese dress, then religion. Then women use Chinese language and dress, bind feet, then finally Lolo language is dropped, and the next generation is Chinese (pp. 250-51, 368). It is probable that in their southward migration, the Lolo mixed with Mon-Khmer peoples, producing Woni and southern Lolo; Lahu may be descendants of Lolo and Wa; Liso of Lolo and Kachin or Maru. Others have had Lolo language imposed. On the other hand, southern Lolo may have been original stock, and the northern Lolo may be mix with Tibetans (pp. 365-66). Dress and economic activities; locations (389-91 and passim). Vocabularies.

　　　　Lisu live on heights, because they are militarily weak. Chinese soldiers married Lisu and became chiefs. Locations (pp. 36-37, 127-28, 391-392). Vocabulary from

Kachin Hills. Woni (Akha) locations and vocabulary (pp. 393-95 and passim). Maps, photos.

Reviews: 1909, North China Branch of the British Royal Asiatic Society 40: 116-17. H. Cordier, 1909, T'oung Pao 10: 709-13. H. Brenier, 1911, Comité d'Asie-française: 44. H. L. C., 1909, Geographical Journal 33: 75. von Fehlinger, 1909, Mitteilungen k. k. Geographisch und Geologisch Wien 52: 493. C. Sainson, 1909, Journal Asiatique, série 10, 14: 322-25. H. Brenier, 1910, Ecole française d'Extrême-Orient, Bulletin 10,1: 233-53.

Dawson, G. W.
1912   "The Bhamo District," Burma Gazetteer, Rangoon, Office of the Superintendent, Government Printing, Burma. (Reprint 1960.)

Lisu grow opium, practically all consumed locally. They came originally from between the Shweli and the Salween. They practice ancestor worship, grafted onto animism.

Deal, David Michael
1971   National minority policy in southwest China, 1911-1965, doctoral dissertation, Seattle, University of Washington. (Dissertation Abstracts International 32,8: 4510-11A, University Microfilms order No. 72-7334.)

Yi as a case study of cultural change and political integration. 427 pp.

De Francis, John
1951   "National and minority policies," American Academy of Political and Social Science, Annals 277: 146-55.

List of minorities and autonomous areas in China.

Dellinger, David Whitley
- 1967 "Notes on Akha segmental phonemes and tones," <u>Linguistic Circle of Canberra Publications, Series A- Occasional Papers No. 9, Papers in Southeast Asian Linguistics No. 1</u>.
- 1969a <u>Akha: A transformational description</u>, doctoral dissertation, Canberra, Australia National University. xi, 271 pp.
  Akha lexicon, phonological components, structure rules, transformational rules.
- 1969b "Some comments on Akha: Its relationships and structure and a proposal for a writing system, Part 1," in Peter Hinton, ed., <u>Tribesmen and Peasants in North Thailand</u>, Chiang Mai, Tribal Research Centre: 108-12.

Dèng, Zhī-fú
- 1930 "Sì-chūan xī nán zhī yí zú (The foreign tribes of southwest Szechuan)," <u>Chēng-dū dà-xúe shí-xúe zá-zhì</u> (Chengtu University Historical Magazine) <u>2</u>.

Department of Public Welfare, Royal Thai Government (see also Hill Tribe Welfare Division)
- 1962 <u>Report on the socio-economic survey of the hill tribes of northern Thailand,</u> Bangkok, Department of Public Welfare.
  Akha, Lahu, and Lisu included.

Desgodins, Auguste
- 1872 <u>La mission du Thibet de 1855 à 1870 d'après les lettres de M. l'abbé Desgodins</u>, par C. H. Desgodins, Verdun, Charles Laurent, Editeur. iv, 419 pp.
  Lissou brigandage; pay taxes to lama of Tcha-moutong. Concerns the Société des Missions Etrangères.

1873 "Mots principaux des langues de certaines tribus qui habitent les bords du Lan-tsang-kiang, du Loutzekiang et Irrawaddy," Société de Géographie, Bulletin, série 6,5: 144-50.

Dessaint, Alain Y.

1971a "Lisu annotated bibliography," Behavior Science Notes 6,2: 71-94.

Lisu names and their meanings, survey of the information available on their language, history, and ethnography. 173 entries.

1971b "Lisu migration in the Thai highlands," Ethnology 10,3: 329-48.

Lisu changes in residence, the way in which a decision to migrate is reached, and what migration reveals about social structure. After an ethnographic summary, the particular case of the migration that took place in 1969 and 1970 is considered. The reasons for migration included a lack of land, disputes between households, and poor interethnic relations. The decision-making process is analyzed as consisting of three periods: a germination period, precipitating acts leading to migration, and a period of adjustment to the consequences of a decision. Also considered are the sources of information, sources of influence, and perceived alternatives. It is concluded that the Lisu social structure is based upon loose, informal, and unstable household allegiance groups, and that migration offers the opportunity to cooperate with or separate from other individuals and households within the potential social field. The allegiance groups consist of of a number of households which cooperate in economic and ritual activities, and are based on kinship, affinal relations, or simply cooperation with an important man. Four types of migration which occur among the Lisu are defined on the basis of the number of migrants, the distance, and the permanency of change. Map.

1972a Economic organization of the Lisu of the Thai highlands, doctoral dissertation, Honolulu, University of Hawaii. (Not available through University Microfilms.) 216 pp.

Lisu economic organization, social structure, and ethnic relations. Based on a study of the Lisu of northern Thailand, 1968 to 1970, whose economy is based upon the shifting cultivation of opium poppies, hill rice, and maize. An historical and geographic summary emphasizes the importance of migration in Lisu social and economic organization. The motivations, mechanisms, and implications of migration are discussed by means of a detailed consideration of an actual migration in 1969-70. This leads to a consideration of how the Lisu select agricultural land, their technology, agricultural ritual, systems of measurement, and cultural goals, and the means by which they mobilize labor. The following chapter examines the distribution of resources within the Lisu household and village, and the exchange relationships between Lisu and non-Lisu. It is concluded that among the Lisu, migration functions as a means of avoiding interethnic conflict and conflict within the village, and as a means of reallocating labor within the multivillage Lisu community. Labor is in fact the only important manipulatable element in

Lisu economic organization. Each Lisu household has a great degree of choice in forming allegiances with other households, and certain manipulatable mechanisms exist, such as bride service and cooperative labor. The Lisu have utilized a traditional system of agriculture, usually associated with subsistence economy, to adapt to a wider money economy in which they are now inextricably enmeshed. Opium has been used by the Lisu to reinforce their core values of social equality and political anarchy, as well as to attain their more immediate goal of material wealth. The vagaries of opium yields and market prices have reinforced the value that Lisu put on labor and labor relations. It has also helped determine the quality of ethnic relations with their non-Lisu neighbors. Maps.

1972b "Lisu settlement patterns," Siam Society, Journal, 60,1: 195-204.

Lisu village locations, population estimates, problems of ethnic identity, the difficulties of enumeration, Lisu migration into Thailand. The siting of Lisu villages is found to depend upon both physical and social factors: proximity to good opium and rice fields and to water, distance from harassing ethnic groups, proximity to markets and those ethnic groups with which a symbiotic relationship is maintained. Maps.

1972c "The poppies are beautiful this year," Natural History 81,2: 30-37, 92-96.

Lisu ethnographic summary, opium technology, and marketing. Photos.

1975 "Witches, were-tigers, and wat-spirits: Animism in Southeast Asia," in Alain Y. Dessaint and Ernest C.

Migliazza, eds., Anthropology and Linquistics, Dubuque, Kendall/Hunt Publishing Company: 177-78.

    Lisu stories, including the origin of beliefs in spirits, beware of strangers' hospitality, and beware of non-Lisu. Photos.

Dessaint, William Y.
1963   Ethnographical survey of the Lisu in Chiangdao district, London, School of Oriental and African Studies (typescript). 112 pp.

    Lisu of Thailand: settlement patterns, demographic data, ecological factors, and economic systems.

Dessaint, William Y., and Alain Y. Dessaint
1975   "Strategies in opium production," Folk 17: 153-68. Lisu.

Dessirier, Jean
1923   A travers les marches révoltées ouest-chinois, Yun nan-Se-tchouen-Marches thibétaines, Paris, Librairie Plon. 316 pp.

    Lolo force Chinese to retreat, rule over Chinese (pp. 40, 63). Few Lolo are addicted to opium (p. 92). Diary of a member of the Mission Legendre 1910. Photos.

Devakul, M. R. Wutilert: see Hanks, Hanks, and Sharp 1965.

Devéria, Gabriel
1886   La frontière Sino-Annamite, description géographique et ethnographique d'après des documents officiels chinois traduits pour la première fois, Paris, Ernest Leroux. 182 pp.

    Lisou (Li-sie) have lived in Yunnan since the fourth century B.C. (pp. 163-64).

    White Lolo have same food, language, and taxes as

Chinese. Divine by putting wheat in water. Wooden shoulder halter for carrying baskets (pp. 138-39). Black Lolo are the highest class of aboriginals to which chiefs and administrators belong. Locations. Women bind feet, language and food similar to Chinese. New Year's sacrifices of chickens, wine. Lô-man of Ma Touan-lin, Lou-lou of Annals of Nan-chao, Lolo-sse of Mongol Annals (pp. 140-55). Kan Lolo, Hai Lolo (Pa Lolo), Lou-wou Lolo, A-tcho Lolo, Mo-tch'a, and other groups mentioned (pp. 122-68).

Ouo-ni known by various other names (pp. 135-36). Map, drawings. See Cordier 1907: 8-11.

1891 "Les Lolo et les Miao-tze, A propos d'une brochure de M. P. Vial, missionaire apostolique au Yun-nan," Journal Asiatique, série 8,18: 356-69. (Reprint: 1891, Paris, Imprimerie Nationale.)

Lolo (Loulou or Lô-man) chief, Mong-hou, defeated in 224 A.D. by General Tchou Ko-leang. In sixth century, Lolo were divided into White Tsouan (Pe-man) in west and Black (Ou-man) in east. Language divisions: "ou" in north and "a" in south. Ngi-pa (an "a" dialect) has no /u/, /r/ is close to /l/; aspiration of /h/ is soft, many words pronounced with mouth closed, only 300 monosyllabes. Almost no prepositions, all complements to verbs come after subject and before verb. About 1840 signs in Lolo writing, hieroglyphic. About 30% of the spoken language cannot be written. May have originated about 550 A.D. Comparison with Miao writing. See Cordier 1907: 12.

Deydier, Henri
1954   Lokapâla, Génies, totems et sorciers du nord Laos, Paris, Librairie Plon. (Translations 1954, Lokapala: Damonen, Totems und Zauberer von Nord-Laos, Wien, Gallus Verlag. 1967, Lokapala: Demons, totems and sorcerers of northern Laos, Washington, D.C., Army Translation Service.) 242 pp.

Akha of Phong Saly include Akha Pouli, Oma, Phou Sang, and Mou-chi. Maps, photos.

Diao, Richard
1967   "The national minorities and their relations with the Chinese Communist regime," in Peter Kunstadter, ed., Southeast Asian Tribes, Minorities and Nations, Princeton, Princeton University Press: 169-201.

Theory and operation of autonomous minority areas, especially in Tai autonomous areas, which include Hani, Lahu, Lisu, etc.

Diguet, Edouard Jacques Joseph
1908   Les montagnards du Tonkin, Paris, Augustin Challamel. 159 pp. (Extracts: 1908, Revue Coloniale, Jan.: 28-37.)

Lolo mentioned in fourth-century Chinese writings as Tien (White Lolo) and Tsouan (Black Lolo). Lolo of Nam Chieu empire invaded Red River Valley in 860. According to Truong Vinh Ky, the Hac La La (Black Lolo) invaded Tonkin in sixteenth century. The White and Black Lolo, La Qua (Penti Lolo), Phu La, Lati, and Ho Nhi comprise 1% of highland population of Tonkin. Physically the Lolo are the handsomest people in the highlands: more vigorous and intelligent, but also lazy and not good at commerce. Many smoke opium. Extensive description of costumes of the various subgroups (pp. 145-51). Photos.

Ding, Wen-jiang

1935 "Cuan wén cóng kẽ zi xu (Preface to the collection of Lolo characters)," Dì-lǐ xúe-bao (Geographical Bulletin) 2,4.

See 1936, below.

1936 "Cuan wén cóng kẽ (Ts'uan wén ts'ung k'o) (Collection of Lolo characters)," Lì shǐ yǔ yán yán jiu sǔo, Zhong yang yán jiu yuàn (Peking, Institute of History and Philology, Academia Sinica) Special Publication 11.

Lolo (or Tsuan) writing, including a genealogy of the Tsuan family. See Chen 1948a, Dǒng 1940, Fang 1945a and 1945b, Lo 1944a and 1944b, 1945a and 1945c, Ma 1942-44 and 1946, Shiratori 1957, Wen You 1936b.

Diringer, David

1962 Writing, New York, Praeger. (Based on 1937, L'alfabeto nella storia della civilta, Florence, and on 1948 (and later editions), The alphabet: a key to the history of mankind, London and New York.) 607 pp.

Lolo (1951 edition, pp. 141-43).

Di-xúe zá-zhi

1913 "Liáng-shān yí wù diao chá ji (an inquiry into Liangshan Yi affairs)," Dì-xúe zá-zhi (Geographical Magazine) 4,5.

1922 "Si-chuān é biān yí-rén xiàn zhong zhi diao chá (A survey of present conditions of the Yi people of the E or O-pien border area of Szechuan)," Dì-xúe zá zhi (Geographical Magazine) 13,2.

D'Mazure, Thomine (communicated by A. P. Phayre, with notes and
    comments by H. Yule)
    1861   "Memorandum on the countries between Thibet, Yunan and
                   Burmah," Asiatic Society of Bengal, Journal 30,4: 367-83.
                   Among (Louts in Chinese, Guia in Tibetan), below
                Bonga in valley of Louts Kiang pay tribute to Chinese and
                Tibetans. (Yule: probably Nous or Lous of Klaproth's
                map.)
                 Lisou, also in Louts Kiang Valley, "They are said
                to be of very wicked dispositions" (p. 372). (Yule:
                north of Theng-ye-choo on Klaproth's map.)
                 Other tribes mentioned cannot be identified with
                any certainty. Map.
Documentation Francaise, La: see Menguy. 1960.
Dǒng, Yíng, and Xúe Jiàn-húa (or Tung, Ying, and Hsueh Chien-hua)
    1959   "Social reforms in national minority areas in China,"
                 Rén-mín rì-bào (Peking), Aug. 15. (English translation:
                 Survey of the China Mainland Press 2093: 13-23.)
                 Lisu are cited as an example of a primitive class of
                society. Nukiang Lisu autonomous Zhou had in 1945: 10
                factories; 60 primary schools, with 3,000 pupils; and
                one health center. In 1958, it had 600 factories and mines,
                over 700 middle-school students. Illiteracy had been al-
                most eliminated, every xian and xiang has a health
                center, there is a general hospital, and a surplus of grain.
Dǒng, Zùo-bīn (Tǔng, Tsò-pīng)
    1940   "Cūan rén pǔ xì xīn zhèng (New evidence regarding the
                 genealogy of the Ts'uan people)," Mín-zú xúe-yán
                 (Nationalities Research) 2.

Lolo (or Ts'uan) genealogy. See Chen 1948a; Ding 1936, Fang 1945a and 1945b, Lo 1944a and 1944b, 1945; Ma 1942-44 and 1946; Shiratori 1957.

Dreyer, June Elizabeth Teufel
1970 "China's minority nationalities: Traditional and party elites," Pacific Affairs 43,4: 506-30.

Yi. Yunnan warlord Lung Yun was a sinicized Yi. Deposed by Chiang Kai-shek, he was reinstated after 1949, and made a member of the Central People's Government Council and a vice-chairman of the National Defense Council and of the Southwest Military and Administrative Committee. His half-brother, Luttan, was also a vice-chairman and was head of the Military and Administrative Committee for Yunnan. Wang Ch'i-mei, a Szechwan Yi, served on the Party Work Committee in Tibet.

1973 Chinese Communist policy toward indigenous minority nationalities: A study in national integration, doctoral dissertation, Cambridge, Harvard University. (Available from Pusey Library, Harvard University.) iv, 432 pp.

Du, Bin (or Tu, Pin)
1959 "Education for the people of Liangshan Yi nationality," Mínzú Tuánjié (Nationalities Unity) 11. (English translation: Extracts from China Mainland Magazines 203: 31-33.)

Dubernard, l'Abbé
1873 "De Tse-kou à Ta-so (Thibet). Visite aux lyssous," Les Missions Catholiques 5,228: 498,500-01; 229: 512-13.

Lyssou villages near Tse-kou are dependent on Mouquois, Moso chiefs of Ouy-si. Submission to the

Chinese is superficial, with revolts every 5-30 years, in which case they advise the chief by stick with cuts. About 40-50 years ago, a revolt laid waste Lan-tsang-kiang from Ye-tche to Ouy-si. The subsequent pacification was so terrible that the Lyssou were reported exterminated to Peking. In 1871, The Mouquois of Ye-tche was as-sassinated at Hong-pou lamasary; 2,000 of his Lyssou subjects laid waste the surrounding villages in revenge. Mixed Lou-tze and Lyssou villages. Trip to visit Lyssou chief of Ta-so, 8 days from Tse-kou; list of villages. Mou-ma (sorcerer) chases evil spirits with drum and liquor. Slaves treated as members of family. Clothes of hemp or of rich silk stolen from Chinese.

Dubernard, l'Abbé, and Auguste Desgodins

1875 "Les sauvages lyssous du Lou-tze-kiang," Société de Géographie (Paris), Bulletin, série 6,10: 55-66.

    Lyssou, Mosso, and Chinese fighting mediated by Dubernard. Mosso use Lyssou to fight feuds. Mixed Lyssou-Loutze villages. Lyssou polygamy; kidnap prisoners for slaves.

Du Halde, Jean Baptiste

1735 Description géographique, historique, chronologique, politique et physique de l'Empire de la Chine et de la Tartarie chinoise, 4 vols., Paris, P. G. Le Mercier. (English translation 1736, London, J. Watts.)

    Li se or Li sse at 25°33'N on the frontiers of Ava live as semibarbarians in the mountains.

Durrenberger, Edward Paul

1969-70 A socio-medical study of the Lisu of northern Thailand,

1970 Chiang Mai, Tribal Research Centre (mimeographed).
Lisu cosmology, paper read at the American Anthropological Association meeting.

Analyzes Lisu spirits in terms of linguistic categories and relates these to concepts of ecology and political structure.

1971 The ethnography of Lisu Curing, doctoral dissertation, Urbana, University of Illinois. (Dissertation Abstracts International 32,10: 5585B, University Microfilms order no. 72-12, 145.) 343 pp.

Lisu theory of disease and curing. Activities involved in curing, including a case history, the kind of data interpreted and the reasoning processes that lead a Lisu to the course of action taken. Their explanation of how diseases arise and the pantheon of spirits involved. The underlying cause-effect theory of pathogenesis shows why spirits are involved the way that they are and the reasons certain treatment is credited with curative effects. Based on fieldwork in Ban Lum, Chiang Mai Province, Thailand, from Feb. 1969 to July 1970.

1973 The theory of misfortune among the Lisu of northern Thailand, paper read at the American Anthropological Association meeting.

Misfortune, the categories of disease causation that it postulates, and the types of therapy that it implies.

1974 "The regional context of the economy of a Lisu village in northern Thailand," Southeast Asia 3,1: 569-75.

Lisu have five economic focuses: miang (pickled tea), rice, opium, livestock, and motor roads.

1975a   "Lisu occult roles," Bijdragen tot de Taal-, land- en volkenkunde 131,1: 138-46.

The Lisu servitor of the village guardian spirit and the shaman have a contractual relationship with the supernatural. The master of incantations and the medicine woman do not. For all four, the spirit is an alter ego. If the spirit is an aspect of the personality of the person, then that person is a witch or were-animal.

1975b   "The Lisu concept of the soul," Siam Society, Journal 63, 1: 63-71.

Lisu soul may be thought of as positive and body as negative, with analogy to Yin and Yang; then a person would be in a neutral state of health and vigor. If the soul is subtracted, it must be brought back by appeal to certain spirits. After death, a soul goes to the sky (also positive) and thus becomes a spirit.

1975c   "Understanding a misunderstanding: Thai-Lisu relations in northern Thailand," Anthropological Quarterly 48,2: 106-20.

Lisu ideas of obligation to reciprocate (in this case, medicine) differ from Thai ideas. Misunderstandings reinforce negative stereotypes that each has of the other.

1975d   "A soul's journey: A Lisu song from northern Thailand," Asian Folklore Studies 34,1: 35-50.

Lisu song for the recall of a soul: text and explanation.

Dussault (Commandant)

1924   "Les populations du Tonkin occidental et du Haut-Laos," Société de Géographie de Hanoi, Cahiers 5: 1-47.

A Kha (Kha Kho) live at 1,000 to 1,400 meters

altitude. Their numerous subgroups are distinguished by the women's costumes. Unlike other Kha, who are virtually slaves of the Lao, the A Kha are independent. Photos.

Xa Pho (Xa Phong) language is similar to Lolo.

Eales: See Archibald Rose and J. Coggin Brown 1911.

Eberhard, Wolfram

1942 "Kultur und Siedlung der Randvölker Chinas," T'oung Pao 36: Supplement. 506 pp.

Wu-man Volker includes A-che Lolo, A-hsieh Lo-lo, A-hou Lo-lo, Hei Lo-lo, Kan Lo-lo, Ku-tsung, K'u-tś-ung, Lao-wu, Li-su, Lo-lo, etc.

1943 Lokalkulturen im alten China, Vol. 1, Leiden, Supplement to T'oung Pao 37; Vol. 2 Monumenta Serica Monograph Number 3. 447 + 588 pp.

Lolo mentioned.

1968 The local cultures of South and East China, Leiden, E. J. Brill. (Translated by Alide Eberhard.) 522 pp.

Lolo mentioned (pp. 53, 189).

Ecole Française d'Extrême-Orient, L'

1921 "Ethnographie indochinoise," Ecole Française d'Extrême-Orient, Bulletin 21,1: 167-96.

Lolo data based on Lajonquière, Bonifacy, Laufer, Dauffès, Vial, and Liétard.

Edgar, J. Huston

1934 "Language changes in West China," West China Border Research Society, Journal 6: 258-62.

Lolo numerals.

Edkins, Joseph
1871 "A vocabulary of the Miao dialects," Chinese Recorder and Missionary Journal 3: 96-99, 134-49.
  Lolo of Weining from the "topography of the prefectural city Hing-i."

Egerod, Søren, and Inga-Lill Hansson
1974 "An Akha conversation on death and funeral," Acta Orientalia 36: 225-84.
  Akha of Mae Chan district, Thailand. Comments on death and funeral customs in Akha and English translation. Basic phonology, grammar, and word list.

Eickstedt, Egon von
1944 Rassendynamik von Ostasien; China and Japan: Tai und Kmer von der Urzeit bis heute, Berlin, Walter de Gruyter & Co. 648 pp.
  Lolo, Li-su: Distribution, physical features, history, relations and affinities with other groups, writing (pp. 162-78). Maps, photos.

Eink, Z.
1968 "The hidden life of the Akha: Birth, marriage and death," Standard Bangkok Magazine, Aug. 4: 8-11.
  Akha highly structured society related to respect for tradition and ancestors. Gateway as symbolic barrier between human and spirit worlds.

Embree, John Fee, and William Leroy Thomas, Jr.
1950a Ethnic groups of northern southeast Asia, New Haven, Yale University, Southeast Asia Studies (mimeographed).
1950b Bibliography of the peoples and cultures of mainland South-

east Asia, New Haven, Yale University, Southeast Asia Studies. 821 pp.

Encyclopedia Britannica
1973 "Kaw," Encyclopedia Britannica 13: 256.

Enriquez, Colin Metcalf Dallas
1918 A Burmese loneliness, Calcutta, n.p. 283 pp.
Akha mentioned.
1921 "The Yawyins or Lisu," Burma Research Society, Journal 11: 70-74.
Lisu distribution (especially within Burma), names (name given at birth never used), death customs (dead given money to travel over mountains and cross rivers), legend according to which they are offspring of a Chinese female and Nat Palaung. Lisu are influenced by the Chinese, but probably come from eastern Tibet and are affiliated with the Lolo.
1923a A Burmese arcady, London, Seeley, Service. 282 pp.
Lisu clan names. Map, photo.
1923b "Story of the migrations," Burma Research Society, Journal 13.
Migrations into Burma of Mon-Khmer, Tibeto-Burman, and Tai-Chinese: speed, economic causes, British influence.
1924 Races of Burma, Delhi, Manager of Publications. (Second edition 1933.) 98 pp.
Lisu may become Chinese and vice-versa. Lisu clan names (similar to those found in Thailand today). Photos.

Evans-Pritchard, Sir Edward: see Skipton 1973.
Fàn, Yì-tían
 1931 "Tán-tán jiang biān gǔ-zōng (A talk about the River Guzong)," Yún-nán bàn-yuè-kān (Yunnan Bimonthly) 3.
   Guzong, a Yi subgroup?

Fang, Jwang-You (pinyin: Fāng, Zhǎng-yǒu)
 1945a "Léi-bō píng-shān mò-chuān děng xiàn tǔ sī jiā pǔ (Genealogies of the headmen of Leipo, Pingshan, Mochuan and other counties)," Biān-zhèng gōng-lùn (Frontier Affairs) 4, 4-6.
 1945b (Genealogies of nine headmen of the Man Yi Sz (Lolo district), Biān-zhèng gōng-lùn (Frontier Affairs) 4, 7: 20-40.
   Lolo genealogies (as deep as 24 generations), years of accession, and other data on Chinese-recognized chiefs.
 1945c "Liáng-shān luǒ zú xi pǔ (Genealogies of the Lo tribe of Liang Shan)," Biān-zhèng gōng-lùn (Frontier Affairs) 4, 9-12: 1-20.
   Lolo of Liang Shan genealogies, including that of the main branch, Gu Hou Zhong. Gathered May 1939. See also Chén 1948a, Dīng 1936, Dǒng 1940, Lo 1944a, and 1944 b, 1945a; Ma 1942-44, 1946; Shiratori 1957.

Farjenel, Fernand (avec notes de Chavannes et Senart)
 1910 "Le serment des 37 tribus Lolos," Journal Asiatique, 10 série, 15, 3: 574-84.
   Lolo: A translation of the Chetch'eng inscription differing from that of Chavannes 1909a and 1909b, concerning Chinese pacification of Lolo chiefs.

Fei, Hsiao-tung (Pinyin: Fei, Xiao-dong)
    1951-52   "The minority peoples in Kweichow," China Monthly Review 121,6: 289-94; 122,1: 54-63.

        I: 1.5 million, including 100,000 in Kweichow. T'ussu headman system instituted by Han; positions of three T'ussu in Kweichow canceled by Ming; two reinstated without real power by Ch'ing. After 1949, "most of the T u Mu (Lolo headmen) became bandits" (p. 57). Although land rents were only 10-20% of harvest, tenants were exploited by landlords in other ways. Now they have stopped excessive exploitation. In Liang Shan, slave labor still exists. Outside this mountain redoubt, Han landlords acquired Lolo land and exacted rents in labor or in kind. Photos, sketches.

    1952   "China minority nationalities," Far Eastern Economic Review 13,3: 89-91.

        Old Yi feuds ended. Regional autonomy, economic development.

Fei, Hsiao-tung, and Lin, Yáo-húa (Pinyin: Fei, Xiao-dong, and Lin, Yáo-húa)
    1956   "A study of the social nature of the minority nationalities," Rén-mín Rì-bào, Aug. 14. (English translation: Current Background 430: 18-25.)

        Yi of Ta Liang Shan cited as an example of slave-level society. Castes included Black Yi (15% of the population), serfs who owned slaves, serfs, and slaves.

Feingold, David
    1968   "Networks of identity; Ethnic designations and kin groupings among the Johgwo Akha of northern Thailand," Abstract, Proceedings of the VIIIth International

Congress of Anthropological and Ethnological Sciences, Tokyo and Kyoto.

1969a   What kind of Akha are you? paper read at the American Anthropological Association meeting, New Orleans.

1969b   The politics of space: Field allocation among the Akha of northern Thailand, paper read at the Association for the Advancement of Science meeting, Boston.

Akha: The greater the percentage of women and children in the household work force, the greater the tendency to emphasize opium production.

1970   Consensual settlements in Akha law, paper read at the American Anthropological Association meeting, San Diego.

1973a   Minorities in Thailand: A comparative perspective, paper read at the Association for Asian Studies meeting, Chicago.

1973b   The well-done medium: Trance performance in Akha society, paper read at the American Anthropological Association meeting, New Orleans (to be published in a collection edited by Vivian Garrison and Vincent Crapanzano).

Akha spirit medium is self-selected diagnostician. Validation of her role is examined in interaction with the audience during her trance.

1973c   On knowing who you are: Intra-ethnic distinctions among the Akha of northern Thailand, paper read at the IXth International Congress of Anthropological and Ethnological Sciences, Chicago (to be published in David J. Banks, ed., Changing Identities in Modern Southeast Asia (World Anthropology), Chicago, Aldine Publishing Co.).

1974 Loafing through life: The evasion of social responsibility among the Akha of northern Thailand, paper read at the American Anthropological Association meeting, Mexico.

Feng, Han-yi, and John Knight Shryock
1938 "The historical origins of the Lolo, "Harvard Journal of Asiatic Studies 3: 103-27.

"Lolo" first appeared in Yuan period, soon identified with "lulu" (eastern Ts'uan barbarians, fifth to ninth centuries); possible derivations of "Lolo" reviewed. Nan-chao Yeh-shih (Ming) lists 11 Lolo tribes subject to Nan-chao. History of An clan of northwestern Kweichow (based on Tu-shih fang-yu chi-yao, 1624-80, and Yen-chiao chi-wen by T'ien Ju-ch'eng, 1560). Man-shu indicates Lolo are eastern Ts'uan, but not western; it says they cremate their dead, and keep the ears in vases. Eastern Ts'uan area of Ssuch'uan rose in revolt in 1723-25, when direct Chinese administration was forced upon them. Independent Lolo of Chien-ch'ang Valley early came under influence of Chinese, because it was an important route, but those of Ta-liang shan remained independent until almost the end of the Ch-ing period, despite attempts to subdue them in 1723-35 and 1796-1820. Ch'ou Ta-wu freed thousands of Chinese captives in 1870. Chao Ehr-feng built a road and some garrisons in 1909, prohibited slavery, and established Chinese administrative districts.

Fenouil, Jean Joseph
1862 "Missions de la Chine. Extrait d'une lettre de M. Fenouil. . . ," Annales de la Propagation de la Foi

34: 319-34. (Reprinted in Cordier 1907: 43-51; English translation in Baber 1882: 118-24.)

Y-Jin are administered, but Man-Tse of Leang-Chan have never been subdued. On the way to visit there in 1861, Fenouil was attacked by Man-Tse, his servants killed, and kept prisoner for 48 hours.

Fergusson, W. N.

1910 "Mr. Fergusson's map of the Lolo country," Geographical Journal 36,4: 438-39, 512.

Map of southern Se-chuan by a missionary in Chengtu 1906-07. See also map of northern Se-chuan in "The Tribes of North-western Se-chuan," Geographical Journal 32,6: 594-97, 648.

1911 Adventure, sport and travel on the Tibetan steppes, London, Constable and Company, Ltd. 343 pp.

Lolo kidnap Chinese and rob travelers in spite of troops and blockhouses. A force of 3,400 Chinese decapitated several Lolo slaves in retaliation, but fled in fear from real battle. A few weeks later, John W. Brooke entered Lololand and was murdered by A-heo tribe (?). Lolo cremate dead, bury ashes in jar, write name on paper and place in basket; a great price is paid to retrieve body of dead Lolo. In 10th month, a great fair is held and ponies raced. Women have high status, especially in stopping quarrels. Nosu are originally inhabitants of Assam, driven north by Bengali. Of same stock are Corean and ancient Japanese, certainly not Tibetan. Old Lolo capital is southeast of Chingchi hsien. Based on travels with

C. H. Meares and J. Brooke, 1907-08. Map, photos.

Février, James Germain
1948 Histoire de l'ecriture, Paris, n.p.
Lolo (pp. 82-83).

Fides Agency
1942 "Un peuple non-chinois en Chine: les Lolos," Les Missions Catholiques 74,3364: 168-71.
Lolo character, costumes, classes, slavery, kidnapping. Photos.

Fitzgerald, Charles Patrick
1941 The tower of five glories, London, The Cresset Press. 280 pp.
Li Su is one of the largest, most scattered tribes in Yunnan, found west and northwest of Min Chia, whose markets they sometimes frequent. Rarely cultivate rice. Lolo means "basket" and is loosely applied to any non-Han, e.g. those southeast of Ta Li in Ting Hsi Ling range may actually be Lisu.

Flatz, G., C. Pik, and S. Sringham
1965 "Haemoglobin E and B-thalassaemia: their distribution in Thailand," Annals of Human Genetics 29,2: 151-70.
Correlation of HbB prevalence to occurrence of malaria and to fertility in women.

Flatz, G., and S. Sringham
1964 "Glucose-6-Phosphate dehydrogenese deficiency in different ethnic groups in Thailand," Annals of Human Genetics 27,4: 315-18.
Deficiency of G-6-PD correlates more with incidence of malaria than with ethnic affiliation.

>   Limitations and value of C-6-PD in genetical studies of migration.

Fletcher, H. G.
1927   Tengyueh: Route book of travels in neighbourhood, Hints for travellers, Market day dates, and notes on Yunnan pronunciation, etc., Shanghai, Statistical Department of the Inspectorate General of Customs, China, The Maritime Customs. III. Miscellaneous Series: No. 36. 162 pp.

>   Liso (p. 42). Liso-Kachin Village (p. 49). Lisaw of Su-tien (P. 61). Flowery Lisaw of Pajao (Hua chiao ho) (P. 63). Map.

Fleurelle, de
1910   "La legénde du déluge chez les Lolos," Société de Géographie de l'Est, Bulletin 31,4: 254-55. (Reprinted in 1911, Revue Indochinoise avril: 400-01; 1911, A travers le Monde 17: 79.)

>   Lolo legend tells of three brothers warned of coming flood by an old man who tells eldest to build a boat of iron, second to build one of copper, and youngest one of wood. Youngest brother and his sister survive. To determine whether they may marry, they roll rocks from opposite sides of valley to see if they meet. De Fleurelle was a member of d'Ollone's expedition.

Forrest, George
1908   "Journey on upper Salwin, October-December, 1905," Geographical Journal 32: 239-66.

>   Lissoo: Forrest was a botanist who accompanied

consul George Litton on his expedition up the Salween from Tengyueh. The map is probably erroneous, and they probably did not get further north than 26°45'N. The Southern Lissoo marry Chinese and are nominally under Chinese control. They are called Han-ti or Han-jen to distinguish them from the wild northern Lissoo. Forrest passed through several Lissoo villages, including one with 90 houses. He met a shaman who had led a rebellion against the Chinese. The Lissoo raise maize, hemp, tobacco, buckwheat; they make fermented drinks from millet and maize. They worship spirits, especially ancestral. He believes they are undoubtedly from southeastern Tibet. Map, photos.

1910 "The land of the crossbow," National Geographic 21: 132-56.

    Lissoo ox hide shields. Trade. Forrest witnessed a dispute between two villages over the theft of some maize. Map, photos.

Franck, Harry A.

1925 Roving through Southern China, New York & London, The Century Company. xxi, 649 pp.

    Nosu or I-bien called "Lolo" because of basket in which they keep dead souls. They now bury rather than cremate. Fine-featured Nosu are lords who sometimes mistreat their Chinese and Miao serfs and slaves. Photos.

François, Charles

1904 "Notes sur les Lo-lo du Kien-tchang," Société d'Anthropologie de Paris, Bulletin et Mémoires, 5e série, 5: 637-47.

Lolo hate Chinese. Lolo distribution, divisions, customs, dress. See Cordier 1907: 83-84.

Franjola, Matthew

1972　　"Have cheroot, will travel," Far Eastern Economic Review 76,15: 12-13.

Akha and Laho fight in the Kokang Brigade of the Shan State Army, Burma.

Fraser, James Outram

1922　　Handbook of the Lisu (Yawyin) language, Rangoon, 108 pp. Superintendent, Government Printing, Burma.

Lisu language study, based mainly on Tengyueh and Myitkyina areas. Fraser recognizes six tones and provides a good morphological description and extensive vocabulary. Brief but good ethnographic introduction.

Fraser, James Outram, translator

1938　　The New Testament in Hwa Lisu, Hongkong, China Bible House. (Various reprints.)

Fraser was a Protestant missionary whose script is still used by Christian Lisu. For his biography, see Taylor 1944.

Fu, Mao-ji (or Mao-chi)

1944a　　Phonetics of the Lolo language in the Taliang mountains, Hsichow, n.p. 20 pp.

Lolo distribution, writing, dialects, phonetics.

1944b　　Sikang I-yu hui-hua (Sikang Lolo conversation), Sichang, n.p.

Lolo of Ta-liang mountains language study.

1945a　　A study on the Lolo manuscript Sii-zeu-bo-pa, "The origin of the gods," from the Taliang Mountains,

1945b   A study on the Lolo proverbs in and near the Taliang mountains, Hsichow, Huachung University Monographs on Chinese Studies series II, no. 1. 58 pp.

A study on the Lolo proverbs in and near the Taliang mountains, Hsichow, n.p. 15 pp.

       Lolo arbitrators base decisions on 16 proverbs, which are reproduced here in Lolo characters, phonetic, literal, and free translations (into Chinese).

1951   "The Lolo kinship terms as affected by sex of the speaker," Asia Major, n.s. 2,1: 68-70.

       Lolo of Ta liang shan males use EB, YB, Z; while females use EZ, YZ, B. YB or younger generation are called by name given 5, 7, or 9 days after birth; EB and elder G are called by "style" given when a person begins to speak (nickname?). Widow cannot refuse to marry in H's family, unless she can repay bride-price even if she must marry HF or Hs (by another wife).

1957   "Written languages for China's minorities," People's China 3: 25-31.

Fürer-Haimendorf, Christoph von

1968   "Lisu," Encyclopedia Britannica 14: 102.

Gaide, L.

1903   "Notice ethnographique sur les principales races indigènes de la Chine méridionale (Yun-nam en particulier) et du nord de l'Indo-Chine," Annales d'Hygiene et de Medicine Coloniales 5: 449-94. (Reprinted 1905, Revue Indo-Chinoise, n.s. 3,10-11: 707-16, 787-93.)

       Lolo near Sse-mao include Nissou, Lohè (when sinicized called Ouang Lolo, when independent called

Ya Lohè, and includes the La-hou "clan"), Siang-Tan Hé-lou-jen (completely sinicized). Marriage entails bride-price (5 tael silver) or service (3 years). Dead buried with silver in mouth, in favorable place, with stone raised in front and name inscribed on it. Son uses blood of finger to write parents' names on board in Lolo characters. Boards kept 3 generations, then burned. I-pou (tablets) are venerated for 3 days after death, then 1st and 15th of each month and anniversary days in 3rd and 10th months. They are kept in bamboo baskets. In eastern Yunnan, orchid stems of 7 or 9 knots are used instead of tablets. Rather than a religious system, they have superstitions, bons, bad spirits. Writing, originally ideographic but now phonetic, used for religious manuscripts. Reads top to bottom, left to right. Village chiefs usually literate. Dress. Unmarried women wear one hair-tail, married two (curled around head before children, in chignon in back after having several children). Hounis include Mâbè, Pou-tou, Khado, Si-mou-lou, Lô-mi or black Houni, Pi-yo or white Houni, Peunn-jen. Distribution.

Akha or Kha probably a Houni subtribe, since they have the same origin, vocabulary and physical type. Live on right bank of Mekong. Village gates are decorated with drawings, carvings (human figures with large genitals), or head and skin of a dog holding a wooden rat. Similarities between Lolo, Houni, and Akha are noted (pp. 477-80). Lolo group is gradually migrating southward (pp. 487-88).

K'ou-ts'ong-jen caravans visit Ssemao (pp.484-87). Map.

Garnier, Francis
1873   <u>Voyage</u> <u>d'exploration</u> <u>en</u> <u>Indo-Chine</u>, 4 vols., Paris, Hachette.

    Lisu illustrated wearing roughly-made skin clothing. Language said to be close to Melam.

    Lolo vocabulary from Yuen-kiang; vocabularies of Kato, Mantze, and Kho (<u>2</u>: 509-16).

Gao, Shou-sui
1960   "The Lagu of Yunnan," <u>Minzú</u> <u>Huabào</u> <u>3</u>: 20.

    Lahu before Liberation kept rough records on wood or bamboo. After 1949, a written language was created, 1,500 teachers trained, and 56,000 youths enrolled. Since 1958, 30% of the young population (26,000) have become literate. Photos (by Wang Yao-zhi).

Geddes, William
1965   "The hill tribes of Thailand," <u>SEATO</u> <u>Record</u> <u>4,6</u>: 16-21.

    Akha, Lahu, and Lisu mentioned. Based on four mimeographed lectures presented at the SEATO Seminar on Community Development, Bangkok, July 23, 1965.

Geis, G. J.
1912   "Exogamy among the Lisu tribe," <u>Census</u> <u>of</u> <u>India</u>, <u>1911</u>, <u>9</u> (Burma): 153, Rangoon, Superintendent of Government Printing.

    Lisu clan names and marriage customs.

<u>Geographical Journal</u>
1909   "J. W. Brooke," <u>Geographical</u> <u>Journal</u> <u>33,2</u>: 222-23.

    Died in Lisu country, 1908.

George, E. C. S.
   1915   "Ruby Mines District," Burma Gazetteer, Rangoon, Office of the Superintendent, Government Printing, Burma. (Reprinted in 1961.)

                Lisu settled in this district shortly after its annexation by the British. Coming from China, they selected the highest altitudes for their "wasteful energies," causing formation of treeless savannas. During the previous 10 years, they were forced to adopt other means of livelihood: potatoes (introduced by the British), terrace paddy (borrowed from the Palaung) (pp. 44-45).

Gill, William John
   1880   The river of golden sand, 2 vols., London, J. Murray. (Condensed by Baber in 1883.) 332 pp.

                Lisus, Lusus, or Lissaus.

Gjessing, Gutorm
   1957   "Chinese anthropology and New China's policy towards her minorities," Acta Sociologica 2,1: 45-68.

                Yi newspaper now published. Map.

Goré, Francis
   1939   Trente ans aux portes du Thibet interdit, 1908-1938, Hongkong, Maison du Nazareth. 388 pp.

                Lissou language is affiliated with Lolo, but White and Flowered Lissou have been influenced by Chinese.

Gould, Charles
   1885   Mythical monsters, London, W. H. Allen. (Reprint: 1969, Detroit, Singing Tree Press.) 407 pp.

                Lolo: Three figures, one with Lolo characters

from manuscript of J. Haas (pp. 256-58). See Cordier 1907: 33.

Goullart, Peter

1955   Forgotten kingdom, London, John Murray. 218 pp.

    Black Lolo are energetic people, "the most noble looking people I have seen in my life" (p. 115). Live at 5,000-6,000 feet in Taliang shan. Their hair is gathered through hole at the top of the turbans and hangs as a tail through which the Divine Spirit communicates with man. Dress. Localized clans, each with its prince. Nobles are warriors; all agricultural work is done by White Lolo, who are Chinese or other tribespeople. Marriage between Black and White is forbidden under pain of death. Some emancipated White have been successful as intermediaries between Black and Chinese. High status of women. Food, opium, horse fairs. Lissu quarrel with Black Lolo. Black Lissu are especially ferocious, being outcasts from Ta liang shan. Black Lissu "baroness" near Likiang.

1959   Princes of the black bone: Life in the Tibetan borderland, London, John Murray. (German translation, 1962, by Kurt Wagenseil, Die Schwarzen Lolo zwischen Tibet und China, München, Paul List Verlag.) 221 pp.

    Lolo of Fulin, Dienba, and Mienning in Sikang Province. Black Lolo are aristocratic warriors, and White Lolo are serfs. Clan conflicts. Believe in one god, spirits of nature, and demons. There is no organized priesthood and no temples, but "pimo" keep written lore, diagnose diseases, exorcise demons, and

are experts in ceremonial and medicinal herbs. Many
Lolo have studied or undergone military training in
Chengtu and Chungking. Chinese merchants at Dien Ba
are contemptful of Lolo "barbarians," but also fear
them. They barter salt, sugar, matches, thread, and
firearms for wax, honey, hides, copper, and coffin
planks. Poor relations of Lolo and local Chinese
often erupt in fighting and kidnapping. A Lolo noble,
"Koumou," was said to have been poisoned by a Provincial Army commander a few months after Goullart met
him. The Army trades in opium and plunders Lolo
villages. White Lolo work on Sichang-Fulin highway.

  Goullart was a Russian emigré employed by the
Chinese Industrial Co-operatives. He regularly
traveled on foot, with only a single guide, and had a
knack for meeting "aristocratic" ladies whom he greeted
with a flourish and a "Mesdames." His writing conveys
the feeling of the country and the people, but does not
contain much specific information.

Gourdin, Edouard François
1879 "Le pays de Kien-tchang (Su-tchuen méridional)," Les Missions Catholiques 11,517: 215-18.

  Lolo enslave Chinese, but these continue to
advance in the valleys. Sy-fan. Mo-so. See Cordier
1907: 73-74.

Gourou, Pierre
1951 "Land utilization in upland areas of Indochina," in The Development of Upland Areas in the Far East, 2 vols., New York, Institute of Pacific Relations, 2: 25-

42.
    Lolo of Bao Lac practice dry, permanent, intensive agriculture with plow and manure-an example that should be followed (p. 33).

Graham, David Crockett

1926-29   "The Lolos of Szechwan," West China Branch of the Royal Asiatic Society, Journal 3: 108-11.
    Lolo characteristics, occupations, clans, customs, religion, and sacred language.

1930   "The Lolo of Szechuan Province, China," American Anthropologist 32: 703-05.
    Lolo year begins in 10th moon; holidays in 5th and 8th moons. Sky god provides good crops, victory and blessings, and is symbolized by hair knot above forehead.

1954   Songs and stories of the Ch'uan Miao, Washington, D.C., Smithsonian Institution, Publication 4139, Miscellaneous Collections vol. 123, no. 1. 336 pp.
    Lolo are landlords of Miao (p. 35). Lolo and Miao tales: ancestral rock (p. 17), Lolo thieves (pp. 25, 231), kidnapping of slaves (pp. 29, 33, 129), Lolo and Miao fight the Chinese (pp. 30-33), Lolo and Miao immigrated together (p. 261). Gold and silver followed the Lolo into the Cool Mountains (p. 169), Lolo slaves (p. 165), Lolo women are efficient servants (p. 23).

1955   "A Lolo story: 'The Great God of O-Li-Bi-Zih' by Lin Kuang-tien," Journal of American Folklore 68: 175-99.
    Lolo story is similar to Chinese geomantic tales: supernatural signs indicate that the emperor of a new dynasty is about to be born; the only person who knows

about it tries to bury his ancestors in a propitious place or tries to get the symbols for himself; the plan almost succeeds, but a catastrophe occurs at the last minute. The tale explains how the Lolo rid themselves of cruel Chinese oppression, and explains the reason for wearing hair in a knot above the forehead.

Graham, David Crockett, translator
1931   Seven Lolo sacred books, Foochow and Shanghai. 12 pp.
       Lolo: Two rain chants, five prayers for exorcising demons.

Graham, Shirley
1961   "Minority peoples of China," Freedomways 1,1: 95-104.
       Yi (Nosu and Punosu) mentioned.

Graham, Walter Armstrong
1924   Siam, 2 vols., 3d ed., London, Alexander Moring. (HRAF A01-23, 24.)
       Lishaw section reprinted from the 1912 edition. The Lishaw are said to be related to the Muhso (Lahu), but their customs are almost indistinguishable from those of the Yunnanese.

Gregory, John W., and C. J. Gregory
1924   To the Alps of Chinese Tibet, Philadelphia, J. B. Lippincott. 321 pp.
       Lisu bandits attack salt caravan east of the Mekong. Lisu burn idols, and convert to Christianity near Weisi in 1922.

Grierson, Sir George Abraham, ed.
1903-28 Linguistic survey of India, Calcutta, Office of the Superintendent of Government Printing.
         Volume 1, part 2, includes the following vocabu-

laries: Aka (Kaw) by L. F. Taylor, Lahu by Taylor, Lishaw by Taylor and Scott, Lisu by Fraser, and Lolopho by Liétard.

Grilliéres, G.
1905 "Voyage au Yun-nan et au Thibet Oriental," La Géographie 11,4: 285-92.
Lolo are degenerate, cretins, have goiter, and some cannot even speak.

Gūang, Wèi-rán
1954 A-xì rén de gē (The songs of the Asi), Míng-jiān wén-xúe cóng shū, Rén míng wén-xúe chū bǎn shè (Peking, Folk Literature Series, People's Literature Publishing Company).
A-si Yi. See Yúan 1946, 1953.

Gūang-míng rì-bào (Kǔang-míng Jìh-pào) (Peking)
1957 "Wǔ gúo de shǎo shù mín zú jiān jie-Lǎ hǔ zú (Brief introduction to the minority peoples of our country-The Lahu people)," Jan. 18.
Lahu in Sse mao and Lan Ts'ang special regions number 129,000. "La" derives from "tiger," and "hu" means "place where it is divided." Lahu have gradually migrated south from Tien-ch'ih, where their souls still return. Before liberation, they were exploited by headmen and landlords. Now, they have new tools, irrigation, autumn crops, fertilizers, land reform, medical and educational advances, and new towns, such as Meng Lang Pa.
1959 "The new life of the peoples of Tibetan and Yi nationalities inhabiting Szechwan province following

democratic reforms," May 15. (English translation: Survey of China Mainland Press 2025: 28-30.)

    Yi of Liangshan autonomous Zhou had a 1958 grain harvest of 650 million catties. Half the school-age children are enrolled in school. A Yi cooperative member sacrifices his life to save a lamb from a leopard.

1963 "Hundred year old person, although physically old, her heart is red," Feb. 16.

    Lahu centenarian, who suffered under the old system, was so grateful when given a portrait of Mao and a book of his quotations from the People's Liberation Army that she shouted "Long live Chairman Mao!" She has asked to be taught to read. Under the leadership of the reddest of the red hearts, she has become young again despite her age.

1971 "Use Marxism-Leninism and Mao Ze-dong's thought to train minority nationality cadres," Nov. 22. (English translation: Survey of China Mainland Press 71-48: 117-19.)

    Nuchiang Lisu Autonomous Zhou minorities cadres raise their consciousness in class struggle. 1,500 have been trained since the Cultural Revolution. Now, 90% of the leading cadres are non-Han. Lisu examples cited. 1970 food output was 21% greater than any year previous to the Cultural Revolution.

1972a "Minority nationality education in Lichiang area develops rapidly under the guidance of Chairman Mao's proletarian line of education," Jan. 29. (English translation: <u>Survey of China Mainland Press</u> 72-6: 186-89.)

Yi: Hung ch'iao production brigade in Ninglang Yi autonomous xian consists of 13 teams, including 7 nationalities, and has expanded its educational programs (including the training of non-Han teachers) since the Cultural Revolution.

1972b "Emancipated serfs run schools," Oct. 9. (English translation: <u>Survey of the China Mainland Press</u> 72-43: 68-70.)

Yi of P'ulo commune, Put'o xian, Liangshan Yi autonomous zhou. 92.4% of school-age children attend school.

1973a "Outside cadres in Nujiang Lisu nationality autonomous zhou, Yunnan province, seriously learn the languages of the local minority nationalities," Feb. 7. (English translation: <u>Survey of China Mainland Press</u> 73-8: 56-57.)

70% of outside cadres above commune level are fluent in Lisu, Nu, and/or Tulung.

1973b "CCP Weihsi xian committee in Yunnan province energetically trains teachers of minority nationalities," Mar. 23. (English translation: <u>Survey of China Mainland Press</u> 73-14: 58-59.)

Lisu, Nasi, Pumi live in xian. Of 635 teachers in xian, 397 are minority members (of which, 45% are women).

1973c "Children of Nu nationality grow up healthily and happily," May 31. (English translation: <u>Survey of China Mainland Press</u> 73-24: 105-06.)

Nu of Pichiang and Fuking xian in the Nuchiang-Lili autonomous zhou, Yunnan province, and of Kungshan Tulung-Nu autonomous xian.

Guébriant, de (See also Maitre and d'Ollone 1909.)

1899 "Au Su-tchuen," <u>Les Missions Catholiques</u> <u>31</u>, <u>1549</u>: 64-66; <u>1550</u>: 78-81; <u>1552</u>: 106-08; <u>1553</u>: 117-18; <u>1554</u>: 129-31; <u>1555</u>: 136-39; <u>1556</u>: 152-55.

Lolo have Chinese slaves. Their battle cry often suffices to rout Chinese soldiers. The La family has been toù-ssé for 4-5 centuries. Lolo manuscripts kept by pé-mou. At market, one may see Lolo, Sifan, Li-Sou, Tibetan, Mo-So, Pé êul, Tchong-Kia-tsé. Based on missionary's excursion to Kien-tchang. (See Maitre and d'Ollone 1909.)

1908 "A travers la Chine inconnue. Chez les Lolos," Les Missions Catholiques 40,2026: 164-66; 2027: 172-73; 2029: 199-203; 2030: 207-09; 2031: 221-24.

Lolo: Guébriant crossed Leang-chan with d'Ollone in 1907. 200 Chinese families live at Kiao-kio, traders in the middle of Lolo country; other Chinese fled a century ago. White Lolo (oûa tsé or ngu-má) are serfs, Black Lolo (hé-y) are masters, toù-ssé (dze mô) are chiefs, but many Black Lolo are not on good terms with them. Photos.

Guibaut, André (sometimes misspelled Guibaud)

1937 "Marche de la Mission Guibaut-Liotard de Tali Fou, base de départ, aux marches tibétaines de Loutseukiang (Bahang)," T'oung Pao 33: 295-98. See 1938a, below.

1938a "Au Tibet par la vallée de la Salouen," Harvard Journal of Asiatic Studies 3: 312-36.

Guibaut and Liotard were probably the first Europeans to follow the Salween from $25°35'$ to $28°30'$N (in 1936). They report that a mandarin, his soldiers, and his servants were recently massacred by Lissou, as were earlier English and German travelers. Housing (very similar to present-day Lisu in Thailand). They claim that all Lisu smoke tobacco pipes, but not opium (neither is true of present-day Lisu in Thailand). Map, photos.

1938b "Vers le Tibet par la vallée de la Salouen," La Géographie 69: 37-43.

See 1938a, above.

1940 "Les populations du cours moyen de la Salouen," L'Anthropologie 49: 654-55.

Lissou have Mongoloid-Europoid appearance and resemble the Tibetans of Tsarong.

1947 Ngolo-Setas, Paris J. Susse. 228 pp.

1967 Missions perdues au Tibet, Paris, André Bonne. 267 pp.

Lissou used poison-tipped arrows. Photo shows two Lissou about to be executed for rebellion. Photos.

Guibaut, André, and Louis Victor Liotard

1941 "Les gorges de la Salouen moyenne et les montagnes entre Salouen et Mekong," Annales de Géographie 50: 180-95.

Map, photos.

1945 "Notes de géographie humaine sur la vallée moyenne de la Salouen," Annales de Géographie 53-54: 29-46.

Lissou: some live in established villages, have rice terraces, and use plows pulled by oxen. The Chinese buy skins, bear bile, and stag horn from them in return for iron goods, clothes, and silver. Ethnographic map, photos.

Ha, Bac

1964 "The Ha-nhi tribe and its ten years of progress," Nhan Dan, May 27: 2. (English translation: Joint

Publications Research Service No. 25, 217, Translations of Political and Sociological Information on North Vietnam No. 85, June 22, 1964, pp. 22-30.)

Ha-nhi were contemptuously called "U-ni" by Thai in past. Ten years ago they lived in caves and went naked as a result of Thai oppression. Only 600 remained. Today there are 2,800 in Muong Te district, 77% in 8 cooperatives, and the rest in labor-exchange teams. The most stubborn hold-out was the sorcerer, who only joined a cooperative last year. They are now prospering: last year they sold 38 tons of rice and 5 tons of maize to the government, they have eliminated opium addiction, they have a militia and a theatrical troupe, they have irrigated and terraced fields, 359 can read and write. They now work together with Thai, belong to same Party cells, and even make loans of rice and maize to them. There are 99 Party members and also some in administrative posts and in the army. The executive secretary of one Party cell is a former opium addict. A woman Party member is a cripple, who works as a clerk. See Mong 1957.

Ha, Van Thu
1956   "Historical origin of the peoples of Viet Bac Autonomous Zone," Nhan Dan 842: 3, June 24. (English translation: Joint Publication Research Service D C 198, The ethnic minorities of North Vietnam, July 1, 1958, pp. 5-7.)

Lo-lo of Cao-bang come from China.

Haberlandt, Michael

1922-23 "Ostasien," in G. Buschan, ed., Illustrierte Völkerkunde, Stuttgart: Strecker und Schröder. (Bd. 2, 2 und 3 aufl.: 559-688.) (First edition 1910.)

    Lolo: Short summary section. The "Lisu" of Hainan are not Tibeto-Burman. Photos.

Halpern, Joel M.

1961 Population statistics and associated data, Laos Project Paper No. 3, Los Angeles, University of California (mimeographed).

Hammerton, Sir John Alexander, ed.

1922-24 Peoples of all nations, 7 vols., London, The Fleetway House. 5,436 pp.

    Volume 2 contains photos by Scott of Akha (pp. 1061, 1064, 1072), La'hu (p. 1084), Lihsawa (p.1073); by R. J. Steele of Akha (p. 1081); by Pollard of Nosu (pp. 1330, 1334, 1335, 1336).

Hanks, Jane R.

1964a National security in northern Thailand (mimeographed). 15 pp.

    Thai-tribal relations. Patron-client system of Shan and Akha.

1964b Rite and cosmos: An Akha diary (manuscript). 72 pp.

    Akha, Lahu, and Lisu north of the Mae Kok, Thailand.

1964c The Akha patrilineage, National Science Foundation, Bennington-Cornell Anthropological Survey (mimeographed). 23 pp.

    Akha patronymic linkage names. Occasions for the recital of names of ancestors, heroes, and spirits.

                The patrilineage is the most important institution
                maintaining Akha homogeneity and indicates links with
                Chinese culture. Comparison with lineages in Yunnan.
Hanks, Lucien M.
    1975   Maps of ethnic settlements of Chiengrai Province north
                of the Mae Kok River, Thailand, for 1964, 1969, 1974,
                with gazetteer, Ithaca, Southeast Asia Program, Cornell
                University.
                    Akha, Lahu, and Lisu villages are mapped, and
                information is provided on their population and head-
                men.
Hanks, Lucien M., Jane R. Hanks, and Lauriston Sharp, ed.
    1964   Summary of the data from the Mae Kok area of Thailand,
                with some afterthoughts on upland settlement patterns
                (mimeographed). 36 pp.
                    See 1965, below.
    1965   Ethnographic notes on northern Thailand, Ithaca,
                Cornell University, Southeast Asia Program, Data Paper
                58. xi, 96 pp.
                    Interethnic relations north of the Mae Kok in
                Chiangrai Province. Some villages consist of Lisu,
                Lahu, and other groups, some of whom intermarry. The
                authors seem surprised at finding ethnic intermarriage
                and mixed villages, but these have been noted by
                travelers as early as the nineteenth century. Tale about
                the Lisu brother and sister who saved the world. The
                ethnographic map (1964), issued separately, with in-
                formation on each village, is the best available for
                any part of the area settled by the Lolo group.

Includes the following articles: "Headmanship among the Lahu Na" by M. R. Wutilert Devakul (pp. 31-35), "The brother and sister who save the world: A Lisu folk-tale" by William H. Wohnus and Lucien M. Hanks (pp. 67-71), and "Philadelphia among the Lahu" by Lauriston Sharp (pp. 84-90). See also Hanks 1975, above.

Hanks, Lucien M., Jane R. Hanks, Lauriston Sharp, and Ruth B. Sharp
1964 <u>A report on the tribal peoples in Chiengrai Province north of the Mae Kok River</u>, Bangkok, <u>Siam Society Data Paper 1</u> (mimeographed).
 See Hanks, Hanks, and Sharp 1965.

Hansen, Henny Harald
1960 <u>Some costumes of highland Burma at the Ethnographical Museum of Gothenburg</u>, Göteborg, <u>Etnografiska Museet Etnologiska Studier 24</u>. 81 pp.
 Lisu costume. Photos.

Harris, George L.: see Henderson 1971b.

Hart, Virgil C.
1888 <u>Western China, A journey to the great Buddhist centre of Mount Omei</u>, Boston, Ticknor and Company. 306 pp.
 Lolo: Told by Chinese of warlike Lolo (p. 282).

Haudricourt, André G.
1957-58 "Des consonnes uvulaires en Tibéto-Birman," <u>Société de Linguistique de Paris, Bulletin</u> 53,1: 257-67.
 Yi phonemics based on a comparison of Vial 1909 and Ma Xué-liáng 1951, both of whom note an uvular series distinct from postpalatal series. 105 glyphs with corresponding sounds noted.

Henderson, John W., ed.
1971a   Area handbook for Burma, DA Pam 550-61, Washington, D. C., Foreign Area Studies, American University and Department of Army. (1968 edition edited by T.D. Roberts.)

   Incorrectly considers Akha and Ekaw two different groups (p. 85). Lahu and Lisu mentioned.

1971b   Area handbook for Thailand, DA Pam 550-53, Washington, D.C., Foreign Area Studies, American University and Department of the Army. (Earlier editions: 1956 edited by Lauriston Sharp, Frank J. Moore, and Walter Vella; 1958 edited by Wendell Blanchard, both for Human Relations Area Files; 1963 edited by George L. Harris and 1968 edited by Harvey H. Smith, both for American University.)

   Incorrectly states that the Lisu eldest son lives with parents, while younger sons move away. (It is often the youngest married son who remains with parents, rarely the eldest son.) Akha and Lahu mentioned.

Henry, Augustine (See also Start and Wright 1936.)
1902   "On the Lolos and other tribes of western China," British Association for the Advancement of Science, Report 765-66.

   Summary of Henry 1903, below.

1903   "The Lolos and other tribes of western China," Royal Anthropological Institute, Journal 33: 96-107.

   Woni south of Red River also include Pudu, Mahe, Kado, Aka, and Piza. Linguistically similar to Lolo, but biologically different.

Pula is a dialect of Lolo near Mengtse and Yuanchiang. Pula are only 4-1/2 feet tall and may be aborigines on whom the Lolo imposed their language (as they have on the Muji, Aja, Sansu, A-ch'o, and K'u-ts'ung). Lolo language and script. Lolo soul seen in dreams. Soul leaves body during illness and at death, when it must be witnessed or it can become dangerous. Red cord tied about arm to retain soul. Ancestral tablets made of pieris tree wood (same as that used for the Lolo ark), thatch, bamboo (9 joints for female, 7 for male), written by priest. Three types of evil spirits: ghosts of accidental or unclean deaths, invisible demons, and "slo-ta," unusual phenomena which portend and cause disasters. They must be coaxed and threatened. Twice a year a pig and fowl are sacrificed at the worship stone near the village tree, which houses a dragon-protector. People of each surname group worship a different patriarch, who lives in the sky; they cannot touch or eat their totem. Creation and deluge legends. Songs. Some of the people whom Henry visited and took for Lolo were actually Miao (cf. Start and Wright 1936, where "Lolo" costumes he collected are actually Miao).

Review: Edouard Chavannes, 1903, T'oung Pao série 2 and 4,5: 422-24.

Hertz, William Axel
1912 "Myitkyina District," Burma Gazetteer, Rangoon, Office of the Superintendent, Government Printing, Burma. (Reprinted in 1960.)

>Lisu immigrated into district in large numbers after British annexation. Reports of Yawyin rebellion in Yunnan in 1901-02, which was led by a shaman; Kachin and Lashi were also involved. The Yawyin are included in the figures for the Kachin (pp. 72-74, 102).

Hervey de Saint-Denys, Marie Jean Leon Marquis d': see Ma, Touan-lin

Hestermann, F.
   1915   "Die nicht-chinesische Schrift der Lolo in Yünnan (Südwestchina)," Wiener Zeitschrift für die Kunde des Morgenlandes 29: 231.

>Lolo writing.

Hicks, C. E.
   1910   "The Nou Su people of the neighbourhood of Chao-tung in Yunnan," Chinese Recorder and Missionary Journal 41,3: 210-19.

>Nou-su twin ancestors, Wu-sa and Wu-meng, came to Chao-tung plain and found the P'uh (lao ren) people. The Chinese have pushed the Nou-su across Kinsha River and into the mountains. Land quarrels frequent. Subgroups include Black (Na Su); White (Tu Su); Lake or Red, who are blacksmiths; A-u-tsi, who are feltmakers and basketmakers. Marriage by capture; bride may have to wait 10 years before revisiting her parents. Small bamboo basket contains bamboo tubes, one or two inches long, in which there are pieces of grass and wool representing each ancestor couple. Every three years the basket is burned and a new one made. Hill worship. New Year's Customs. Writings. Summarized in Clarke 1911: 114-16.

Hill Tribe Welfare Division, Department of Public Welfare, Ministry
of the Interior, Royal Thai Government

1965 Facts about the Tribal Research Centre, Bangkok.
73 pp.
Objectives, opening speeches. In Thai.

1967a Report on Buddhist missionary activities among the
hill tribes in 1966, Bangkok. 53 pp.
In Thai.

1967b The development and welfare scheme for the hill tribes
in Thailand (B.E. 2510-2514), Bangkok. 68 pp.
Describes Hill Tribes Research Centre, self-help
land settlements, mobile development and social welfare
field units, budget allocations and estimated achieve-
ments of the development and welfare scheme, hill
tribe-government relations. In Thai.

1968a How the newspapers talk about us, Bangkok.
Suwan Ruenyote and Smith Manusrudee on the self-
help settlement shop at Tak and communication problem
with Lahu and Lisu (in Thai, 19 pp.). Laiad
Piboonsawat on Doi Muzer land settlement near Tak,
which includes Lahu and Lisu villages; livestock
epidemics, communist infiltration (in Thai, 38 pp.).
Anonymous articles in English on "Undefined Loyalties,"
factors separating highlanders and lowland Thai, and
"Languages minus Scripts: educating tribesmen poses
difficult problem for government agencies" (11 pp.).

1968b Report on dissemination of Buddhism among hill tribes
in northern Thailand, Bangkok. 69 pp.
Purposes and operations of Phra Dhammayak and

-130-

Phra Dhammatoute missionary teams. Names of Akha, Lahu, and Lisu volunteers for priesthood in 1967. In Thai.

1970   *In-service orientation on hill tribes, First Symposium*, Bangkok.

Includes cultural summaries on Khe Lisu (16 pp.), Lisu (8 pp. not clear whether these are considered two separate groups--they should not be), Muzer (by C. Audretch, C. Chaffee, J. Jen-uksorn, C. Vongburi, and K. Thong-on, 10 pp.), Lahu (by B. Srisawasdi and D. Jones, reprints, 42 pp.), and classification of the Lahu by S. Wongprasert (3 pp.). In Thai.

Hinton, Harold C.
1955   "The national minorities in China," *Far Eastern Economic Review* 19,11: 321-25, 12: 367-72.

Minority problems and policy. 1953 census, regional autonomy, centralizing forces, limited benefits of "autonomy" or minority status.

Hinton, Peter
1968   "Agricultural development in northern Thailand," *Agricultural Credit Newsletter*.

Lahu swiddening and the need for development. In Thai.

Hinton, Peter, ed.
1969   *Tribesmen and peasants in North Thailand*, Chiang Mai, Tribal Research Centre. 117 pp.

Akha, Lahu, Lisu of Thailand.

See Dellinger (1969b), Kickert (1969), Walker (1975), and Wyss (1969).

Hope, Edward Reginald
1968 "Lisu," in William A. Smalley, ed., Phonemes and Orthography in Eight Marginal Languages of Thailand (mimeographed).
Lisu morpheme types.
1969 Lisu religion (manuscript).
1972 The deep syntax of Lisu sentences: A transformational case grammar, doctoral dissertation, Canberra, Australia National University. xi, 185 pp. (published in 1974, Australian National University Research School of Pacific Studies, Department of Linguistics, Pacific Linguistics, Series B, No. 34, viii, 184 pp.)

Lisu grammar is analyzed in terms of a base, including a set of presuppositions and a focus. The logical relations that hold between the components of the sentences are not related to their relative order, but to logical notions associated with those components; these notions are the case labels. A series of base rules and transformational rules are posited sufficient to generate all of the major Lisu surface structures.

1973 "Non-syntactic constraints on Lisu noun phrase order," Foundations of Language 10: 79-109.

Lisu order of noun phrases in a surface sentence cannot be accounted for adequately in syntactic terms. The unpredictable nature of the placement of subject and object results in ambiguity of meaning, which can be resolved only by reference to context. The constraints on the order of noun phrases are semantic and logical in character, not syntactic. Based on Hope 1972, above.

n.d. <u>Lisu-English, English-Lisu dictionary</u> (manuscript). Not seen.

Hsiao, Sidney Chihti (Pinyin: Xiao, Zhi-di) (assisted by An-chi Wong)
1946 "A first study of the blood groups among some inhabitants of west Yunnan," <u>Royal Anthropological Institute of Great Britain and Ireland, Journal</u> <u>76,1</u>: 51-57.

    Moso of Likiang similar in blood groups to Koko Nor. Min Chia of Tali similar to Hopei, Peking, Mukden. But Mohammedan Min Chia are closer to Mongolians.

Hsin, Wen (Pinyin: Xin, Wen)
1973 "Many nationalities unite against drought," <u>China Reconstructs</u> <u>22,2</u>: 20-21.

    Yi are one of the nationalities in the Kwangsi-Chuang Autonomous Region who solved drought problems by drilling wells. Photos.

Hsin-hua Shè: see New China News Agency (NCNA).

Hsu, Hung-pao (Pinyin: Xu, Hong-bao)
1965 "The Lisus of the Nu River," <u>China Reconstructs</u> <u>14,6</u>: 19-21.

    Lisu grow irrigated rice in Nu River Autonomous Chou, which was established in August 1954. Photos.

Hsu, Itang (or I-t'ang) (Pinyin: Xú Yi-táng)
1932 <u>Les trois grandes races de la province du Yun-nan</u>, Paris, Adrien-Maisonneuve. (Reprint 1932, Librairie russe et française.)

    Translation of selection from <u>Yun-nan tong Zhi</u> by Wang Wen-chao (1894 edition), which itself includes materials reprinted from some 62 earlier sources. Lolo groups include Hei (Black), Po (White, Miao, Hai (Sea), Kan (Land), Sa-mi, A-tcho, Lou-wou, Sa-wan, A-hie, Ko, Pou-la, Ta (Great), Siao (Little). Dress. Holidays. The Hei Lolo were severely "pacified" by Chinese from 1573 to 1620. The Po Lolo wrap the deceased in a wool rug, carry it on a bamboo chair, preceded by seven men, who shoot arrows in the four directions to ward off evil spirits; it is cremated, then a drum is beaten to call the soul (pp. 51-120).

1942 "Léi-bō xíng-jì (Leipo travelogue)," Biān-zhèng gōng-lùn (Frontier Affairs) 2,11-12.

Lolo mentioned.

1944 Léi-bō xiǎo liáng-shān zhī ló-mín (Leipo hsiao liang-shan)(The Lolo of Hsiao Liangshan, Leipo, Southwestern Szechuan, A brief report of an investigation trip to Leipo in the year of 1940), Jīn-líng dà-xúe, Zhōng gúo wén huà yán jiu sǔo cóng kan yi zhǒng (Chengtu, University of Nanking Institute of Chinese Cultural Studies, Series B). 104 pp.

Lolo of Xiao Liangshan, Leibo (Szechwan) came from Yunnan following the defeat of Yang in 1730. They retreated into the Da Liangshan, from which they raided the Chinese in 1802, 1814, and 1839. From 1875 to 1892, they advanced into Xiao Liangshan, and by 1917 most of the eastern portion of Leibo xian was occupied by Lolo. Their villages average 23 families. The typical house of wood, bamboo, and mud has an entrance with carved birds, sun, moon, or prayers,

under which is a wooden guardian eagle blessed by the
"bĭ-mŭ" ("pen mother," shaman); opposite are goats'
horns and chicken feathers remaining from propitiatory
sacrifices. The house may have a kitchen on the east,
a bedroom on the west, and a living room between. In
the northeastern corner is a hearth of three stones,
which must never be touched with the feet, as this will
bring misfortune. Guests of high status are seated
behind the hearth, the host on the right, and lower
status persons nearest the door. Wooden utensils
(including a double-lid toilet bucket), bamboo baskets,
stone tobacco pipes. Staples are maize and buckwheat
pancakes, bean curd, sour and dried vegetables. Rice,
chicken, pork, mutton, and beef are eaten only after
sacrifice. Dress includes blue or black cotton kerchiefs for young girls, and black cotton hats with
ribbons for women. Women also wear earrings with
complicated pendants made by Han. Skirts of four
layers: white, black, red, and blue. Topcoats. At
the age of 5 or 6, a boy lets a strip of hair grow
above the forehead, which is tied into a knot when he
comes of age. Turbans reflect nobility by their size;
white turbans for funerals. The left ear is pierced
once or twice for earrings of beads, coral, amber, or
silver. White or blue topcoats with multicolored
lapels; blue cotton trousers. Both men and women wear
ornaments on their chests: bamboo musical instruments,
spice or needle pouches, charms such as boars' teeth,
tiger claws, bear claws, and a red or blue cotton

pouch in which there are prayers written by the bi-mu. A large outer coat is worn by men. Hunt using dogs, poisoned arrows, or traps. Livestock raising. Both irrigated and swidden agriculture. Land may be acquired by clearing, by inheritance (father to all sons equally), leasing by slaves. Father's sister's daughter marriage preferred. Marriage is generally within one's own class, and may be within one's own clan. Marriage between generations possible. Bridewealth averages 600 to 1,000 taels of silver among chiefs, 300 to 500 among other Black Lolo, and 100 among White. When at least half the bridewealth has been paid, a bi̯-mu̯ examines the two families' horoscopes for an auspicious date for the wedding (they prefer to marry when their age is of an odd number: 13, 15, or 17). After the wedding, the bride lives with her parents until the birth of the first child. Divorce is most frequent during this "waiting-at-home period." Black Lolo especially may take two or more wives. Levirate: widow marries husband's younger brother. Average Black Lolo family is 5.3 and 10 slaves; average White family 6.34. The average annual income of a Black Lolo is 8 times that of a White. Although the Black are the aristocrats and landlords, through corruption and inefficiency they have lost some political power to the White, some of whom were appointed officials during the Ching.

White Lolo, who comprise 89% of the population, are former Han who were captured and made slaves;

many of them have been able to buy their freedom. Some of them are as rich as Black, and all bi-mu, carpenters, and ironworkers are White. The free White and the slaves comprise 98.33% of the population, the Black only 1.67%. There are many rules of etiquette which must be observed between castes. Warfare is announced by a messenger carrying wooden tablet, on which each family makes a notch to signify their participation. The number of notches (odd or even) on each side may be interpreted as an omen. Also read sheep's shoulder bone. In battle, they wear colorful silk and cotton costumes, with hats of woven bamboo with white and yellow cloth. They wear charms and are very superstitious before a battle. Tactics. Women usually mediate an end to wars.

On the 5th, 7th, or 9th day after birth, the bi-mu prays for the baby, cuts its hair, and gives it a name. When a daughter is 13, 15, or 17, she goes through a ceremony performed by her parents and a bi-mu: she changes her hairdo from one to two plaits, and her skirt from two layers to four. The bi-mu chooses an auspicious date and location for cremating the dead. The bi-mu also makes a soul-plate (for honoring the ancestors) of bamboo, wool thread (red for men, green for women) wound around 9 times for men, 7 for women. A chicken is tied to it while the bi-mu recites prayers to rid it of all things unclean; it is then kept near the hearth for one or more years, until the bi-mu takes it to a cave in the mountains.

A rite for sending the spirit to heaven. Three souls: one in the tomb, one roams the world, one is reborn as a man or animal, after going through the otherworld. Spirits and propitiatory rites described. Praying for rain, prognostication, curses, oath taking, superstitions. Bi-mǔ ("pen-mothers") are always men, who usually inherit this office from an uncle; they know how to write and recite prayers. Shi-niang may be men or women who are possessed by the soul of a deceased shi-niang. Both bi-mǔ and shi-niang are White Lolo. Maps. Drawings.

Hsu, Kuang (Pinyin: Xu, Guang)
1975 "Woodcut: A liberated slave of Yi nationality criticizes Lin Piao and Confucius," China Reconstructs 24,4: 3.

Hu, Chang-tu, et al. (Pinyin: Hu, Zhang-du)
1960 China: Its people, its society, its culture, New Haven, HRAF Press. 611 pp.
      Lisu operate iron works in Yunnan.

Hu, Hsien-chin (Pinyin: Hu, Xian-jin)
1938 The four tribes of southern China, Cambridge, Harvard University Library (manuscript).
      Lolo, Yao, Miao, Li: unwarranted generalizations.
1942 "Frontier tribes of southwest China," Far Eastern Survey 11,10: 116-20.
      Nosu, Kachin, Pai-i, and Min-chia would make good fighters against the Japanese. Many are becoming assimilated by the Chinese because they join the bureaucracy. Lung Yin, the governor of Yunnan, is a

Nosu.

Hu, Liang-chen
1957 La société Lolo des Ta-Leang-Chan au sud-ouest de la province de Sseu-Tch'ouan, Doctorat de l'Université de Paris. viii, 551 pp.

Hu, Tan, and Dai Qing-sha
1964 "Hā-ní yǔ yúan-yīn di sōng-jǐn (Vowels with and without stricture in the Hani language), "Zhōng-gúo Yǔ-wén (Chinese Literature) 128: 76-87.

Huang, Chang-lu (sometimes Chang-lo, Ch'ang-lu)
1958a "How the minorities in Yunnan change," Peking Review 24,17: 14-17.

    Lahu: Half of the 130,000 Lahu used to live in a feudal society. Feudal land ownership abolished peacefully in 1955-56. They now produce 477 catties of grain per capita annually, compared to 100-200 in pre-Liberation years.

    Lisu lived in a primitive communal society. They used wooden plows, with blades an inch wide. Since Liberation, they have built 60,000 mou of terraced fields on Kaolikung and Pilohsueh mountains.

    Nu, Tulung, Panglung, Pulang, Chingpo, and Kawa also mentioned.

1958b "Minority nationalities in Yunnan freed from bondage of old customs," Rén-mín rì-bào, Sept. 4. (English translation: Survey of the China Mainland Press, 1859: 11-13.)

    Hani and Yi of Yuankiang, who were at first hesitant to use manure, have renounced their beliefs in spirits for the Communist Party.

1959a   "A new village on the banks of the Nu Chiang in Yunnan," Mínzú Túanjíe (Nationalities solidarity). (English translation: Joint Publications Research Service DC 860: 20-25.)

       Nu and Lisu village with 134 families, dining hall, nursery, stable, old people's home. Chih-tzu lo brigade of Pi-lo People's Commune formed their first mutual aid team in 1955. Former Nu slave marvels at improvements.

1959b   "6,000,000 minority people in Yunnan province advance at flying speed with the help of Han people," Kunming, New China News Agency, June 11. (English translation: Survey of the China Mainland Press 2038: 35-36.)

       Nuchiang Lisu Autonomous Zhou, previously the poorest mountain area in Yunnan, is now self-sufficient in grains and produces iron, steel, and tools. Author is NCNA correspondent.

1965   "Yunnan's minority peoples on the socialist road," Peking Review 23: 22-25.

       Lisu of Nuchiang Autonomous Zhou trebled grain output in 4 of 5 counties in their first 10 years, 440 households of Santai Mountain (including Chingpo and Penglung as well as Lisu) increased grain production 6 times since Liberation. Members of Sunglin People's Commune remember Kuomintang (Nationalist Chinese) raids; one in 1949 took 100 lives. After Liberation, every former slave and serf received 1.5 to 3 mu of land, and every 3 households received an ox.

Huáng, Tiě, Yáng Zhǐ-yǒng, and Liú Yǐ, ed.
1954　　　Ā shī mǎ, n.p., Zhōng gúo chīng nián chū bǎn shè
　　　　　(Young China Publication Company).
　　　　　　Shani legend in Chinese. See Gladys Yang
　　　　　1955a and 1955b.

Huard, P.
1939　　　"L'endémie goitreuse dans la Chine du Sud-Ouest et en
　　　　　Indochine française," L'Institut Indochinois pour
　　　　　l'Etude de l'Homme, Bulletin 3,1: 113-15.
　　　　　　Akha goiter.

Hudspith, J. Edwin
1969　　　Tribal highways and byways: A church growth study in
　　　　　North Thailand, thesis, Fuller Theological Seminary.
　　　　　363 pp.
　　　　　　Akha, Lahu, and Lisu religious beliefs and how
　　　　　they may be used (as highways) to further the growth
　　　　　of Christian churches among them.

Hutton, James H.
1962　　　"Lisu," Encylopedia Britannica.
　　　　　　Erroneous in most respects. Claims Lisu belong
　　　　　to Haddon's "protomorphus," with Caucasian affinities.
　　　　　See Fürer-Haimendorf 1968.

Intharaksa, Chana
1970　　　"Arunjarung thi Paapee (Dawn at Paapee)," Chiang
　　　　　Mai 10-14: 60-61.
　　　　　　Lisu living near Pa Pae, Mae Taeng district,
　　　　　Chiang Mai Province, Thailand. Photos. In Thai.

Investigation Group, Revolutionary Committee, Liangshan Yi Autonomous
　　　Zhou, Szechwan, and Revolutionary Committee, Meiko Xian, Szechwan

1971	"Chairman Mao's brilliant 'May 7 directive' illuminates emancipated slaves' road to running schools," New China News Agency, Oct. 16. (English translation: Survey of the China Mainland Press 71-44: 11-14.)

Yi former serfs of Walikou commune, Meiku Xian have started own school, linking education and labor for all ages to study Mao thought, cultural and scientific subjects. In 1960, Liu Shao-chi and his agents said that education had proceeded beyond economic base and chased some students out of school.

Its, Rudol'f F.

1968	Proiskhozhdenie narodov Iuzhnogo Kitaia: Ocherki etnicheskoi istorii chzhuan, miao, i itszu (The formation of the peoples of South China: Notes on the ethnic history of the Chuan, Miao and Yi). Institut etnografii imeni N. N. Mikluho-Maklaia, Akademii nauk SSSR.

Cited in Leonard H. D. Gordon and Frank J. Shulman, eds., Doctoral dissertations on China, A bibliography of studies in western languages, 1945-1970 (Seattle and London, University of Washington Press, 1972).

Izikowitz, Karl Gustav

1939	"Traps from the Lamet and the Puli Akhá," Ethnos 4: 2-20.

Akha near Muong Sing use deadfall, simple snares, spring-pole snares, spear traps, and bird nets. Illustrations.

1943	"Quelques notes sur le costume des Puli-Akha," Ethnos

     8,4: 133-52.

     Akha dress and ornaments described and compared to those of other Asian peoples, including Lissu. Photos.

1951   Lamet: Hill peasants in French Indo-China, Götebørg, Ethnografiska Museet, Ethnologiska Studier No. 17. 375 pp.

     Akha mentioned for comparative purposes. Photos

Jaafar, Syed Jamal: see Anthony R. Walker, ed., 1975.

Jack, Robert Logan

1904   The back blocks of China, London, Edward Arnold. (Reprint 1969, New York, Greenwood Press.) 269 pp.

     Lolo murder Chinese and steal their cattle (p. 97). Lolo costume (pp. 100-01), housing (pp. 116, 129-30), village and feud described (pp. 118-19), mixed Sifan-Lolo village (p. 110). Map, photos.

Jacobs, Oma Lee

1970   Bibliography on the Akha, Bangkok, Battelle Memorial Institute, Thailand Information Center. 45 pp.

     Akha: About 80 entries.

Jamieson, C. E.

1923   "The aborigines of West China," China Journal of Science and Arts 1,4: 376-83.

     Lolo exorcist shuts eyes and places forefinger on page of exorcist book; the figure it falls on must be sacrificed (photograph of book). Black Lolo are the only aborigines represented on horseback in Chinese drawings. They introduced horses to Kweichow. They were appointed by Chinese to rule over White Lolo and

Flowered Miao in third century. Chang Ying says that they were originally called Ko-lo from the age of that name.

Jamieson, E.
1909   Habits and customs of the Muhsos (Black and Red) also known as Lahus, Ethnographical Survey of India, Burma, No. 3, Rangoon, Office of the Superintendent of Government Printing, Burma. 6 pp.

Lahu came from southwestern China and now inhabit Wa country, Kengtung, Trans-Salween, Mongpan, and Mongpai (Siam). They are related to Kwis of Kengtung. Black Lahu offer to house nat every 12 days. Red Lahu offer on full and waning moon, but tinged with Buddhism. Woman has high status: customarily groom goes to live near bride's father; if woman divorces she pays 8 rupees, but if man initiates divorce he pays 15. Dress. Cremation. Ordeals: picking lead from fire, chewing mouthful of rice: guilty if grains not properly broken. Only trade item is opium.

Jén-mín jih-pào: see Rén-mín rì-bào.

Jensen, Hans
1935   Die Schrift in Vergangenheit und Gegenwart, Glückstadt und Hamburg, n.p. (Third edition: 1969, Berlin, Deutscher Verlag der Wissenschaften.) 607 pp.
          Lolo (pp. 144-47).

Jì, Jié-fēi
1944   "Nán-shāo jiàn gúo shǐ mò (The rise and fall of Nanchao)," Biān-zhèng gōng-lùn (Frontier Affairs) 3,4.

Jì, Xī-chén (or Jì Syī-chén or Chi, Hsi-chên)

-144-

1958   Liáng-shān yí zú di fei yué (The Liang Shan Yi tribe's Great Leap Forward), Peking, Kē Sywé pǔ jí (General Science Publishers). 138 pp.

    Yi: Liang Shan Autonomous Region, established in 1955, has a population of 970,000, of whom 706,000 are Yi. The Yi's first ancestor was Chywe Li He Gu Hou. During Chou they were called "Pù," during three kingdoms "Nán Mán," during Chin and Sui "Lyāo." Some say that during Tang dynasty, Black Yi came from the north in search of pasture and conquered the agricultural White Yi. But according to Tang records, the Yi tribe of Nan Syao Gwo of Yunnan entered Szechwan in 671, 674-75 A.D., occupying the area around Chengtu, where they enslaved artisans and peasants. Before Liberation, the Black Yi, who comprised 5% of the population, owned 60-70% of the arable land, 80% of the slaves and provisions, 40-60% of the horses, cattle, and sheep. The slaves, who made up 70% of the population, owned 5% of the arable land and paid the Black Yi land rents in labor (30-80 days a year) or goods (50-60% of the harvest); traditional gifts when a Black Yi married, died, built a house, or was ill; aided them in feuds; and repaid debts. Four classes of slaves: Chyu Nwo, who had bought freedom; Ān Jyā Wa Dz, who lived separately from their masters and may have had their own slaves (San Tao Wa Dz); and Gwo Yā, who lived in their masters' houses. Slaves took their masters' surnames. There are over 100 territorially-based clans with elected or hereditary leaders owning

-145-

clan pastures and forests. Clans were equal in status and always feuding; a sponsor was necessary for a Yi traveling through another clan's land. The over-all headmen appointed by the Han in Yuan, Ming, and Ching dynasties were never effective. Because of poor agricultural techniques and lack of motivation, harvests were poor; opium was grown on the best land. At husband's death, a wife had to marry a relative of her dead husband. Spirit doctors were not Black Yi; they selected New Year's Day, which therefore varied from clan to clan. Calendar based on 10 months of 16 days each. Long sections on improvements since Liberation.

Ji-niu-bu Ha (or Chi-niu-pu Ha)
1971 "Chairman Mao's revolutionary line is the lifeline of emancipated slaves," Hóng-qí (Red Flag), Jan. 1. (English translation: Survey of the China Mainland Magazines 71-01: 26-33. Excerpts: New China News Agency, Peking, Jan. 15, 1971; English translation: Survey of the China Mainland Press 71-03: 173-76.)

Yi: Author is former slave and head of Revolutionary leading group of Walikou cooperative, Meiku Xian, Liangshan Yi Autonomous zhou, Szechwan. His cooperative has 65 households, 248 people, power plant, brick and tile kiln, lime kiln, water mill, and new, tile-roofed houses. Hailaishihku attended Third National People's Congress in 1964 as Yi representative. Revolutionary leading group was formed in 1968, during struggle between two classes, 1958-68. Sabotage by former slave owners and followers of Liu Shao-chi (1962), who alleged that minorities are backward and special. Many quotes from Mao.

Jiang, Dìng-liáng (Jyang, Yìng-Lyáng, or Chiang, Ting-liang)

1938   Kàng zhàn zhōng di xī-nán mín-zú (The people of the southwest during the anti-Japanese war), n.p. 43 pp.

1948a   Xī-nán biān-jiāng mín-zú lùn-cóng (Hsi-nan pien-chiang min-tsu lun-ts'ung) (Articles on border tribes in the south-west), Canton, Hǎi Jū University Press.

    Yi: Article 1: "K'un-ming ching nei te I-min (The Yi people within the limits of Kunming city)," states that the Yi form a community in Kunming, despite lack of official recognition. Originally from northwestern China, they have spirit doctors, scriptures, temples to various deities, and they observe the torch festival on the 24-25th days of the 6th month. Women are free to choose husbands, do most of the work, and therefore have high status--sometimes a woman is head of the household. They love to drink.

Article 4: "(The headman system among the Hai Yi of western Yunnan)," may refer to the Pai-i or the Yi. Ten grades of headmen were established in Yuan dynasty; since the positions were hereditary, they became virtual monarchs and appointed their relatives to other positions. Administrative unit remained the village, whose chief relayed the headman's orders to the people.

Article 7: "(Ju Ke Lyang and the Nan Man):" Ju is still revered today by Han and Yi for pacifying the Yi by capturing their chief, Meng Hwo, 7 times.

Article 8: "(The written languages of the southwest

	border regions):" during late Han, the Yi were known as Jyang, and their language as Bai Lang Wen (white wolf language).
1948b	Liáng-shān yí-zú di nú lì zhì dù (The slave system of the Liang-shan Yi), n.p. 79 pp.
	Yi population estimates, kin terms, and clans. Map, photos.
Jiang, Yong	
1958	"Women of the national minorities in Yunnan make Great Leap Forward," Gūang-míng rì-bào, Aug. 21. (English translation: Survey of the China Mainland Press, 1854: 15-18.)
	Hani song praises new roads and carts, which free women from heavy carrying.
Johnston, Sir Reginald Fleming	
1908	From Peking to Mandalay, A journey from North China to Burma through Tibetan Ssuch'uan and Yunnan, London, John Murray. (Reprint 1972, Taipei, Ch'eng Wen Publishing Company.) 460 pp.
	Liso linguistically closer to Burmese, but live with Moso in Yung-ning district. Both are contemptful of the Lolo. As noted by Orléans, these and many other groups have a tradition that they originally came from the area around Nanking (pp. 281-82, 291-92).
	Lolo robbers (pp. 146, 235). Lolo struggles with Chinese (p. 120). Twenty-three Lolo families have lived at Pa-U-Rong since 1850. A few use Tibetan characters to write in Lolo. Their deities reside on mountains. Dead wear white veils and are thrown into

Yalung River. Inheritance goes to eldest son, but if there is none, one may be adopted, or the inheritance may be given to the lamas (pp. 186-90). Bonin and Vial identify Lolo with Man-tzu. T. W. Kingsmill claims that they are both descendants of Mauryas, mixed with Bod and Kiang of Tibet (pp. 273-76, 286).

Moso call themselves Lashi or Nashi (pp. 281-82).

Jones, Delmos J.

1966 The tribe, the village and over-generalization: Example of the Black Lahu, Report for the National Research Council, Bangkok. 26 pp.

Lahu villages differ from one another.

1967 Cultural variation among six Lahu villages, Northern Thailand, doctoral dissertation, Ithaca, Cornell University. (Dissertation Abstracts 28: 2242B, University Microfilms order no. 6713,916.)

Lahu villages differ from one another. Review: Hans Spielmann, 1968, Siam Society, Journal 56,2: 295-97.

1968 "The multivillage community: Village segmentation and coalescence in northern Thailand," Behavior Science Notes 3,3: 149-74.

The effective social unit among the Lahu and other highlanders in Southeast Asia is a group of villages linked by history, migration, kinship, etc.

Jones, P. H. M.

1966 "Civilising influence," Far Eastern Economic Review 54,7: 394-97.

Yi, Lisu, Nu, Kutsung, Tulung, and other minorities

in China developing and becoming communist. Photos.
Jui: see Ruey, Yih-fu.
Jùn, Dé
1935   "Chūan-nán mǎ biān yí-rén zhī gài kuàng (The general condition of the Yi of the Ma border area in southern Szechuan)," Kāng-zàng qián-bāng (Sikang-Tibet Pioneer) 2,9.

JUSMAG Psychological Operations School
1967   A target analysis of the major hill tribes of northern Thailand (mimeographed). 19 pp.
        Akha, Lahu, Lisu. Village locations, maps, historical background, attitudes toward government, weapons, leaders, Communist influence.

JUSMAG Seventh Psychological Operations Group
1968   The Akha tribal group in north Thailand (mimeographed). 19 pp.
        Akha cultural summary. Map.

Kacha-ananda, Chob
1971   "The Akha swinging ceremony," Siam Society, Journal 59,1: 119-28.
        Akha ceremony observed at Saen Chai, Thailand, in August 1967. First day ancestors honored, chickens sacrificed. Second day two village swings built, also household swings for children. Third day feast on pigs and an ox. Fourth day swinging. See Urbani 1974.

Kandre, Peter
1967   "Autonomy and integration of social systems: The Iu Mien ("Yao" or "Man") mountain population and their neighbors," in Peter Kunstadter, ed., Southeast Asian

Tribes, Minorities and Nations, Princeton, Princeton University Press, 2: 583-638.

Akha, Lahu, Lisu mentioned.

Kanthathatbamrung, Manat

1965 *Assistance to the northern hill tribes provided by the Border Patrol Police*, thesis, Bangkok, Thammasat University Institute of Public Administration. 154 pp.

Akha, Lahu, Lisu: differences between these cultures and Thai culture; problems with opium, nomadism and opium. Government policies toward these problems, also husbandry and agricultural promotion, security. Border Patrol Police activities in these areas. In Thai.

1967 *Welfare and management activities of Border police among the hill tribes in northern Thailand*, Bangkok, Thammasat University Department of Public Administration. 89 pp.

English version of his 1965 volume, above.

Kao, Hua-nien

1955 "Yang-wu Hāní yǔ chu-tan (Preliminary investigation of the Hani language of Yang-wu), *"Zhōng-shān dà-xué xué-bào* (Scholarly reports of Chung-shan University).

1958 *Í-yǔ yǔ-fǎ yén-chìu* (A study of the grammar of the Yi language), Peking, Scientific Publishing Company. 161 pp.

Nasu grammar, texts, word list.

Kasemsri, M. L. Pichitwong

1973 "Muser chief gives Burmese the slip," *Bangkok Post*, Feb. 19: 5.

Muser (Lahu) spiritual leader Pu Caw Lon (Thai spelling: Pu Chong Luang) escaped Burmese attack. He declares war on Burmese. Photos. See Thamsakati 1973, Thavisin 1973.

Katsura, Makio

1965a Interim report of field research on the Akha language No. 1, Report to the National Research Council, Bangkok. 5 pp.

1965b Interim report of field research on the Akha language No. 2, Report to the National Research Council, Bangkok. 10 pp.

1966a "Akago no genchi chōsa yori (Notes on a survey of the Akha language in Thailand)," Tōnan Ajia Kenkyū (Southeast Asian Studies) 3, 3: 195-99.
Akha. In Japanese.

1966b "Akago Aru isson hōgen no onso (The phonemes of the Alu dialect of Akha)," Tōnan Ajia Kenkyū (Southeast Asian Studies) 4,1: 122-32.
Akha. In Japanese.

1968a "Futatabi kitatai yori - Lahu-nago no genchi chosa (Notes on a field survey of the Lahu-na language in northern Thailand)," Tōnan Ajia Kenkyū (Southeast Asian Studies) 6, 2: 211-20.
Lahu-na. In Japanese.

1968b "Rafu-Na go no onso taikei: Rafu-Na go no kijutsu (Lahu-na phonemics - A descriptive study of the Lahu-na language in northern Thailand)," Tōnan Ajia Kenkyū (Southeast Asian Studies) 6, 3: 113-37.
Lahu-na. In Japanese.

1968c "Akago no on-in kōzō oyobi keitai kōzō no gairyaku (An outline of the phonological and morphological structure of the Akha language in northern Thailand)," Tōnan Ajia Kenkyū (Southeast Asian Studies) 6, 4: 220-40.

                Akha. In Japanese.

1970   "An outline of the structure of the Akha language (Part I) - Introduction and phonemics," <u>Tōnan Ajia Kenkyū</u> (Southeast Asian Studies) <u>8</u>, <u>1</u>: 16-35.

                Akha. In English.

Kauffmann, Hans-Eberhard

1934   "Landwirtschaft bei den Bergvölkern von Assam und nord-Burma," <u>Zeitschrift für Ethnologie</u> 66, 1-3: 15-111.

                Akha, Lahu, Lisu, Lolo, Mosso: Crops, livestock, tools, division of labor by sex. Maps.

1966   "Beobachtungen im Lisu-dorf Tham Ngob, Nordthailand, <u>Wiener Völkerkundliche Mitteilungen</u> <u>8</u>: 55-68.

                Lisu village in Fang district, Chiang Mai Province, Thailand, housing, dress, spirits, marriage, graves. Description based on a weekend visit.

Kĕ, Xìang-Fēng: see Ko, Siang-feng.

Keen, F. G. B.

1973   <u>Upland tenure and land use in north Thailand</u>, Bangkok, Southeast Asia Treaty Organization. 172 pp.

                Lahu and Lisu mentioned.

Kerr, Arthur Francis George

1923   "Report of the Botanical Section of the Ministry of Commerce, September 1st 1920 to December 31st 1922," <u>The Record</u> (Board of Commercial Development, Siam) <u>8</u>: 8-16, <u>9</u>: 3-12 (English edition).

                Black Musô village of about 100 houses near Doi Pahom Pok, Fang district, Chiang Mai Province, Thailand. Musô cultivate peaches. Their clearings are overgrown with weeds and bushes. Tiger attacking their ponies. Musô extend as far south as 17°30'N (Tak). Map.

Kerr, Arthur Francis George, and Erik Seidenfaden
1950 "Ethnology," in <u>Thailand, Nature and Industry</u>, Volume 1, Bangkok, Department of Commercial Intelligence, Ministry of Commerce.
  Musso divided into Red and Black.
  Lissu and Ko (Akha) photos.

Kia Tan: see Pelliot 1904.

Kickert, Robert W.
1966 <u>Cornell University-Bennington College Field Research Project Report</u> (manuscript). 18 pp.
  Akha, Lahu, and Lisu north of Mae Kok, Chiangrai Province, Thailand. Migrations, ethnic relations, relations with Thai Border Police, government policies, and security problems.
  See Hanks, Hanks, and Sharp 1964, 1965; Hanks, Hanks, Sharp, and Sharp 1964.

1967 <u>The Akha of A'du</u>, Report to the United States Army Advanced Research Projects Agency, Research and Development Center, Thailand. 50 pp.
  Akha of A'du village, Mae Chan district, Chiangrai Province, Thailand. Interim field research report. Demography, surname groups, village stability, leaders. Map, photos.

1969 "Akha village structure," in Peter Hinton, ed., <u>Tribesmen and Peasants in North Thailand</u>, Chiang Mai, Tribal Research Centre: 35-40.
  Akha of Chiangrai Province, Thailand: villages, households, descent, rank spiritualists, settlement

of disputes.

Kingdon-Ward, Francis: see Ward, Francis Kingdon.

Kingsmill, Thomas W.

1900-01 "Han Wu Ti, and the aboriginal tribes on the south western frontier of China," China Review 25, 111: 103-09.

    Yelang (Nashi?) and Mimo (Moso) mentioned as southwestern I in Shiki in the time of Wu (140-86 B.C.).

Ko, Siang-feng (or Hsiang-feng) (Pinyin: Kē Xiāng-fēng)

1938 "Lólo wén zì zhī chū bù yán jiū (A preliminary study on the written language of the Lolos)," Jīn-líng Xué-bào (Nanking Journal) 8, 1-2: 23-25.

    Lolo writing. In Chinese.

1949 "Marriage among the Independent Lolos of western China," American Journal of Sociology 54: 487-96.

    Lolo of Liang-shan in 1939-40 remained robbers and kidnappers of local Chinese, despite repeated attempts to conquer them from the time of Chu-keh Liang's invasion in 225-26 A.D. They have destroyed roads built in their territory. Black Lolo are feudal lords, who differ physically from the White Lolo serfs and slaves. Chang Long-ching estimated 2,225 Black and 14,733 White families in eastern Liang Shan in 1934. Western part has about the same population. Ren Chentong estimated the average Black family at 5.3 plus 10 slaves, and the average White family at 6.34, for a total population of 23,850 Black, 45,000 slaves, and 190,000 White. Chinese traders bring salt, cloth, and cotton for hides and drugs; they are often members of secret societies, which afford them protection. Equality of Lolo men and women. Marriage between Black and White is forbidden. Small exogamous lineages. Bride-price. After marriage ceremony, the wife returns to her parents' home for one or two years.

Ku, Yen-wu (Pinyin: Gu, Yan-wu)

1823 T'ien-hsia chun-kuo li-ping shu, n.p. 64 vols. (Numerous reprints.) Historical geography.

Lisu and Wei of Yun-lung zhou wear long hemp gowns. Women wear white clothes. In Chinese.

Kuang-ming Jih-pao: see Guang-ming ri-bao.

Kuhn, Isobel

1947 Nests above the abyss, London and Philadelphia, China Inland Mission. 254 pp.

Lisu of Yunnan. Photos.

1956 Ascent to the tribes, Chicago, Moody Press. 315 pp.

Lisu: Kuhn and her family missionized in Yunnan from 1929 to 1949 and in Thailand from 1952 to 1954 for the China Inland Mission (now the Overseas Missionary Fellowship). Despite the fact that she was fluent in the Lisu language, her books display considerable ignorance of them, and especially of Lisu religion. She regularly greets Lisu strangers by announcing that she has a message from God for them, urges those she knows better to destroy their "demon" shelf, refuses to watch "demon" dances, is openly shocked by the vulgarity of their love songs, and flagrantly distrusts the "witchdoctors." Fortunately, her successors are much better informed. This book is partly about the brief stay of OMF missionaries at Thango, Fang district (cf. Kauffmann 1966). Photos.

1957 By searching, London, China Inland Mission. 128 pp.

1959 In the arena, London, Overseas Missionary Fellowship. 222 pp.

1960 Stones of fire, Chicago, Moody Press. 224 pp.
 Lisu of Yunnan.

Kunstadter, Peter, ed.

1967 Southeast Asia tribes, minorities and nations, 2 vols., Princeton, Princeton University Press. 902 pp.

"China: Introduction" (pp. 149-67): Minorities listed with Chinese character, populations, distribution, occupations, religion, language, autonomous areas.

"Thailand: Introduction" (369-400): List of minorities, populations, locations. Various organizations concerned with minorities.

"Burma: Introduction" (pp. 75-91). List of minorities, populations, and locations.

"Vietnam: Introduction" (pp. 677-702). List of minorities. Maps, photos. See Diao 1967, Kandre 1967.

Lajonquière: see Lunet de Lajonquière.

Lamjuan

1969 Chaaw Khǎw (Hill peoples), Bangkok, Sǎmnákphim Bandaansaana. 271 pp.

Akha, Lahu, Lisu: Superficial notes extracted from newspapers. In Thai. Photos.

Larnlue, Aroon

1970 "Hill tribes: problems and programs," Bangkok World,

Apr. 5: 17.

Akha, Lahu, Lisu: Refugee centers and other government programs.

Lasher, Robert
1963 Report: The 12th Mobile Information Team field trip, visits to 46 villages in Mae Hongsorn, Chiang Mai and Tak provinces, March 26-April 12, 1963, Bangkok, United States Information Service Research Division. 34 pp.

Akha, Lahu, Lisu villages. Maps, photos.

Lasker, Bruno
1950 Human bondage in southeast Asia, Chapel Hill, University of North Carolina Press. 406 pp.

Lolo mentioned as keeping slaves.

Laufer, Berthold
1916 "The Si-hia language," T'oung Pao 17, 1: 1-126.

Lo-lo and Mo-so closely related to Si-hia in vocabulary (pp. 30-57), prevalence of vowel /i/ and dipthongs (especially /ou/) and lack of final explosive consonants (pp. 107-15).

Layton, Dora H.
1968 "The road to Huai Fuang," Sawaddi 6, 4: 10-12, 26-27.

Akha, Lahu, and Lisu villages in Chiangrai Province affected by Border Patrol Police, Seabees, and Hill Tribes Handicraft program.

Lê, Thành Khôi
1955 Le Việt-Nam, Histoire et civilisation, Paris, Editions de Minuit. 542 pp.

Lolo live at all altitudes; 12,000 live in Lai-châu, Lào-kay, and Yên-bái. Includes Black and

-158-

White Lolo, Fou-la, Xa-pho, and Ho-nhi. Grow opium. Maspero supposes a common ancestral culture for Thai, Lolo, Meo, and Chinese (pp. 44-48).

Lê, Van Hao
1971   "Les études et les recherches ethnologiques au Nord Viet Nam," Etudes Vietnamiennes 32: 9-54. (Also published in English: "Ethnological studies and research in North Viet Nam," Vietnamese Studies 32.)

Coong, Si La (or Kha Pe), Co Sung (or La Hu), Bo Kho Pa (or Lao), and U Ni (or Ha Nhi), all Tibeto-Burman groups, were reported by Vuong Hoang Tuyen in his 1966 study, "Geographical distribution of ethnic minorities in North Viet Nam." The Lo Lo, Pu Piao, Cao Lan, and Nhang Ka (or Khang) have also been studied by Vietnamese scholars (pp. 17-19).

Leach, Edmund
1954   Political systems of highland Burma, London, Bell. (Various reprints, including London School of Economics Monographs on Social Anthropology and Boston, Beacon Press.) (HRAF AP1-26.) 324 pp.

Lisu may live with or marry non-Lisu, especially Kachin or Chinese. They may change ethnic identity. Some have class stratification.

LeBar, Frank M., Gerald C. Hickey, and John K. Musgrave
1964   Ethnic groups of mainland southeast Asia, New Haven, Human Relations Area Files Press. 288 pp.

Best and most recent gazetteer type of summary. Some errors: Lisu are in fact found as far south as the provinces of Kamphaeng Phet and Phitsunalok; the population figures based on Young are too high;

alcohol is made from rice and millet as well as from maize; the existence of patrilineal clans is ignored; "maw-pi" is Thai for the Lisu ne pha. The ethnographic map is very useful, but it does not show the Lisu near the Chiangrai-Burma border, in the Kengtung and the Putao areas, nor (now) in the Tirap and the Phitsunalok areas.

LeBar, Frank M., and Adrienne Suddard, eds.
1960   Laos, Its people, its society, its culture, New Haven, HRAF Press (revised 1967). 294 pp.

         Ho (descendants of Chinese traders and Lolo women) number a few thousand in mountains (pp. 36, 43).

         Kho (A'Kha) live in villages of 40-50 households. Village is autonomous, and hereditary headman has limited power (pp. 43, 72).

Leclère, André
1900   "Géographie générale des provinces chinoises voisines du Tonkin," La Géographie 1, 4: 267-88.

         Lolo of Yunnan: brief sketch. Unmarried girls live together in special house. Women have great freedom. Map, photo. See Cordier 1907: 78-81.

Lee, Chin Yang
1941   "Writer finds Yunnan-Burma border region a paradise for adventures," China Weekly Review 96, 8: 260-63.

         Lisu appear only on market days at Mang shih.

Lefèvre-Pontalis, Pierre
1892   "Notes sur quelques populations du nord de l'Indo-Chine," Journal Asiatique, série 8, 19: 237-69.

         Lolo and Ou-Nhi may pass as Chinese. Lolo manuscripts were collected by Vacle. Vocabularies:

White Lolo of Poufang, Ouhni of Poufang, Minkia of Xieng-hung.

1902   Mission Pavie, Indo-Chine 1879-1895, Géographie et Voyages, vol. 5. Voyages dans le Haut Laos et sur les frontières de Chine et de Birmanie, Paris, Ernest Leroux.

Ou-Nhi seem to be most ancient population of Panna d'Ipang, but Lolo have also been there a long time. Yao are newcomers. Ou-Nhi are said to be related to Kha (this is erroneous), but men wear Chinese dress and try to be considered Chinese (pp. 27-28, 34).

Lolo village near Ipang grows tea. Description of dress (pp. 27-28).

Mou-seu have villages in high inaccessible spots such as the Nam Ngao area. Dress. Photos. (pages 150, 154, 160, 296-97, 301-03.)

Legendre, Aimé-François

1905   Le Far-West Chinois, Deux années au Setchouen, Paris, Plon-Nourrit et Cie. 546 pp.

Lolo are Aryans, but have mixed with Mongols, Chinese, aborigines, etc. They worship natural elements. Lolo of Foulin (where P. Martin missionized) and Gue-Leou-Ka. Map, photos.

1909a   "Far West Chinois, Races aborigènes, Les Lolos, Etude ethnologique et anthropologique," T'oung Pao, série 2, 10: 341-80, 399-444, 603-05. (Reprint 1909, Leiden, E. J. Brill, 151 pp.)

Lolo food, houses. Sharp senses, not outwardly emotional, warrior morality. Children, high status of women. Esthetics, costumes, music.

1909b "Les Lolos," Comité Asie-française, Bulletin, Nov. 14: 487-96.

1910a "Les Lolos (Etude anthropologique)," Société d'Anthropologie de Paris, Bulletins et Mémoires, série 6, 1: 77-94. (Extract 1910, Société Géographique de l'Est, Bulletin, n.s. 31: 221-25.)
Lolo anthropometric data.

1910b "Far-West Chinois - Aborigenes: Lolos," Societe d'Anthropologie de Paris, Bulletins et Memoires, serie 6, 1, 6: 520-22.
Lolo anthropometric data on 10 individuals from Ta Tou Ho Basin (Oua Tou Vo massif), which are similar to the 19 of Ngan Ning presented in Legendre 1910a.

1910c Le Far-West Chinois, Kientchang et Lolotie, Chinois-Lolos-Sifans, Impressions de voyage, étude géographique, sociale et économique, Paris, Plon-Nourrit et Cie. 471 pp.
Lolo language resembles Sifan and Tibetan. Food, houses, physical and moral traits, high status of women, hereditary power, three castes, property, law. Religion based on supplication of evil spirits. Agriculture, blacksmiths. Dislike of Han: the name "Lolo" alone is enough to strike terror in Chinese hearts. Chinese are masters only in Ngan-Ning Valley of Lolo country. Description of vendetta in chapter 23. Most information on Lolo is summarized in chapters 38 and 39 (much of this is a repetition of Legendre 1909a). Legendre was a military doctor in Setchouen from 1907 to 1909, during which time he visited Kientchang, and (with Père de Guébriant) Ta Leang Shan. Map,

photos.

1910d "Far West Chinois - Kientchang - Les Lolos," <u>Revue de l'Ecole d'Anthropologie</u> <u>20</u>: 185-205. (English translation 1912, "The Lolos of Kientchang, Western China," <u>Smithsonian Institution Annual Report</u>, 1911: 569-86.)

Lolo of Ta Liang Shan raid and feud constantly. Houses. Description of a surprise attack in 1907, in which Lolo lit fires at corners of village. Prefer marriage with mother's mother family. Scapulimancy with goat or sheep: if crack forms cross it is a good sign, but if fine cracks cut across, further rites must be performed. Patient eats heart of sacrificed animal, blood is offered to God and patient's family eats rest. Three origin stories: (1) couple fall from heaven; (2) male appears and gives birth to bear and monkey; (3) several people fall from heaven and one couple has 10 sons and daughters. Two deluge legends: (1) brother and sister who survive flood give birth to Hsifan, Lolo, and Chinese; (2) brother and sister give birth to bear, monkey, and man. Dead are placed in mortuary box in fetal position and burned. No ancestor cult. Dress. Food. Most powerful tribe is Lo Hong, with 10,000-20,000 fighters. Most villages are autonomous groups of 10-20 households. Photos.

1913a <u>Au Yunnan, et dans le massif du Kin-ho</u> (<u>Fleuve d'Or</u>) Paris, Plon-Nourrit et Cie. xii, 433 pp.

Lisso (Lisu) and Lolo continued to grow opium in 1910 after it had been banned elsewhere in Yunnan (p. 6). Rebel Lisu defeat Chinese troops, who are forced

-163-

                   to plead for mercy (pp. 52-53). Visited several Lisu villages, including Protestant converts. Claims Lisu will not sacrifice young animals, only old ones. They practice apiculture. Map, photos.

1913b   "Voyage d'exploration au Yunnan central et septentrional, Populations: Chinois et aborigènes," Société d'Anthropologie de Paris, Bulletins et Mémoires, série 6, 4, 5: 447-57.

                   Lolo, Lissou, and Lo Wou of Yunnan are timid and peaceful, unlike those of Ta Liang Shan. Dress, agriculture, houses, food, sickness. 90% of population suffers from goiter; other prevalent diseases include malaria, smallpox, leprosy, typhoid fever, and tuberculosis.

Legendre, Aimé-Francois, with Paul Lemoine
    1910   "Généralités sur la géologie des pays Lolos," Bulletin du Museum.

                   Not seen.

Léi, Bó-lún
    1921   "Ló lo rén mín fēng tǔ zhì (An account of the customs and environment of the Lolo)," Dì-lǐ zá-zhì (Geographical Magazine) 12, 1.

Léi, Jīn-liú
    1944   "Yún-nán jí jiāng lólo de zǔ xiān cóng bài (Ancestral worship among the Lolo of the Ji River area in Yunnan)," Bian-zhèng gōng-lùn (Frontier Affairs) 3, 9.

Lepage: see Vissière 1914.

Leparoux
    1905   "Information diverses, Yunnan," Les Missions

Catholiques 37,1888: 375.

    Man-tseu (Lolo?) rob missionary.

Leroi-Gourhan, André, and Jean Poirier, with André-Georges Haudricourt and Georges Condominas.

1953   Ethnologie de l'union française (Territoires extérieurs), Tome second: Asie, Océanie, Amérique, Paris, Presses Universitaires de France. 1083 pp.

    Akha: 4,500 in Laos.

    Lolo: 12,000 in northwestern Tonkin and 5,000 in Laos (called Ho).

    La-ti, La-que, and Ke-lao: 1,000 in northwestern Vietnam.

    Based on Abadie 1924; Diguet 1908; Izikowitz 1939, 1943; and Roux 1924 (pp. 649-51).

LeRoux, P.

1935   "Mort du R. P. Henri Biron, tué en Lolotie," Les Missions Catholiques 67; 3234: 562-64.

    Biron missionized among the Lolo from 1931 to 1935.

Lesserteur, M.

1878   "De quelques tribus sauvages de la Chine et de l'Indo-Chine. II. Les Tou-jen (Kouang-si)," Les Missions Catholiques 10, 473: 309-11.

    Tou-jen resemble the Tchoung-kia-tsé or Y-jên of Kouy-tchéou. Their language is similar to Siamese. They would seem to be a Tai people.

Lévi-strauss, Claude

1949   Les structures élémentaires de la parenté, Paris, Presses Universitaires de France. (Second edition, 1967, Paris, Mouton. English translation, The elementary structures of kinship, (1969, London, Eyre & Spottiswoode.) 639 pp.

Lolo kinship, high bride-prices, initial period when wife lives with her parents, right of female succession, intervention of women in feuds, levirate, ultimogeniture in movable property--all shared with Kachin--but hierarchical positions about hearth, prohibition of marriage between elder brother and younger brother's wife, distinction of junior and senior lines--all shared with Manchu. Erroneously states that White Bones are senior caste and Black Bones are junior (actually White Lolo are junior).

Lewis, Elaine T.
1969 "The linguistically rich Akhas," Sawaddi 7, 3: 8-10, 28.

Akha say of their language "yawku nya" ("complete, satisfying, perfect"), reflecting its complex phonemic character and semantic richness. Photos.

1974 "New Year - Lahu Style," Sawaddi, Nov.-Dec.: 14-16.

Lahu Christian village (Gosay) near Doi Tung, Chiangrai, has over 80 households, mostly Black. Headman owns small truck. At midnight of New Year, guns are fired, and youths draw new water to ritually clean the hands and feet of elders. A pine or other sapling is planted in the middle of the dancing area. Rice cakes and pork are presented to the headman and elders. Photos (by Paul Lewis).

Lewis, Paul W.
1968a Akha-English dictionary, Ithaca, Cornell University

Southeast Asia Program, Data Paper Number 70. 363 pp. Review: James Matisoff, 1969, Journal of Asian Studies 28, 3: 644-45.

1968b "Akha phonology," Anthropological Linguistics 10, 2: 8-18. (Reprinted in Lewis 1969-70, below.)

1968c "The role and function of the Akha 'village priest,'" Behavior Science Notes 3, 4: 249-62.

Akha village priest, his selection and ordination by elders, responsibilites for ceremonies, sacred places, births, deaths, village matters, and fines. His relations with the spirit priest, blacksmith, headman, and shaman. The priest is a stabilizing force in Akha culture, but syncretism has occurred, for example the offerings to the lords of land and water are borrowed from Shan ritual. It is becoming more difficult to recruit priests.

1969 "The rice theme in the Akha culture," Journal of Sociology and Anthropology (Chiang Mai University) 2, 2.

1969-70 Ethnographic notes on the Akhas of Burma, 4 vols., New Haven, Human Relations Area Files, HRAFlex Books AO4-001, AO4-002. 876 pp.

Akha of Kengtung area, Burma, from 1951 to 1966. Best for its descriptions of religious and curing ceremonies, religious specialists, beliefs, life cycle customs, language, and such related topics as proverbs, names, and kinship. Less comprehensive coverage is given to agriculture, hunting, husbandry, food, housing, settlements, property, justice, sexual behavior, family, and other aspects of social and economic organization. The principal limitation of the data is that they were acquired through interviews with informants from several different villages, rather than through participant-observation.

Reviews: Alain Y. Dessaint, 1972, American Anthropologist 72: 852-53, and Journal of Asian and African Studies 7: 313-15.

1970a Introducing the hill tribes of Thailand, Chiang Mai, Chiang Mai University, Faculty of Social Sciences (mimeographed). 102 pp.

Akha, Lahu, Lisu cultural patterns.

1970b Recommendations for the hill tribes of Thailand (manuscript). 10 pp.

Akha, Lahu, and Lisu face three major problems: opium, food, education. They fear leaving the highlands, but they need paddy land.

1970c The hill tribes of Thailand, Chiang Mai, American Baptist Mission. 3 pp.

Organizations in Chiang Mai supporting tribal programs.

1973 "Tone in the Akha language," Anthropological Linguistics 15, 4: 181-88.

Akha tonal changes are described and seen as having developed in order to give more contrast. Three song types: (1) those in which words are important and receive proper tones; (2) tune-oriented songs, in which words are nonsense or of modern meaning and (3) nonvocal music, in which meaning is communicated through the use of tones associated with words.

1974 "An Akha for a day," Sawaddi, Nov.-Dec.: 6, 21-24.

Akha everyday activities. Photos.

Lewis, Paul W., ed.
1969   Lahu li sha tan (Lahu magazine), periodical published in Chiang Mai by the Lahu-Akha-Lisu Association of Churches.

1970   Lahu ya htai hkaw hen tu ve li (Thai study book for Lahus), 2 vols., Chiang Mai, Lahu-Akha-Lisu Association of Churches.

Lewis, Paul W., Yohan, and Ca Ui, translators
1966   G'ui sha ve Li hpu aw suh (New Testament in Lahu), Rangoon, Bible Society of Burma. (1962 edition issued by the British and Foreign Bible Society.)

Li, Can
1937   "Yun-nan bian chu de liang zhong miao-zu bai-yi yu ye-ren (two kinds of Miao tribes, the White Yi and Ye or Wild Men, of the border areas of Yunnan)," Wen-hua jian-she (Cultural Reconstruction) 3, 7.
        Yi and Lisu.

Li Cheng-tchoang: see Siguret.

Li, Hong-de
1958   "The Hani sweep away 1,000-year old practices," Guang-ming ri-bao, Nov. 12. (English translation: Survey of the China Mainland Press, 1928: 21-23.)
        Hani offered pigs and chickens every Dragon day (every 12 days) to high priest, who exploited people. Debates and cooperation led to the abolition of this and other wasteful superstitions, such as spirit propitiation, erection of dragon gates (the old gates were used to build lavatories and pig sties). Dragon mountain, where dead were buried, is no longer taboo.

Li, Lĭn-zăn
n.d. The dragon king sutra in Mosso hieroglyphics (manuscript). 16 pp.

Mosso text, one of 22 collected, concerns a dragon king who escaped to the high mountains to avoid the world, and yet came into conflict with men. Because of his emphasis on cleanliness, when the Mosso sacrifice to the dragon they must go through a cleansing ceremony, and shamans must keep a vegetarian diet (the dragon cannot stand the sight of blood). Copied and translated by He-tsai in Bai-de-ge village, Wei Syi county, Yunnan.

Lĭ, Xù-huá
1935-36 "Dà liáng shān zhī luó-ló mín zú (The Lolo tribes of Greater Liangshan)," Hé bĕi dì yī bó wù yuàn huà bào (First Museum of Hopei Pictorial): 102-103, 106-107.

Li, Yu-i, Fei Hsiao-tung, and Chang Tse-i (edited by Fei Hsiao-tung)
   (Pinyin: Li, You-yi, Fei Xiao-dong, and Zhang, Ze-yi)
1943 Three types of rural economy in Yunnan, New York, Institute of Pacific Relations (mimeographed). 35 pp.

"Weits'un, A mixed community of Chinese and Lolos," by Li. Lolo natives retreated to arid region during Ming (ca. 1380), and in 1467 the native chief was superseded by a Chinese official. The land has since been regarded as the private property of his family. Pressured by high taxes, the Lolo killed most of the Chinese lords in 1847-72. Though pacified and forced to return the land, the Lolo had put an end to the feudal system. Eventually some even bought land. In the traditional serf system, the land was divided among 42 families, each paying dues in kind, plus 15 days' service a year and building materials. They were not free to leave the village without permission. Lot size differed, because a family could cultivate additional unused land. Rent was the same for each lot; it is now 1% to 3.3% of the harvest. After the revolt, only rent was collected, not services. Details of land ownership, cultivation, rent, and income. After revolt, the Chinese became absentee landlords and had difficulty in collecting rents, therefore they were eager to sell. Lolo pay in installments and may pay interest rates of 40-50% in kind. Differences in standards of living correspond not with wealth, but with ethnic differences. Lolo have lower standard of living, despite their thrift and industry, because they inspire to own land. Rich Lolo include opium dealer, brewers, stockbreeder, rice merchants, and Catholic steward. Village is located in Lunan Valley, 180 kilometers south of Kunming.

Liao, Yu-tao
1940 "The torch festival among the Lolo," Xin Ning-yuan (Xi-chang) 1,3.
  In Chinese. See Chao 1950.

Lichiang Regional Chinese Communist Party Committee
1973 "Actively train national minority cadre," Hóng-qī (Red Flag), Mar. 3. (English translation: Survey of China Mainland Magazines 73-3: 18-22.)
  I, Lisu, Nahsi, Nu, Pumi, Tulung areas: 50% of cadres are minority members (67% of leading cadres). Recommends promoting unity between minority and Han cadres.

Liétard, Alfred

1904 "Le district des Lolos A-chi," Les Missions Catholiques 36, 1811: 93-96; 1812: 105-08; 1813: 117-20.
 Lolo buy paddies from Chinese opium addicts. A-chi belong to langue d'o (Vial's "ou"). The writing given them on dough has been lost. After 15, they sleep in groups in granaries. Love songs. Shell money. Chinese collect rents and services and generally oppress Lolo. Catholic evangelization begun in 1888 by Vial at Lou-Mey-y, followed by Kircher (1894-98) and Lietard (1898-). Now have 12 schools. In addition to A-chi, there are A-djay, A-li, and Tsi-cho Lolo. Map, by de Gorostarzu (p. 95). Photos. See Cordier 1907: 82-83.

1909a "Notions de grammaire Lo-lo, Dialecte A-hi," Ecole Française d'Extrême-Orient, Bulletin 9, 2: 285-314.
 "Lo-lo" originally applied only to Lo-lo-p'o, now extended to many groups. Sounds, adjectives, numbers, pronouns, verbs, adverbs, postpositions, phrase construction.
 Review: 1910, Les Missions Catholiques 42, 2126: 108.

1909b "Notes sur les dialectes Lo-lo," Ecole Française d'Extrême-Orient, Bulletin 9, 3: 549-72.
 A-hi, Lo-lo-p'o, P'u-p'a, and Co-ko (both by Bonifacy 1908), Li-p'a or Li-su of Pin-tch'ouan-tcheou on the right bank of the Yangtze, Li-su-p'a (by Théodore Monbeig) vocabularies with French and Tibetan translations. List of Chinese loanwords in A-hi. Text of "Prodigal Son" in A-hi, Lo-lo-p'o, and Tibetan.

1911-12　　"Essai de dictionnaire Lo-lo-Français, Dialecte A-hi," T'oung Pao, série 2, 12: 1-37, 123-56, 316-46, 544-58. "Vocabulaire Français-Lolo," 13: 1-42.

　　　　　Lolo word lists and texts. Lietard was a missionary for the Société des Missions Etrangères de Paris at Lan-gni-tsin, Lou-lou-tcheou, from 1898 to 1904.

1912　　"Au Yun-nan, Min-kia et La-ma jen," Anthropos 7: 677-705.

　　　　　Li-sou, Lo-lo, La-ma jen, Mo-so, Min-kia vocabularies.

1913　　Au Yun-Nan, Les Lolo p'o: Une tribu des aborigènes de la Chine meridionale, Münster, Aschendorff. (Reprint: 1913, Anthropos-Bibliothek 1, 5.) viii, 272 p.

　　　　　Lolo are known by many different names, leading to confusion: Man-tse ("sons of barbarians"), I-jen or I-kia ("foreigners" and more especially Lolo in Yunnan and Thai in Kweichow), Pen-ti jen (when Lolo or Minkia intermarry with Chinese). Hé kou t'eou is the Chinese term applied to noble caste (meaning Black Bones), but it is sometimes used for all independent Lolo, whose correct name is Seu Lo-lo (raw Lolo, in contrast with Chou Lolo, cooked Lolo). Various etymologies of "Lolo." Three Lolo dialects: (1) "a" Lisou p'a (2) "o" Lo-lo p'o, and (3) "ou" Ko-p'ou. Locations of Lisou and Lolo. History: Lolo have probably inhabited Liang Shan since the early part of our era, and at least since tenth century, according to Chinese. Villages range from 10 to 120 families (average 30-40), but Lisou have individual houses near their fields. Houses may be built around courtyard. Grow maize, rice, wheat, buckwheat, sorghum. Agricultural calendar. Use shoulder board to carry baskets. In plains, they use foot-operated rice mortars. Goats, sheep, pigs, fowl, cattle, horses. Hunting, fishing with poison. Dress. Most iron goods are bought from Chinese in exchange for hemp blankets, musk oil. Games include tops, pitching seed in hole, tiger protecting stones, see-saw, dance. Songs with Lolo and French texts (pp. 111-24). Baber's and Devéria's contention that Lolo worship a White Horse is result of confusion over the Chinese writing of pi-mo. They believe in a Creator (whom they mostly ignore), practice simple ancestor worship, and believe in spirits that can cause disease. Two types of sorcerers: one literate. A son will make wooden figures of his dead father and mother; they are kept in the roof thatch until the son's death, when they are burnt by the grandson. During epidemics, the Lolo or Lisou sorcerer may walk a ladder of knives. Many methods of divination are originally Chinese, as are spirit names, but formulas are in Lolo. Deluge legend (pp. 140-42). Ceremonies. Marriage, bride-price. Patronymics were derived from Chinese and are unimportant in marriage (often a whole village took the same name). Medicines include nicotine for toothaches, gall of goat for eyeache, pig's lung for goiter. In Szechwan, the dead are still cremated, but elsewhere they are buried in coffins. Lamentation chanted by women (pp. 172-78). T'ou-seu headman system. Caste system. Language: sounds, tones, Chinese influences, particles, substantives, adjectives, pronouns, verbs, adverbs, postpositions, conjunctions, syntax, writing (pp. 195-267).

Review: F. Heger, 1914, Anthropologische Gesellschaft in Wien, Mitteilungen 44: 73-74.

1947 "Chants populaires des Lo-lo p'o (Yunnan)," Bulletin de l'Université l'Aurore (Shanghai), série 3, 8, 2: 266-74.

Lolo: Nine songs extracted from Liétard 1913 (pp. 111-24), Lolo text and translation. Two types: love or story. Verse has 5 measures; rhythm starts low, then becomes piercing.

Lǐn, Huì-xiáng, and Lú Zuò-fú

1931 "Ló-lo bīao běn tú shūo (Illustrations of the Lolo)," Shè huì kē xúe yán jiū sǔo, Zhōng-yāng yán jiū yùan (Bulletin of the Social Science Research Institute, Academia Sinica) 3.

Lín, Kuang-tien: see Graham, David, 1955; Lǐng Guāng-dìan 1950.
Lín, Yaò-húa (or Yàu-hwa or Yueh-hwa)

1944a "A brief account of Yenching expedition to the Lolo community," West China Border Research Society, Journal, series A, 15: 41-46.

Lolo live alongside Chinese in Hsi-ning, Hsiao liang shan. On the way from here to Lei-po, 40 miles south, Lin had to call on militia twice for protection. Chinese are killed and kidnapped by Lolo nearly every evening. Went to Ta liang shan, along with two Lolo guarantors, but there were several misunderstandings and extortions. Spent a total of 50 days among Lolo

	in summer 1943. Map.
1944b	"Dà liáng shān lólo zú jīe jí zhì du (Class systems among the Lolo on Ta Liang Shan)" <u>Bian-zheng gong-lun</u> (Frontier Affairs) 3, 9: 22-41.

Lolo call themselves Yi, and are divided into Black, White, and Han Wa ("Chinese youths" who eventually become Lolo). Black Lolo are Mongoloid, have Mongoloid eyefold, dark skin, hooked nose, big ears. In Chinese.

| 1944c | "Social life of the aboriginal groups in and around Yunnan," <u>West China Border Research Society, Journal, series A, 15</u>: 47-56. (Reprint 1944, West China Union University Museum offprint number 6.) |

Lolo, including Aka, Liso, Lohei (Lahu), Woni. Locations, populations, houses. Classes. Lolo bride payment consists of silver, cattle, weapons, slaves, paid in installments. After the first night, bride and groom live separately for one or two years. Widow remarries husband's brother or nephew. Feuds. Hostility with Chinese. Those Lolo who have moved south into Yunnan have intermarried with Chinese; some have become Chinese. Lolo chiefs may rule over some Miao.

| 1944d | "Dà xĭao liáng shān kǎo chá jì (Exploration of Greater and Lesser Liangshan)," <u>Bian-zheng gong-lun</u> (Frontier Affairs) 3, 5-6. |

Lolo mentioned.

| 1946 | "Kinship system of the Lolo," <u>Harvard Journal of Asiatic Studies 9</u>: 81-100. |

Liang-shan Lolo. Data collected 1943. Fireplace

(Kuo-chwang) is center for cooking, eating, entertaining. Partial avoidance between elder brother and younger brother's wife; husband's father and son's wife never eat together, talk, or look each other in the face. Levirate. Parallel-cousin marriage prohibited. Cross-cousin marriage preferred (mother's brother is called "father-in-law"). Bride lives with her parents until first pregnancy. Kin terms in Lolo, Chinese, phonetic, and English.

1947 Liáng shān yī jīa (Liang-shan I Chia) (The Lolo of Liang Shan), Shāng wù yìng shū guǎn shè huì xúe cóng kān (Shanghai, Commercial Press). (Translated by Ju-shu Pan, 1961, New Haven, Human Relations Area Files Press.) 159 pp.

Da-liang shan and Xiao-liang shan. Data collected July-Sep. 1943. Populations. History. Lolo and Han trade and have shifting frontiers. Chinese control towns, but Lolo control much of the countryside. Since the founding of the Republic, Chinese garrisons have been reduced, and the Lolo have attacked many towns and disrupted communications. At Lei-po, much of the population has left because of Lolo attacks. Those who remain (including sinicized Lolo) are constantly on the defensive. Small bands of Lolo plunder one house at a time and take captives. The only way to travel is with a Lolo protector. Subdivisions of Lolo, locations. Each clan occupies several villages of up to 50 households each. Clan leadership depends on personal ability in fighting and organization. Kin terms. Cross-cousin marriage. Houses. Dress.

-177-

Exogamous clans. Children of mixed Black and White marriages are called "yellow bones" and considered pariahs. Polygyny is rare, only among nobles. Betrothal gift 500-800 ounces of silver for Black, 100-200 for White, none for slaves. May originally have been pastoral, since they look down on agriculture. White Lolo, who make up 80-90% of population, grow maize and buckwheat; minimum swidden per person half an acre; 40-60% of harvest is paid to Black landowners. Opium is traded for guns and silver from Chinese; temporary Han laborers are imported during opium planting and harvesting. Movable property is inherited equally by children; male slaves go to sons, female slaves to daughters; fields to sons, house to youngest son. Caste system; in multiclan villages, White may be subject to several nobles; slaves are mostly captured Han. Constant feuding; strategy is usually surprise attack, and after one or two persons are killed, a temporary truce is called. Women sometimes talk the men out of a battle. Animists. Pi-mu is both priest and magician, always male, and usually a White Lolo; tutorial is usually father to son or uncle to nephew. Divination. Ceremonies in third, seventh, and tenth months to drive away evil spirits from household. Magic against enemies. Cremation. One, three, or five years after death, an expensive ceremony is held to release the departed soul. Interdictions, ordeals, covenants.

Lindgren, Ted D.
1967 A comparative study of the Area V Border Police Patrol

teacher and the remote area villager in northern
Thailand: Their perceived role of each other in a
remote area civic action program (manuscript). 22 pp.

Akha, Lahu, Lisu. Border police teachers, schools, extracurricular activities, attitudes on sending children to school.

Ling, Bing
1961   Zhōng miàn tai yin biān min qín (Customs of border peoples of China, Burma, Thailand and India), Hong Kong, World Book Store.

Lisu are possibly Aryans; clothing, crossbows, poison, houses, gods and spirits, marriage, birth.

Ling, Chŭn-shēng
1938   "Táng-dài yún-nán de wū-mán yǔ bái-mán kǎo (Research on the Wuman and Baiman of Yunnan during the T'ang dynasty)," Lì shǐ yǔ yán yán jiū suǒ, Zhōng yāng yán jiū yuan (Bulletin of the Institute of History and Philology, Academia Sinica) Rén lèi xué jí (Anthropology issue) 1, 1.

1953   "Dōng-nán yǎ de fù zǐ lián míng zhì (The patronymic linkage systems of Southeast Asia)," Dà-lù zá-zhì (Continental Magazine) 1.

See Shiratori 1957.

Ling, Gǔang-dìan (or Kuang-tien) (See also David Crockett Graham, 1955.)

1948   "Hēi yí hé bái yí (Black Yi and White Yi)," Biān-zhèng gōng-lùn (Frontier Affairs) 7, 2.

1950   Yí-zú min jiān gù shi (Lolo tales), Peking, n.p. 169 pp.

Linguistic Survey of Burma
1917   Preparatory stage or linguistic census, Rangoon,

Superintendent, Government Printing. 79 pp.

Litton, George John

1904a   Report on a journey to the north of Tengyueh sub-
         prefecture (manuscript).

1904b   Report on a journey to Tibetan Yunnan (manuscript).

1906   Report on the upper Salween (manuscript).
         See Forrest 1908.

Liu, Chun (Pinyin: Liu, Zhun)

1954   "National minorities enjoy regional autonomy,"
         People's China 1, 1: 9-14.
         Yi have organized a militia.

Liu, Chungshee Hsien (Pinyin: Liu, Zhong-she-xian)

1932   "On a newly discovered Lolo Ms. from Szechuan, China,"
         Man 32: 235-37.
         Figure.

1937   "A Lolo manuscript in the Bodleian library, Oxford,"
         Man 37: 39-40.

Liu, Hsiu-yeh (Pinyin: Liu, Xiu-ye)

1940-41 "Selected bibliography of Yunnan and of tribes of
         southwest China," Quarterly Bulletin of Chinese
         Bibliography, n.s. 1: 83-113, 333-48, 450-68; 2: 199-
         225.

Liú, Yáo-hàn

1954   "Nán-shào tóng zhì zhě méng shì jiā zú shǔ yì zú zhī
         xīn zhèng (New evidences showing that the Meng ruling
         family of Nanchao to be Yi)," Lì-shǐ yán-jiū (Histori-
         cal Research).

Líu, Yǐ: see Huáng, Tíe, et al., eds.

Lo, Ch'ang-p'ei (Pinyin: Ló Cháng-péi)

1944a   "Lùn zàng miǎn zú de fù zǐ lián mín zhì (A discussion of the patronymic linkage system of the Tibeto-Burman tribes)," Biān-jiāng rén-wén (Border Culture and Humanities) 1, 3.

See 1944b, below.

1944b "Zài lùn zàng miǎn zú de fù zǐ lián mín zhì (Further discussions on the family naming system among the Tibeto-Burman tribes)," Biān-zhèng gōng-lùn (Frontier Affairs) 3, 9: 19-21.

The son takes the last one or two syllables of father's name. There are four patterns: ABC-CDE-EFG--GHI; AYB-BYC-CYD-DYE; ABCD-CDEF-EFGH; and YAYB-YBYC-YCYD. Genealogies of A-he and Lo-hong clans. White Lolo had no surnames until the birth of A Myau, whereupon Myau became their surname. See Lo 1944a, 1945a and 1945c, Ma 1942-44, Ruey 1950, Shiratori 1957.

1945a "The genealogical patronymic linkage system of the Tibeto-Burman-speaking tribes," Harvard Journal of Asiatic Studies 8, 3-4: 349-63.

Lolo, Woni, and Aka (as well as Moso and Burman) genealogies illustrate naming system in which last one or two syllables of father's name are repeated in son's name. See also 1944a, 1944b, and 1945c.

1945b "Gòng-shān nù yǔ chū tàn xù lùn (Preliminary survey of the Nu language of Gong Mountain)," Biān-zhèng gōng-lùn (Frontier Affairs) 3, 12.

1945c "Sān lùn zàng miǎn zú de fù zǐ lián mín zhì (Third discussion on the patronymic linkage system of the Tibeto-Burman tribes)," Biān-jiāng rén-wén (Border Culture and Humanities) 2, 1.

See 1944b, above.

1945d "A preliminary study on the Trung language of Kung Shan," Harvard Journal of Asiatic Studies 8, 3-4: 343-48.

Trung (or Ch'iu-Chi in Chinese) probably belongs to the Lolo-Moso group, close to Nung. Located 97°50' -98°50' E, 27°-28° N. Phonemes, six tones, word order, classifiers, affixes. See Matisoff 1972a.

1950 First survey of the Lo-i language of Lien-shan, Peking.

Not seen, but apparently Lolo. In Chinese.

Logan, J. R.
1858 "The West Himalaic or Tibetan tribes of Asam [sic]," Journal of the Indian Archipelago and Eastern Asia, n.s. 2: 68-151.

Li-se probably eastern Sing-Phos (p. 92).

Lowis, Cecil Champain
1919 The tribes of Burma, Rangoon, Office of the Superintendent, Government Printing, Burma. (First edition 1910. Reprint 1949.) 109 pp.

Lowy, Rennold L.
1947 "Adventures in Lololand," National Geographic 91, 1: 105-18.

Lolo said to hold U.S. flyers as slaves in eastern Sikang and western Szechwan. Lolo raided Chungsopa, carrying off young men and girls. Black Lolo chief and "queen" of Tienpa rule 300 White families. Photos of women's costumes, etc.

Luce, Gordon Hannington
1968 "Burma languages," Burma Research Society, Journal 51, 1: 29-34.

Lisu (Lolo) is one of the groups of Tibeto-Burman languages. Probably originally pastoralists of northwestern China, part of Ch'iang ("goat-men"), squeezed out by Chinese agriculturalists and Tibetan hunters.

Lunet de Lajonquière, Etienne Edmond

1904 *Ethnographie des territoires militaires*, Hanoi, Schneider. 258 pp.

Lolo have been in Bao-lac for several centuries; they are not migratory, like the Man and Meo. Number 1,800 (18,000 is a misprint, p. 243). They retain their physical type, dress, and language, but they no longer have writing, and they have adopted many beliefs and ceremonies of their neighbors, truly "dénationalisées" (p. 250). Based on information gathered by Diguet, Bonifacy, Révérony, and Fesch. Map.

Review: Cl. E. Maitre, 1905, *Ecole française d'Extrême-Orient, Bulletin 5*: 199-207.

1906 *Ethnographie du Tonkin septentrional*, Paris, Ernest Leroux, Editeur. 384 pp.

Lolo, including P'ou-la or Fou-la, Houo-Ni, Pen-ti-lolo, Kan-tao-lolo, Xa-pho. Populations, locations. Names, physical features, houses, dress, agriculture, marriage, birth, funerals. Girls in puberty cannot eat pork, chicken, duck, or dog. Live mixed with Meo, and may have a Lolo, Meo, or Tho chief. Vocabularies. Map, photos.

Review by Gaide, 1906, *Ecole française d'Extrême-Orient, Bulletin 6, 3-4*: 348-50.

Lyall, Leslie T.
1965   A passion for the impossible: The China Inland Mission, 1865-1965, London, Hodder and Stoughton. 190 pp.

Lisu in Yunnan were first missionized through Miao in 1907; the following year the Lisu missionized among the Lahu. Fraser arrived to work among Lisu in 1910. By 1918, 60,000 Lisu were baptized. John Kuhn arrived in 1928. In 1943, Lisu church was organized, with elected deacons and central council. In 1944, a Lisu gospel magazine was begun.

Nosu reached in 1910. The center of 30 Nosu churches was Salowu.

Attempt to reach the Tuli, related to Lisu, failed.

Mǎ, Cháng-shòu (or Cháng-shèo)
1942-44   "The genealogical table of the Lo los at Liangshan, Western Szechuan," Bian-jiang yén-jiu lùn-cóng (Frontier Studies) 44, 4: 51-83.

Lolo usually do not have written genealogies, but they engage in oral competitions, reciting long genealogies; the naming method, whereby the last part of the father's name is repeated, also aids memorization. It is a disgrace to make mistakes in one's own genealogy, and an insult to do so in another's. Only recently have the Lolo adopted family names like the Han (either Chinese surnames or place names), so that members of one clan may have different surnames, or members of different clans may have the same. Originally, the Black Lolo were divided into Gu Heu and Chu Ni, but eventually they intermarried.

From these two, the present-day clans and subclans evolved, and these remain the basic social units. Most famous of the early Lolo was A T'u, who settled in the Jau Tung region of northeastern Yunnan. One headman identified him with Gu Heu, and his brother with Chu Ni: the former led his people into eastern Liang Shan, and the latter into the western part. Gu Heu's descendants are more numerous, more warlike, and more influential. See Chén 1948a, Dǐng 1936, Dǒng 1940, Fang 1945a and 1945b, Lo 1944a and 1944b, 1945b, and Shiratori 1957.

1946 "Liáng shān ló-yí de zú pǔ (The genealogy of the Lolo of Liangshan)," Mín-zú xué-yán (Nationalities Research) 5.

See 1942-44, above.

Ma, Touan-lin (or Tuan-lin) (Pinyin: Ma, Duan-lin), translated with commentary by Le Marquis d'Hervey de Saint-Denys

1876-83 Ethnographie des peuples étrangers a la Chine, ouvrage composé au XIIIe siècle de notre ère, 2 vols., Genève, H. Georg Libraire-Editeur (2d vol. H. George-Th. Mueller); Paris, Ernest Leroux; London, Trübner and Co. 520 + 626 pp.

A translation with commentary of parts of Wên Hsien Thung Khao, published in 1319. Extremely difficult to identify the groups mentioned by Ma with present-day peoples. Y mentioned 1: 5; 2: 122, 126, 167.

Mǎ, Xúe-liang (or Hsüeh-liang)

1931 "Lǔo mín de jì sì yán jìu (A study of Lolo religious rites)," Xúe-yúan (Source of Knowledge) 2, 2.

1940   "Sǎ ní yǔ 'Pzlp'slbzlfvzl' xiǎo kǎo (A brief examination of the Sani language)," Zhōng-gúo wén-hùa yán-jiù sǔo (Chengtu, University of Nanking, Institute of Chinese Cultural Studies) 1, 2.
       See 1951, below.

1944   "Hēi yí fēng sù zhī yì-chú hùo sùi (A custom of the Black Yi to eliminate disasters and evil spirits)," Bīan-zhèng gōng-lùn (Frontier Affairs) 3, 9.

1947   "Cóng lúo-ló shì zú míng chēng zhōng sǔo jìan de tú téng zhì dù (The 'tu-teng' system as seen from the tribal names of the Lolo)," Bīan-zhèng gōng-lùn (Frontier Affairs), 6, 4.

1948a "Ló wén zùo jǐ xīan yào gōng jīng yì zhù (Lo-wen 'Tso-chi, hsien-yao, kung-sheng ching'i-chu) (A witchcraft book, 'On Performing rites, offering medicines, and sacrificing beasts')," Lì shǐ yǔ yán yán jiù sùo, Zhōng yāng yán jiù yùan (Bulletin of the Institute of History and Philology, Academia Sinica) 20: 577-666, Special Studies 3, no. 3.
       Lü-Ch'üan, a Lolo dialect: transcription, translation, and commentary on a sacred book.

1948b "Lúo-ló zú de zhāo hún hé fàng gǔ (Lolo spiritualism and witchcraft)," Bīan-zhèng gōng-lùn (Frontier Affairs) 7, 2.

1949   "Lúo wén zùo zhāi jīng yì zhù (Annotations on Lolo sutras)," Lì shǐ yú yán yán jiù sùo, Zhōng yāng yán jiù yùan (Bulletin of the Institue of History and Philology, Academia Sinica) 14.

1951   Sǎ-ní yì-yǔ yán-jiū (A study of Sani, an I dialect), Peking, Yǔ yán xúe zhūan kān dì 2 zhǒng, Linguistics

Special Series Number 2), Publication of the Chinese Scientific Institute, Advanced Studies Publishing House. 371 pp.

Sani, a Yi dialect: sounds (using International Phonetic Alphabet), grammar, word list, glyph list, texts. See Haudricourt 1957-58.

1954 "Minority languages of China," China Reconstructs 3,3: 37-41.

1955 "New script for China's minorities," China Reconstructs 4,2: 10.

1962 "New scripts for China's minorities," China Reconstructs 11,8: 24-27.

Lisu script in use by 1958. Central Institute of Nationalities at Peking offers courses in Lisu.

Ma, Yao

1958 "National minorities in direct transition areas in Yunnan leaping forward toward socialism," Guang-ming ri-bao (Peking), November 15.

Lisu exploitation of poor by rich has been done away with, as have wasteful sacrifices to the spirits. The Lisu, who formerly had an incipient class society, are rapidly moving toward socialism.

Macey, P.

1907 "Etudes ethnographiques sur les Kha," Revue Indochinoise: 240-49, 479-83, 520-52, 781-86, 868-74.

Akha vocabulary.

MacFarquhar, Roderick

1959 "The minorities," New Leader 42,23: 17-21.

Yi took from October 1956 to March 1958 to liberate 10,000 slaves in Ninglang, Yunnan.

Madrolle, Claudius

1898 Les peuples et les langues de la Chine méridionale,

<u>Parlers de l'île d'Hainan et de la presqu'île de
Loui-tcheou</u> (Louei-tsiou) <u>suivis de quelques
expressions des peuples originaires des régions
voisines du Tibet</u>, Paris, Challamel. 15 pp.

Lolo vocabularies from Szechuan and Yunnan.

1908 "Quelques peuplades lo-lo," <u>T'oung Pao, série 2, 9</u>: 529-76.

Lolo and Lisou distribution, names, dress. Vocabularies: K'o (Akha), Lisou by Monbeig, Lolopho by Liétard.

1925 <u>Indochine du Nord, Tonkin, Annam, Laos, Yunnan, Kouang-tcheou Wan,</u> Paris, Librairie Hachette. (Third edition, 1932. English translation: 1939, <u>Indochina: Cochin china, Annam, Yünnan, Cambodia, Tonkin, Laos, Siam,</u> Paris, Société d'Editions Géographiques, Maritimes et Coloniales.) 384 pp.

Lolo number 450 in Ha-giang; Pou-la 360 in Ha-giang, 320 in Lao-kay, and 6,500 in So'n-la; K'i-lao 350 in Ha-giang, 500 in Lao-kay; Heu-yi 230 in Ha-giang; Wou-ni 600 in Lao-kay and 3,100 in Lai-chau (pp. 35ff, 58-59). In Laos (Luang Prabang and Fifth Territory), Lolo include Kho, Mu-so', Wou-ni, and Allo, and number 16,500. Wou-ni live near Muang So, Allo in Sip-song Pana; A-ka (Ko) include 7 subgroups (pp. 67, 73, 151, 315). Lolo villages in Yunnan mentioned (pp. 355-56). This Guide Madrolle is in the best tradition of French tourist guides, an overlooked but extremely useful source of information on distribution of ethnic groups. Photos.

Maire, Henri
1882 "Yun-Nan (Chine). Lettre de M. Henri Maire, missionnaire apostolique au Yun-Nan, à M. Obert, curé de Mandeure. La mission des Lolos-Visite de Mgr. Fenouil. Journée du missionnaire," Les Missions Catholiques 14, 699: 505-07.

Lolo houses. Entire villages have been converted: 300 catechized and 255 baptized this year.

Maitre, Claude-E.
1908 "Correspondance," Ecole Française d'Extrême-Orient, Bulletin 8, 3-4: 616-26.

Questions d'Ollone's claim of being the first to traverse Lolo country, in light of Bonin's previous voyage. Notes contradictions between d'Ollone's depiction of it as a dangerous country and de Guébriant's account of it as peaceful. See Maitre and d'Ollone 1909.

Maitre, Claude E., and Henri Marie Gustave Vicomte d'Ollone
1909 "Correspondance," Ecole Française d'Extrême-Orient, Bulletin 9, 4: 832-36.

d'Ollone cites Bonin 1899 and 1907, acknowledging that de Guébriant and d'Ollone crossed Lolo country before Bonin. Cites de Guébriant 1899 to show that Bonin crossed country inhabited by Chinese. Maitre concedes this point, but re-emphasizes the differences between d'Ollone's and de Guébriant's accounts, citing de Guébriant in Echo de Chine, Nov. 4, 1908: 869-71, where he cautions against thinking of Lolo as cruel savages simply because of their murder of Brooke.

See Maitre 1908.

Manndorff, Hans

1962 "Angewandte Völkerkunde bei den Bergstämmen von Nordthailand," Mitteilungen der Anthropologischen Gesellschaft in Wien 92: 313-15.

    Akha, Lahu, Lisu: general survey of opium growing highlanders in North Thailand.

1962-63 "Bericht uber einen völkerkundlichen Forschungsaufenthalt in Nordthailand, vom. 1. September 1961 bis 30. Juni 1962,: Archiv für Völkerkunde 17-18: 157-60.

    Akha, Lahu, Lisu: Summary of a survey trip.

1963 "Probleme bei der Einführung der staatlichen Verwaltung unter den Bergstämmen von Nordthailand," Sociologus 13, 1: 15-31. (English translation: "Problems for the introduction of government administration among the mountain tribes of northern Thailand," Trans. J3029A, Washington, D.C., U.S. Army Translation Service.)

    Akha, Lahu, Lisu: Thai government aims to end slash-and-burn cultivation, migration, and opium growing.

1965 "Beobachtungen über die Südwanderung einiger hinterindischer Bergstämme," Mitteilungen der Anthropologischen Gesellschaft in Wien 95: 82-91. (English translation, 1967, "Observations of the southward migration of some Indochinese mountain tribes," Trans. J1978, Washington, D.C., U.S. Army Translation Service.)

    Lahu and Lisu southward movement to Tak; migration routes. Vertical distribution of ethnic groups from highest to lowest altitudes: Lisu, Lahu

Nyi, Lahu Na, Akha, Lahu Shehleh, Lahu Shi.

1966 "Veränderungen in den Beziehungen zwischen Tieflandbevölkerung und Bergstämmen in Nordthailand," Sociologus 16, 2: 157-73.

Akha, Lahu, Lisu relations with lowland Thai have traditionally been mutual noninterference. However, with increasing population, Thailand is concerned that slash-and-burn agriculture will cause land depletion, erosion, and flooding, and wishes to stop opium cultivation. The integration of highlanders can best be achieved by building upon (rather than upsetting) past relations: e.g. confirm local headmen, use locals for agricultural education programs.

1970 "Einige Bemerkungen über die Lahu Nordthailands, über das Neujahrsfest Kin Wah und den Hochgott G'dscha," Mitteilungen der Anthropologischen Gesellschaft in Wien 100: 332-39.

Lahu number 15,000 in Thailand. Subgroups. Pawku as religious authority. New Year's at Doi Paka, Fang, in 1965.

1971 "Beobachtungen über die Lisu Nordthailands, über die Verehrung der Nat und die Zeremonien Zur Neujahrszeit," in J. Szabadfalvi and Z. Ujváry, eds., Studia Ethnographica et Folkloristica in honorem Bela Gunda, Budapest, n.p. (pp. 141-155).

Lisu of Thailand: Spirits and spirit specialists. A description of the New Year's celebrations at Doi Nalow, Chiang Dao district, Chiang Mai Province, in 1952. Photos.

Manndorff, Hans, F. Scholz, and E. Volprecht
1964-65   Encyclopaedia Cinematographica Films, Numbers: 1239 Dances at the New Year (Black Lahu), 1240 Husking rice with a stamp mill (Black Lahu), 1241 Removing the seed from cotton with a special machine (Akha), 1242 Shaking up and fulling cotton (Akha), 1243 Spinning cotton (Akha), 1244 Preparation of a woven cotton rope (Akha), 1245 Weaving cotton on a treadloom (Akha), 1246 Making a bark mat (Akha), 1247 Manufacturing a bamboo board (Akha), 1249 Building a house (Akha), 1250 Forging a chopping knife (Akha), 1251 Making a sheath for a chopping knife (Akha), 1252 Weaving a basket with a lid (Akha), 1271 Weaving straps for shoulder bags (Black Lahu), 1283 Chewing betel nuts (Black Lahu), 1284 Making an ornamental string from feathers (Akha), 1285 Braiding an ornamental chain from cotton and seed pearls (Akha), 1286 Men's dance (Akha), 1287 Girls' dances (Akha), 1301 Dog sacrifice at house building (Akha), 1302 Sword dance (Akha), 1303 Dances at the New Year (Lisu), Vienna, Encyclopaedia Cinematographica Films.

    Silent films; most are black and white. Some have explanatory booklets.

Matisoff, James A.
1966   The phonology of the Lahu (Muhsur) language, Report to the National Research Council of Thailand, Bangkok (mimeographed). 37 pp.
1967   A grammar of the Lahu language, doctoral dissertation, Berkeley, University of California. (Dissertation

Abstracts 28: 1419A, University Microfilms order no. 67-11,648.) 697 pp.

Black Lahu spoken in Christian villages of Chiang Mai. A structural analysis in the transformational style. (1) Phonology: syllable structure, initial consonants, vocalic nucleus, finals, tones, junctures, morpho-phonemic phenomena that shed light on earlier stages of language. (2) Sentence types: morphemes are assigned to form classes including "unrestricted particles." (3) Noun-phrase: noun subtypes both autonomous and limited, compounding, reduplication, elaboration, nominal nuclei (quantified, genitivized, determined, and extensive), noun-particles, unrestricted particles in nonfinal noun phrases, constraints on possible sequences of noun phrases. (4) Verb-phrase: three subtypes of verbs, verb-concatenation, adverbs, verbal particles, relationships between several types of particles in final verb-phrases. Conjunctions and interjections. (5) Compound sentences. (6) Various optional transformations by means of which "kernel" sentences are operated upon to produce complex sentences: nominalization transformational, relative transformational, and citative transformational. Permutational transformations characteristic of colloquial speech. See his 1973b, below.

1969a   "Lahu and Proto-Lolo-Burmese," Ann Arbor, Mich., Occasional Papers of the Wolfenden Society on Tibeto-Burman Linguistics 1: 117-221.

Lahu phonology, rejection of Burling's (1967) analysis. Cognates of the name "Lahu." Aspects of the Proto-Lolo-Burmese initial system: PLB velars and Tibetan dentals, Lahu voiced stops, Loloish and PLB resonant system, a laryngeal residue. Initial clusters: "intrinsic" vs. "fusional." Lahu and the PLB rhymes. The Lahu high-rising tone and glottal dissimilation. (See his 1970, below.)

Review: 1970, R.B. Jones, Journal of Asian Studies 30, 1: 230-31.

1969b "Verb concatenation in Lahu: the syntax and semantics of 'simple' juxtapostion," Acta Linguistica Hafniensia 12, 1: 69-120.

Lahu verbs may be strung together by simple juxtapositon to form complex verb phrases, raising some questions on the interrelations of semantics and grammar. There is a well-defined class of cases wherein the evidence indicates that it is the inherent semantic features of individual verbs that actually determine the structural descriptions of concatenations.

1969c "Lahu bilingual humor," Acta Linguistica Hafniensia 12,2: 171-206.

Black Lahu stories of misunderstandings with Shan and Yellow Lahu due to the fortuitous resemblance of a foreign word to a Lahu one. Prerequisites for Black Lahu bilingual humor: a long-standing cultural intimacy, a sufficient degree of otherness. It is the Lahu who tries to speak Shan; it is almost always the Lahu who is the butt of the joke (status hierarchy is Shan highest, Black Lahu, Yellow Lahu).

1970a "Glottal dissimilation and the Lahu high-rising tone: a tonogenetic case-study," American Oriental Society,

Journal 90, 1: 13-44.

    Lahu high-rising tone does not show any simple correspondences to tones in other Lolo-Burmese languages. It can be demonstrated that it is a secondary development within Lahu, furnishing a striking confirmation of the assumption that tones arise in general through the influence of consonants in syllable-final or syllable-initial position.

1970b   Parallelism and quartenary tropes in Lahu religious poetry, paper presented at the Third Annual Conference on Sino-Tibetan Reconstruction, Cornell University.

    Not seen.

1971   "The tonal split in Loloish checked syllables," Urbana, Occasional Papers of the Wolfenden Society on Tibeto-Burman Linguistics 2. 44 pp.

    The two-way tonal split in Loloish checked syllables explored in a dozen languages.

    Review: Kun Chang, 1972, Journal of Asian Studies 31, 4: 988.

1972a   The Loloish tonal split revisited, Berkeley, University of California, Center for South and Southeast Asia Studies, Research Monograph No. 7. 88 pp.

    Revision of his 1970a and 1971, above. The tonal split depends ultimately on the voicing or voicelessness of the root-initial consonants as complicated by the various proto-prefixes that could be preposed to the root. Confirmatory evidence includes about 200 cognate sets.

1972b   "Lahu nominalization, relativization, and genitivization," in John Kimball, ed., Syntax and Semantics, vol. 1: 237-57, New York, Seminar Press.

Lahu particle "ve" serves as marker of genitive constructions, relative clauses and clause nominalizer.

1973a   "Tonogenesis in Southeast Asia," in Larry M. Hyman, ed., Consonant Types and Tone, Southern California Occasional Papers in Linguistics 1: 71-95.

The role of laryngeal final consonants and syllable-initial voicing vs. voicelessness in the generation of tonal phenomena. The interrelationship among monosyllabicity, intersegmental feature-sharing, and compensatory tone. The tonal situation at the Proto-Sino-Tibetan and Proto-Tibeto-Burman levels, and the areal diffusion of tones in Southeast Asia, and the utility of tone-systems for the establishment of genetic relations among languages.

1973b   The grammar of Lahu, Berkeley, University of California Press, Publication in Linguistics No. 75. 673 pp.

Revision of his 1967, above.

1973c   Problems and progress in Lolo-Burmese: Quo Vadimus? paper circulated at the Sixth International Conference on Sino-Tibetan Language and Linguistic Studies, San Diego. 36 pp.

n.d.(a)   "The tones of Jinghpaw and Lolo-Burmese: common origin vs. independent development," Acta Linguistica Hafniensa (in press).

n.d.(b)   Lahu-English and English-Lahu dictionary (in preparation).

Matsuzaki, Hisakazu

1947   Byōzoku to Rorozoku (The Miao and Lolo of South China), Tokyo, Nikkō Shoin. 239 pp.

In Japanese.

Maung Shwe Wa
1963 *Burma Baptist Chronicle*, Book 1, Rangoon, Board of Publications, Burma Baptist Convention. 269 pp.

Lahu first contacted by Baptist missionaries, Mr. and Mrs. Cushing, when they traveled to Kengtung in 1869 (p. 208). Mr. and Mrs. Paul Lewis ran a Bible School at Pangwai for Lahu and Akha (p. 232). There are 20,203 members of Lahu-Wa Baptist churches, which operate 120 schools and a seminary (p. 268). See Crider 1963, Saw Aung Din and E. E. Sowards 1963.

McCarthy, James
1902 *Surveying and exploring in Siam*, London, James Murray. 215 pp.

Lahu mentioned in North Thailand, 1881-93. Maps.

McCoy, Alfred W. (with Cathleen B. Read and Leonard P. Adams, II)
1972 *The politics of heroin in southeast Asia*, New York, Harper & Row. 464 pp.

Lahu used for intelligence and guerrilla activities by the United States, through the Young missionary family. Attempt to unite Lahu with U Nu's United National Liberation Front against the Burmese government. Maps.

McGilvary, Daniel
1912 *A half-century among the Siamese and Lao*, London and New York, Fleming H. Revell Company. 435 pp.

Musso (Lahu) mentioned by this Presbyterian missionary, who lived in North Thailand from 1867. He notes their use of opium along the Mê Kok range.

Meares, C. H.
    1909a   "The death of Mr. J. W. Brooke in Western China," Geographical Journal 34, 3: 340-41.

    1909b   "Mr. J. W. Brooke's journeys in western Sze-chuan," Geographical Journal 34, 6: 614-18, 704.

               Lolo occupy highlands near Fulin on Tung River, from which they raid the Chinese. Brooke went into Lololand, where he was murdered. Map. See Starr 1911.

Meillier
    1918   "Note," Ecole française d'Extrême-Orient, Bulletin 18, 10: 55.

               Lolo armor from Kien-tchang donated to Museum of the School.

Meillet, Antoine, and Marcel Samuel Raphael Cohen, eds.
    1952   Les langues du monde, 2 vols., Paris, Centre National de la Recherche Scientifique (1st ed., 1924, Paris, Librairie Ancienne Edouard Champion). 1294 pp.

               Lolo has no final consonant and no initial consonant clusters. Lolo has 5 tones, Lisu 6 (pp. 554-55). First edition mentions hu-ni as part of the Lo-lo group (p. 369). Map XII.

Menguy, Marc
    1960   "Les minorités ethniques de la Chine continentale," La Documentation Française, Notes et Etudes Documentaires, Série Politique 220, numero 2639, fevrier 27. 32 pp.

               List of minorities (including Lisou, Lahou, Hani, Yi, Akka), populations, historical relations, constitutional status, regional autonomy, economic status, socialist transformation, political line toward minority culture. Centralist policy via Party and minority organizations. Lou-han is a Yi frequently cited in the press, the former head of an expeditionary corps to Tonkin in 1945, and now governor of Yunnan. Maps.

Měng-zàng xún-kān

1935 "Jīn shā jiāng liú yù zhī luo-lo (The Lolo of the Jinsha or Yangtze River Valley)," Měng-zàng xún-kān (Mongolian-Tibetan Quarterly) 98.

Mesny, William

1884 "Lettre de W. Mesny à M. Henri Cordier sur le Ms. Lolo de Chang-hai datée 16 juillet 1883," Revue de l'Extrême-Orient 2,4: 582-84.

Lolo writing, collected from chief called Ngan. See Cordier 1907: 36-37.

Metford, Beatrix

1935 Where China meets Burma, London and Glasgow, Blackie & Son. 231 pp.

Lisu dress, hunting, crops, animism, ancestor worship, birth, marriage and death customs, housing. The dead are given 9 grains of rice and 9 pieces of silver to aid them in crossing 9 hills and 9 streams on 9 paths (7 of each for women). Flowery Lisu of Burma. Photos.

Review: Erik Seidenfaden, 1937, Siam Society, Journal 29: 151-53. Notes the Caucasian features of some Lisu.

Meyer, Roland Théodore

1930 Le Laos-Indochine française-Exposition Coloniale International, Hanoi, Imprimerie d'Extrême-Orient. 111 pp.

Khas-ko mentioned (pp. 24,26).

Mickey, Margaret P.

1948 A bibliography of south and southwest China, with special reference to the non-Chinese peoples and their relation to the peoples of adjacent areas, works in western languages, New York, Viking Fund. (1961, Ann Arbor, Mich., University Microfilms.) 161 pp.

Mieyaa, Pierre

1972 "Cinquantenaire de la mission du Yunnan, 1922-1972," Feuilles Missionnaires 69: 1-13.

  Lahu near Chang-in were missionized by the Pères de Bétharram from 1935, and were later persecuted for their Christianity by the Chinese.

1973 "Un Apôtre: Le Père Jean-Pierre Oxibar," Feuilles Missionaires 71: 7-14; 72: 14-20; 73: 17-25.

  Lahou south of Tali were missionized by Oxibar from 1935 to 1950. Known as "L'Apôtre des Lahous." Photos. See Saint-Guily 1964.

Military Research and Development Center, Bangkok

1968 Ethnographic map of Thailand, Bangkok, Military Research and Development Center.

Mínzú Huàbào (Nationalities Pictorial)

1958 "Lā gū," Mínzú Huàbào no. 9: 13-19.

  Lahu during the Great Leap Forward carried out water conservation projects and set up fertilizer plants and agricultural machinery workshops to produce new tools and equipment. Since Liberation, the Lahu have built iron works, hydroelectric plants, textile factories, highways; they have made greater use of natural resources, eliminated diseases, and developed films, radio, education, and a written language. Photos.

1963   Photograph, Mínzú Huàbào no. 8: cover.
       Photo of Lisu and soldier.

1965   "Young artist was a former slave-Ah Ge," Mínzú Huàbào no. 7: 32.
       Yi of Liang Shan Autonomous Zhou: 18-year old Ah Ge, a wood carver, was a slave before the Liberation. Her family escaped once, but was recaptured; her grandparents were killed and the family dispersed. She graduated after five years at the Szechuan Arts Academy, and is now working at the Chinese Artists Association, Szechuan Branch. Her mother is a member of a cooperative, her brother teaches, and her sister is a cadre. Photos show some of her works depicting pre-Liberation life.

1966   Photograph, Mínzú Huàbào no. 1: 6-7.
       Photo of Lisu studying Mao's work in Thai-Chingpo Autonomous Zhou.

Mínzú Tuánjiē (Nationalities Unity)

1959   "Flying leaps in education in Liang Shan," Mínzú Tuánjiē no. 11: 28.
       Yi of Liang Shan in 1959 had 847 schools, 11 middle schools, 56,000 pupils (half the school-age population), 2,800 teachers (mostly Han).

1965   "Lisu female paper worker," Mínzú Tuánjiē no. 5-6: 55.
       Lisu model worker.

Missions Catholiques, Les

1881-82 "Mon district et huit ans de séjour au Yun-nan (Chine). Recit d'un missionaire," Les Missions Catholiques 13,

-201-

                635: 365-68, 636: 377-80, 637: 390-01, 638: 404-06,
639: 416-17, 640: 427-29, 641: 437-40, 642: 452-54,
643: 463-65, 644: 472-74, 645: 486-89, 646: 501-03,
647: 512-14, 648: 521-24, 649: 534-37, 650: 546-48,
652: 571-73, 653: 585-87, 654: 593-97, 655: 610-12,
656: 617-19; 14,658: 17-20, 659: 29-32, 660: 44-46,
661: 58-60, 662: 66-69, 663: 82-84, 664: 92-93.

        Man-tsé (Yi) of Léang-Chan are immoral and polygamous, and they have raided the lowlands each year for the past 15 years. Other Lolos are under Chinese Thou-ssé (pp. 377-91). Visit to Lolo chief (pp. 546-48). Man-tsé scare (pp. 618-19). Buys Lolo land near Pé-chy-ngay (p. 29). Lolos converted (pp. 58-60). Map (p. 366), photos. (especially pp. 405,529).

1938   "Conversions en masse au Yunnan," Les Missions Catholiques 70; 3297: 430.

        Lahou converted, but now persecuted by authorities.

Mitsumori, Sadao
1945   Biruma, shan no shizen to minzoku (Land and peoples of Burma and the Shan States), Tokyo, Nihon Hyōronsha. 273 pp.

        Lisu: Distribution, dress, life cycle. (Based mostly on Rose and Coggin Brown 1911.) Yawyin of Shan States are not genuine Kachin. d'Orléans claims they had a kingdom in eastern Tibet in the latter part of the tenth century.

        Akka, Lahu mentioned.

Mitton, Geraldine Edith (Lady Scott), ed.
1936   Scott of the Shan hills, orders and impressions, London,

John Murray. xii, 348 pp.

>Muhso or Muso (Lahu) have septs (p. 167), have inhabited area east of Kengtung for several generations (pp. 212-13).

>References to other works by Sir James G. Scott.

Monbeig: see Liétard 1909b, Madrolle 1908.

Mong, Luc

1957 "The Houni people," Nhan Dan 1200: 3, June 21. (English translation: Joint Publications Research Service DC198, The ethnic minorities of North Vietnam, July 1, 1958, pp. 11-13.)

>Houni live in Chungchai and Sin-phinh in 13 hamlets, each with 11 to 90 inhabitants. Total of 603 in 1,800 square kilometers. The government has not levied taxes and has sent relief supplies of rice and cloth. Houni have only one buffalo for three families, and they do not grow sufficient rice. Kuomintang bandits still active in area. They cultivate and smoke opium, and are in poor health. Suggestions for economic, agricultural, medical, and educational aid. See Ha Bac 1964.

Mongkhonrat: see Lamjuan.

Mongolian-Tibetan Quarterly: see Měng-zàng xún-kān.

Monpeyrat, J.

1905 "Notes sur les Mousseux de la province de Muong-sing (Haut-Laos occidental)," Revue Indochinoise, n.s. 4: 1614-23. (First published 1904, Revue Coloniale: 373-85.)

>Mousseux (Lahu) vocabulary.

Moore, W. Robert

1934 "Among the plains and hill people of Siam, " National Geographic 55,5: 563-70.
    Messu (Lahu) and Lissu color photos.

1963 "Burma, gentle neighbor of India and Red China," National Geographic 123,2: 153-99.
    Lisu present at a Kachin festival in Myitkyina. Photos.

Morrock, Richard

1972 "Minority nationalities in China," Journal of Contemporary Asia 2: 181-91.
    Akha, Lahu, Lisu, Norsu (Yi) mentioned. Abolition of slavery among Norsu.

Morse, Robert H. (See also Bangkok Post 1973a, Boh 1967, Voegelin and Voegelin 1965.)

1962 Hierarchiacal levels of Rawang phonology, M.A. thesis, Indiana University. 90 pp.
    Lisu have influenced the Tangsarr clan of the Rawang (p. 24) and some Rawang east of the Salween (p. 33). Map.

1974 "Lisu of Thailand," Sawaddi, Nov.-Dec.: 17-20, 31, and cover.
    Lisu include White, Black, and Red (Yunnan), Flowery (Shan States), and Lushih (Thailand). Houses vary, include log cabins (western Yunnan), adobe (eastern Yunnan), bamboo longhouses (Burma), and square frame structures, with dirt floors (Thailand). At Nokate, a man has 4 wives in one house, also 30 children and 43 grandchildren (of which 16 and 11 have died, respectively). Lisu adapt well and are pragmatists.

Moseley, George V.H., III
- 1967a "Voices in the minority," Far Eastern Economic Review 55, 9: 405-07.
- 1967b "The right to be different," Far Eastern Economic Review 55, 10: 462-64.

    Akha, Lahu, and Lisu are oriented toward Chinese culture, therefore attempts by Thai government to change their lives will lead to trouble. Both China and the West "brainwash" minorities by giving them no alternative but to follow their policies: the West offers material goods, China offers equality with the majority. Photos.

- 1967c The party and the national question in China, Cambridge and London, Harvard University Press. 186 pp.

    Chinese official positions toward minorities.

- 1973 The consolidation of the South China frontier, Berkeley, University of California Press. 192 pp.

    Chinese attitudes toward minorities in historical perspective. The best work available on this subject.

Mueller, Herbert
- 1913 "Beiträge zur ethnographie der Lolo," Baessler Archiv 3,1: 38-68.

    Lolo names, locations, subgroups, writing. Catalogue description of the Weiss collection at the Museum für Völkerkunde, Berlin: dress, weapons, pipes, utensils. Map, illustrations.

Murchie, G. W.
- 1969 Communist Suppression Operations Command Hill Tribe leaflet program, Bangkok, Communist Suppression Operations Command, Psychological Operations Division. 6 pp.

Propaganda leaflets were distributed to troubled areas in northern Thailand. Three examples. In Thai and English.

Nabangxang, Chum, and Charas Mahawat
1964 History, geography, archaeology and hill tribes in northern Thailand, Bangkok, n.p. 274 pp.
Akha, Lahu, Lisu summary descriptions. In Thai.

National Geographic Society
1971 The peoples of southeast Asia (map), Washington, D.C., National Geographic Society.
Colorful map, with illustrations and distribution of major ethnic groups.

Nature
1888 "The non-Chinese races of China," Nature 38, 980: 345-46.
Lolo is a corruption of Lulu, name of a former chief. They call themselves Nersu. Other names. Physical appearance. Vocabulary. Based on Bourne 1888.

New China News Agency, (NCNA), Chaochueh (Pinyin: Zhaojue)
1956a "7,000 in Liangshan Yi area welcome 2nd Group Central Comfort Mission," Nov. 17 (English translation: Survey of the China Mainland Press 1427: 16.)
1956b "Ex-slaves live in own houses in Yi area, Szechwan," Nov. 28 (English translation: Survey of the China Mainland Press 1423: 21.)

New China News Agengy, (NCNA), Chengtu (Pinyin: Chengdu)
1956a "First teachers' school built in Liangshan Yi nationality Autonomous Zhou (Szechwan)," Sep. 10 (English translation: Survey of the China Mainland Press 1369: 25, 1386: 8-9.)

-206-

1956b "Government comforting mission leaves Chengtu for various autonomous areas. Second Group of Comfort Mission arrives O-pian. Fourth Group of Central Comfort Mission reaches Sichang," Nov. 10 (English translation: Survey of the China Mainland Press 1427: 14-17.)
        Yi visited by government teams. See 1956e, below.

1956c "United front expanded in nationalities areas in Szechwan Province," Nov. 17 (English translation: Survey of the China Mainland Press 1427: 12.)
        Yi "upper circle personages" make contributions to socialism.

1956d "Local minority nationals promoted to responsible positions in Szechwan," Nov. 22 (English translation: Survey of the China Mainland Press 1427: 12-13.)
        Yi.

1956e "15,000 attend rally held in Sichang by Central Comfort Mission, Fourth Group. Fourth Group of Central Comfort Mission meets nationalities in Sichang," Nov. 20 (English translation: Survey of the China Mainland Press 1427: 19-20.)
        Yi. See 1956b, above.

1958a "Unprecedented bumper crops harvested in the former grain-short Tibetan and Yi areas of Szechwan," Oct. 14 (English translation: Survey of the China Mainland Press 1883: 37-38.)
        Yi of Liangshan Autonomous Zhou harvested 700 million catties, about 300 per mou, or 750-1,000 per individual.

1958b "Liangshan Yi nationality Autonomous Zhou (Szechwan) develops diversified economy," Dec. 24 (English translation: Survey of the China Mainland Press 1941: 3-4.)

Yi now exploit forests, herbs, groundnuts, paddy rice, wheat, and fish, in addition to maize and buckwheat.

1959a "Production develops in former slave-owning areas in Szechwan," May 22. (English translation: Survey of the China Mainland Press 2025: 34-35.)

Yi of Liangshan turned out 2,000 tons of iron. 87% of Yi belong to cooperatives.

1959b "China's minority people have better food," Jul. 17 (English translation: Survey of the China Mainland Press 2061: 33.)

Yi of Liangshan.

1959c "Industry springs up in Southwest China national minority area," July 19. (English translation: Survey of the China Mainland Press 2062: 45.)

Yi and Tibetan areas have over 100 new factories in Szechwan.

1959d "Ex-slaves in southwest China become workers," Sep. 17. (English translation: Survey of the China Mainland Press 2101: 31-32.)

Yi of Liangshan have improved agriculture, education, health, and transport, and have 2,000 mines and factories.

1963a "Former women slaves and serfs in southwest China receive college education," Mar. 1. (English translation: Survey of the China Mainland Press 2932: 15-16.)

Yi women study at Southwest Institute for Nationalities.

1963b "Commerce develops among former slaves in southwest China," Nov. 30. (English translation: Survey of the China Mainland Press 3112: 18.)

                Yi of Liangshan: 41% of the 1,700 workers in state trading departments are Yi.

1963c   "Former slaves in Southwest China revolutionize farming," Dec. 17. (English translation: Survey of the China Mainland Press 3124: 15.)

                Yi of Liangshan achieved self-sufficiency in 1960.

1964a   "Southwest China theatrical festival by former slaves," Jun. 29 (English translation: Survey of the China Mainland Press 3251: 22.)

                Yi of Liangshan use folk songs and dances in new plays depicting Yi enthusiasm for agricultural collectives.

1964b   "Large numbers of former slaves join Communist Party in southwest China," July 1. (English translation: Survey of the China Mainland Press 3252: 7.)

                Yi of Liangshan comprise 90% (7,800) of the Communist Party members in the area.

1965a   "Former women slaves advance farm production in southwest China area," Mar. 3. (English translation: Survey of the China Mainland Press 3411: 24.)

                Yi of Liangshan: 2 of the 100 women holding official positions.

1965b   "Former slaves become industrial workers in southwest China," Apr. 30. (English translation: Survey of the China Mainland Press 3451: 20.)

                Yi of Liangshan engage in generating power, metallurgy, tool making, vehicle repair, paper making, and motor transport.

1965c   "Children of southwest China slaves become fine citizens," May 30. (English translation: Survey of the China Mainland Press 3471: 10.)

                Yi of Meika xian include 700 children of former

slaves brought up by the state and now engaging in
socialist construction.

1965d   "Southwest China minority people transforming farming methods," July 18. (English translation: Survey of the China Mainland Press 3502: 12.)

Yi practice terracing, irrigation, manuring, seed selection, and use experimental plots and new tools.

1965e   "Former slaves make a success of agricultural cooperation," July 19 (English translation: Survey of the China Mainland Press 3503: 13.)

Yi of Wanigou cooperative in Liangshan doublecrop wheat and buckwheat, and grain production is now half a ton per capita.

1965f   "First generation of trained doctors among former Yi slaves," July 23. (English translation: Survey of the China Mainland Press 3506: 14.)

Yi of Liangshan: 240 of the 1,100 doctors there are Yi.

1965g   "Southwest China minority areas achieve self-sufficiency in grain," Sep. 22. (English translation: Survey of the China Mainland Press 3545: 17-18.)

Yi of Liangshan have doubled grain output in past 10 years due to new agricultural methods. 90% of the Yi are in agricultural cooperatives.

1966   "Bumper harvest in southwest China minority areas," Oct. 30. (English translation: Survey of the China Mainland Press 3814: 25-26.)

Yi of Liangshan. No statistics.

1971   "Southwest China minority area expands educational opportunities," Dec. 12 (English translation: Survey of the China Mainland Press 71-51: 102-03.)

Yi of Liangshan have 2,300 schools. There were 1,100 by 1960, but Liu Shao-chi and his followers
closed down half of them. Houkuomu town has a May 7

school.
1973 "Southwest China minority people become army cadres," Apr. 12.(English translation: Survey of the China Mainland Press 73-17: 88.)
  Yi of Liangshan make up over one-third of the battalion and regiment cadres in militia.

New China News Agency, (NCNA), Kunming
1955a "Transport conditions in Lisu nationality Autonomous Area on Salween River improved," May 12. (English translation: Survey of the China Mainland Press 1052: 21-22.)
  Lisu now have 3 post roads across Pilo Snow Mountains.
1955b "Peasants in Lisu nationality Autonomous Area, Yunnan, carry out spring plowing," May 17 (English translation: Survey of the China Mainland Press 1055: 30.)
  Lisu are being helped by production work teams (from Communist Party committees, state trade organs, bank, and sanatoria), labor model rallies to exchange experiences gained in the 1954 bumper crop harvest, and financial aid from Yunnan Provincial People's Council.
1955c "Middle school opened in Nu Kiang Lisu nationality Autonomous Area, Yunnan," Sep. 29.(English translation: Survey of the China Mainland Press 1144: 13.)
1956a "Song and dance performances for border people," June 20.(English translation: Survey of the China Mainland Press 1316: 25.)
  Hani and Lahu among those attending performances by a Thai touring group.

1956b   "Yunnan strengthens nationalities work in high mountain areas," July 8. (English translation: Survey of the China Mainland Press 1335: 19-20.)
        Lisu, Yi, and other minorities are basically unchanged and need more attention.

1956c   "Land reform in minority areas in Yunnan," Oct. 6 (English translation: Survey of the China Mainland Press 1387: 8.)
        Hani, Lahu, and Yi areas undergo land reform.

1956d   "Fifth Group of Central Comfort Mission visits Yi and Tibetan people in Yunnan," Nov. 14. (English translation: Survey of the China Mainland Press 1427: 20.)

1958a   "Primitive national minorities of Yunnan frontiers expedite direct transition to socialist society," May 19. (English translation: Survey of the China Mainland Press 1783: 11-13.)
        Lisu were the first people to realize cooperativization.

1958b   "Bumper harvests of grain crops," Oct. 2. (English translation: Survey of the China Mainland Press 1874: 15.)
        Lisu of Nukiang Autonomous Zhou produced 2,500 catties of grain per capita.

1958c   "The Yi people of Hsiaoliang Mountains reap an unprecedented bumper crop after crushing the shackles of slavery," Oct. 9. (English translation: Survey of the China Mainland Press 1878: 30.)
        Yi of Ninglang Autonomous Xian produced 150 million catties of grain (1,600 per capita), using 100,000 catties of manure per mou.

1958d   "A big leap forward in cultural and educational enterprises emerges in minority areas of Yunnan province," Oct. 15. (English translation: Survey of the China Mainland Press 1883: 39.)

Yi of Ch'uhsiung autonomous zhou have eliminated illiteracy. South Yunnan University has been founded in Hungho Hani-Yi autonomous zhou.

1958e   "New development of nationalities relations in Tehung Area," Nov. 14. (English translation: Survey of the China Mainland Press 1918: 30-31.)

Lisu cooperative includes Thai, Chingpo, Han and others.

1958f   "Remote minority area develops industry in Yunnan," Nov. 22. (English translation: Survey of the China Mainland Press 1902: 33-34.)

Lisu make up 75% of the population of Nukiang autonomous zhou, established in August 1954. Over 10,000 workers man over 600 factories and mines, 130 steel furnaces, and 150 iron smelting furnaces, to turn out 70 tons of steel and 250 tons of iron, making the area self-sufficient. 60 kinds of new tools have been developed.

1958g   "Tremendous success in small minority area," Nov. 25. (English translation: Survey of the China Mainland Press 1904: 30.)

Lisu, Nu, Lemo, and Tulung are among the 120,000 inhabitants living along the Nu River. Due to irrigation and the use of 72 tons of manure per hectare, grain output has increased from 100 kilograms to 1.25 tons per capita. 86% belongs to cooperatives.

	Industrial and educational progress.
1958h	"Abundance of grain creates problems for Lisu people," Dec. 19.(English translation: <u>Survey</u> <u>of</u> <u>the</u> <u>China</u> <u>Mainland</u> <u>Press</u> <u>1921</u>: 9-10.)
	Lisu have increased irrigation works, paddy fields, manuring, new farming methods. This winter's harvest was four times last year's. Average 800 kilo grain per person leading to storage, grinding, and preparation problems. Lisu song praises changes.
1958i	"Investigations into the history of Yunnan minorities," Dec. 21.(English translation: <u>Survey</u> <u>of</u> <u>the</u> <u>China</u> <u>Mainland</u> <u>Press</u> <u>1921</u>: 12.)
	Central Institute of Nationalities and other institutions are investigating the history of minorities, including the Lisu.
1959a	"Draft of the 'Language Annals' of seven nationalities in frontier regions of Yunnan completed," Mar. 17. (English translation: <u>Survey</u> <u>of</u> <u>the</u> <u>China</u> <u>Mainland</u> <u>Press</u> <u>1982</u>: 20-21.)
	Lisu included.
1959b	"Autonomous area in southwest China plans big leap forward," May 10.(English translation: <u>Survey</u> <u>of</u> <u>the</u> <u>China</u> <u>Mainland</u> <u>Press</u> <u>2014</u>: 32-33.)
	Hani and Yi of the Upper Red River, where 70% of the 1.88 million inhabitants were landless and 2% were feudal lords, underwent land reforms in 1956.
1959c	"Yunnan's minority areas leap forward," May 18. (English translation: <u>Survey</u> <u>of</u> <u>the</u> <u>China</u> <u>Mainland</u> <u>Press</u> <u>2018</u>: 13-14.)
	Lisu Autonomous Zhou receives 90% of its annual

budget from the State.
1959d   "Rice planting completed in southwest China Autonomous Xian. " July 6. (English translation: Survey of the China Mainland Press 2052: 27.)

Lahu of Lantsang planted 67% more paddy this month than last year.

1959e   "Five nationalities run successful commune in Southwest China," Dec. 1. (English translation: Survey of the China Mainland Press 2150: 29-30.)

Yi, Lisu, Pai, Hui, and Han included among the 9,500 households of Fengmi People's Commune, Tali Pai Autonomous Area. Lisu and Yi helped build a dam across Polo River, although they will not benefit from it directly, since they live in the hills. Agricultural and industrial progress.

1960a   "Multi-national literature in southwest China province," Apr. 5. (English translation: Survey of the China Mainland Press 2235: 36.)

Yi novel, "The Merry Kinsha River," by L. Chiao, describes the changes in the Yi area. A culture history of the Yi has also been compiled.

1960b   "Ma Cheng-ch'ang, good guide of the Pula people (Yi nationality)," Oct. 10. (English translation: Survey of the China Mainland Press 2362: 13-15.)

Pula, a Yi people, were urged to build irrigation works, roads, and schools in Nanshan, Red River Commune, Yuankiang Xian. Written by NCNA correspondent Yeh Tzu-chien.

1961   "Study of minority peoples in Southwest China Province," Mar. 9. (English translation: Survey of the China Mainland Press 2456: 17.)

Yi epic, describing the origin and struggles of the Yi ancestors, has been translated into Chinese.

1963a "Gathering of the various Lahu tribes at Lan Tsang, in Yunnan Province, to celebrate the tenth anniversary of the founding of the Autonomous Xian," Apr. 12.

Lahu joined by Hani, Yi, Bulang, Tai, Hwei He, Jingpho at Meng Lang Ba on April 7. Executive officer Li Gwang-hwa, a Lahu, addressed the 5,000 people and pointed out the advances made by the Xian's 100,000 Lahu and China's 190,000 Lahu.

1963b "Southwest China national minority region prospers," May 14. (English translation: Survey of the China Mainland Press 2982: 16-17.)

Lahu of Monlengba, seat of Lantsang autonomous xian, with 10,000 inhabitants, have made progress.

1964a "A network of highways built in Yunnan," Feb. 7. (English translation: Survey of the China Mainland Press 3169: 10-12.)

Lisu of Nukiang autonomous zhou have saved 780,000 labor units since they no longer have to act as porters, thanks to a new all-weather road to Kunming.

1964b "Tenth anniversary of southwest China autonomous xian celebrated," May 22. (English translation: Survey of the China Mainland Press 3227: 16.)

Hani, Lahu, Yi, and 9 other nationalities included in Kiangcheng Hani-Yi autonomous zhou. 80% of the 40,000 inhabitants are in agricultural cooperatives.

1964c "State helps national minorities in southwest China," July 5. (English translation: Survey of the China

Mainland Press 3255: 23-24.)

Lisu of Nukiang autonomous zhou have received farm tools and cattle from state.

1964d   "Southwest China minority area self-sufficient in handicraft articles," Sep. 16. (English translation: Survey of the China Mainland Press 3302: 18-19.)

Lisu and others of Teh-hung Tai-Chingpo autonomous zhou make own tools, aided by 200 Han instructors.

1964e   "Fraternal solidarity among nationalities in southwest China province," Oct. 12. (English translation: Survey of the China Mainland Press 3319: 19-20.)

Yi, Hui, Miao, and Han of Hsuanwei Xian have increased their grain output five times since 1949.

Hani and Lahu have been aided by the Tai in improving agriculture.

1964f   "Southwest China minority area celebrates tenth anniversary," Dec. 7. (English translation: Survey of the China Mainland Press 3354: 11-12.)

Lisu of Nukiang autonomous zhou have been self-sufficient in grain since 1962, they have doubled cultivated area to 3,733 hectares, and yields are 70% above those of 1953.

1964g   "Progress in a southwest China national minority area," Dec. 11. (English translation: Survey of the China Mainland Press 3357: 17-18.)

Lisu of Nukiang Autonomous Zhou have made great improvements. Pre-Liberation, traders demanded a chicken for a single needle. Now three bridges cross the Nu River, and goods are reasonably priced. Lisu account for half of the 220,000 inhabitants, which includes 16 other nationalities. Pei Ah-chien, chairman of the zhou, was deputy to the third National People's Congress and was elected to the Presidium in 1964.

1964h "Thriving agricultural cooperative of Lisu people in Southwest China," Dec. 19.(English translation: Survey of the China Mainland Press 3363: 18-19.)

Lisu of Nipolo agricultural cooperative, who used to pay 24 different kinds of taxes and often ate bark and grassroots, have increased their grain harvest fivefold, to 450 kilo per capita.

1965a "New life for long exiled Chinese minority peasant," Jan. 11.(English translation: Survey of the China Mainland Press 3378: 19-20.)

Lisu family returns home after having taken refuge from Kuomintang and reactionaries.

1965b "Hilly Yi people's commune in Yunnan thrives," July 26.(English translation: Survey of the China Mainland Press 1508: 14-15.)

Yi of Lungshan extend irrigation to 110 hectares. The 300 families also sell fruits, fish, and timber.

1965c "Nanchien Yi Autonomous Xian, Yunnan Province, inaugurated," Dec. 2.(English translation: Survey of the China Mainland Press 3593: 18.)

Lisu, Yi, and 8 other nationalities included in 113,000 inhabitants (48,900 Yi), south of Tali.

1968 "Southwest China minority people creatively study, apply Mao Tse-tung's thought," Dec. 15.(English translation: Survey of the China Mainland Press 4323:

18-19.)

Lisu of Nukiang Autonomous Zhou have set up over 8,000 Mao thought study classes.

1969a "Medical team serves minority nationalities in Yunnan Province," June 5.(English translation: Survey of the China Mainland Press 4434: 17-19.)

Lisu given medical help.

1969b "Family study classes in Mao Tse-tung thought thrive in minority national production brigade in Southwest China," Aug. 1.(English translation: Survey of the China Mainland Press 4471: 19-20.)

Lisu of Otolo production brigade, Tungfanghung commune, on Kaolikung Mountain.

1970a "Southwest China minority area expands industry rapidly," May 12.(English translation: Survey of the China Mainland Press 4660: 89-90.)

Hani-Yi Autonomous Zhou.

1970b "South China commune transforms mountain villages in true revolutionary spirit," July 19.(English translation: Survey of the China Mainland Press 70-30: 91-93.)

Lisu of Liuten commune, Yungsheng xian, in Xiao liang shan, practice irrigation.

1971 "Minority lumbermen mature politically in southwest China," Nov. 14.(English translation: Survey of the China Mainland Press 71-47: 99-100.)

Yi of Ninglang have a forestry bureau (with 300 workers) that has built 152 km. of road, 80 km. of telegraph lines, leveled storage areas, constructed transport lines and overhead cable in the past 18 months.

1972a   "Southwest China minority people and schools," Feb. 8. (English translation: Survey of the China Mainland Press 72-8: 70-71.)

    Lisu, Nahsi, Yi, and others of Lichiang have new schools. Ningland Yi autonomous xian.

1972b   "Southwest China border area trains industrial workers of minority nationalities," July 1. (English translation: Survey of the China Mainland Press 72-28: 149-50.)

    Hani, Yi, and other minorities constitute half the industrial workers of Hungho Hani-Yi autonomous zhou, with 270 state enterprises and 500 workshops.

1972c   "Minority area in southwest China prospers," July 8. (English translation: Survey of the China Mainland Press 72-29: 103-04.)

    Yi, Yao, Miao, Chuang, and Han live in Tayaoshan.

1972d   "Multi-national commune prospers in southwest China border area," Sep. 6. (English translation: Survey of the China Mainland Press 72-38: 67-68.)

    Lisu and others of Pienkukang commune, Nukiang Lisu autonomous zhou.

1972e   "Southwest China minority area improves health work," Oct. 16. (English translation: Survey of the China

Mainland Press 72-44: 16.)

Lisu, Tulung, Nu, Nahsi, Yi, Chingpo, Tibetan of Nukiang Lisu autonomous zhou have 41 medical and health institutions staffed by 449. 80 qualified doctors and many barefoot doctors have been trained from minorities.

1973   "Cultural life in southwest China minority area," Aug. 27. (English translation: Survey of the China Mainland Press 73-36: 167.)

Lisu-Chingpo-Tai-Han newspaper of Teh-hung Tai-Chingpo autonomous zhou has a circulation of 10,000.

New China News Agency (NCNA), Kweiyang (Pinyin: Guiyang)

1959   "Plenty of children among minority people of Southwest China," May 27. (English translation: Survey of the China Mainland Press 2024: 16-17.)

Yi and Kweichow's 11 other minorities increased 9.6% to 4.36 million from 1953 to 1958, due to improved conditions.

1973   "Southwest China autonomous xian increases supplies to minority peoples," Jan. 22. (English translation: Survey of the China Mainland Press 73-6: 24-25.)

Yi like the laces, silk handkerchiefs, and sashes with floral designs that are provided by trading company in Weining xian, Kweichow.

New China News Agency (NCNA), Peking (Pinyin: Beijing)

1956a   "Deputy of Lisu addresses June 27 session of National People's Congress," June 27. (English translation: Survey of the China Mainland Press 1321: 6-7.)

Lisu deputy Pei Ah-chien asks for new written Lisu language, roads, and bridges for Nukiang autonomous zhou.

1956b "Yi deputy on end of slavery at June 29th session of National People's Congress," June 29. (English translation: Survey of the China Mainland Press 1323: 6.)

Yi deputy Wang Hai-min.

1958a "Crop increases in minority areas," Oct 16. (English translation: Survey of the China Mainland Press 1879: 23-24.)

Lisu of Nukiang autonomous zhou harvested 180,000 tons of grain, a sevenfold increase over last year, and an average of 1.2 tons per person, more than twice the national average.

1958b "From slavery to socialism for Yi people in Szechwan," Dec. 15. (English translation: Survey of the China Mainland Press 1921: 10-11.)

1959a "Name list of the National People's Congress Nationalities Committee," Apr. 28. (English translation: Survey of the China Mainland Press 2008: 2-4.)

Lahu delegate: Li Kuang-hua; Lisu: Fu I-chih. (Fu was re-elected to the committee in 1965. He was deputy to the Second National People's Congress in 1959.)

1959b "Progress of Yi people of southwest China minority area," Aug 15. (English translation: Survey of the China Mainland Press 2080: 35-36.)

Yi of Liang shan autonomous zhou, Szechwan, have 33 communes, over 1,000 cooperatives, 4,700 factories and mines, and 13,900 members of the Youth League and Young Pioneers.

1959c   "National minorities," Sep. 1.(English translation: Survey of the China Mainland Press 2095: 17-20.)

         Lisu, Penglung, and Chingpo join in Santashan cooperative.

1968   "People's Liberation Army frontier guards arm national minority people with Mao Tse-tung's thought," May 7.(English translation: Survey of the China Mainland Press 4176: 24-28.)

         Tulung.

1972   "Multi-national southwest China people unite to build border areas," Nov. 30.(English translation: Survey of the China Mainland Press 72-50: 19-20.)

         Yi, Puyi, and Chuang unite to build a power station.

Newsweek

1946   "Slaves of the Lolo," Newsweek 28, 15: 37, Oct. 7.

         Lolo rumored to be holding U.S. flyers as slaves. In 1944, several airmen were ransomed from them. Photo.

Ng, Ronald C. Y.

1971   "Population explosion in the north Thai hills," Geographical Magazine 43: 255-63.

         Akha, Lahu, Lisu mentioned. Erroneously states that Lisu live in villages of a hundred or more houses, whereas there are only two such villages of the 60 Lisu villages in northern Thailand. Photos, map.

Ngoenyuang, Sanit, and Wichit Khumsap

1969   Yaw-Iko-Musoe (Yao-Akha-Lahu), Bangkok, n.p.

         Akha, Lahu: Introductory summaries.

Nguyen Van Huyen
1934 Introduction a l'étude de l'habitation sur pilotis dans l'Asie du Sud-est, Paris, Librairie Orientaliste Paul Geuthner. xxiii, 222 pp.

    Lolo of Bao Lac, Vietnam, have houses on stilts, poorer ones on ground (p. 33).

Nhom Nghien Cuu Dan Toc (Cua Uy-Ban Dan-Toc), Minority Peoples Study Group (of the Committee of Minority Peoples)
1959 Cac dan toc thieu So O Viet-Nam (Minority peoples of Viet-Nam), Hanoi, Nha Xuat Ban Van Hoa.

    Lolo mentioned.

Nishida, Tatsuo
1965-66 "Aka-go no onso taikei (The Phonemic system of Akha. A preliminary report on the Akha language, a language of a hill tribe in northern Thailand)," Onso Kagaku Kenkyū (Studia Phonologica) (Kyoto) 4: 1-37.

1966a "Bisugo no kenkyū: Taikoku hokubu ni okeru Bisuzoku no gengo no yobiteki kenkyu (A preliminary study of the Bisu language)," Tōnan Ajia Kenkyū (Southeast Asian Studies) 4,1: 65-87.

    Bisu has not been reported as an ethnic group by anyone else. In Japanese.

1966b "Taikoku hokubu no gengo chosa ni tsuite (Some notes on a linguistic survey in northern Thailand)," Tōnan Ajia Kenkyū (Southeast Asian Studies) 3,3: 117-29.

    In Japanese.

1966-67 "Bisugo no keitō (The Lineage of Bisu. A comparative study of the Bisu, Akha and Burmese languages I-II),"

Tōnan Ajia Kenkyū (Southeast Asian Studies) 4,3: 42-68, 5: 52-68.
In Japanese.

1967a "Taikoku Tahku ken ni okeru Risu-zoku no kotoba no yobi hōkoku (A preliminary study on the Lisu language in Tak province)," Tōnan Ajia Kenkyū (Southeast Asian Studies) 5,2: 48-79 (276-307).
Lisu phonology, based on a week's study in the same village as Roop (1970). In Japanese.

1967b A short report on the linguistic survey of hill tribes in Thailand, Report to the National Research Council, Bangkok. 2 pp.
Bisu, Akha, Lisu, Lahu.

1968a "Lisu-go no hikaku kenkyū I-II (A comparative study of the Lisu language I-II)," Tōnan Ajia Kenkyū (Southeast Asian Studies) 6,1: 2-35, 2: 19-47 (261-89).
In Japanese.

1968b "Roro-Biruma-go hikaku kenkyū ni okeru mondai (Some problems in proto Lolo-Burmese)," Tōnan Ajia Kenkyū (Southeast Asian Studies) 4,4: 198-219.
In Japanese.

1969 "Rafu-shi-go no kenkyū: Taikoku Chenrai-ken ni okeru Rafu-shi-zoku no kotoba no yobi-hokoku (A preliminary study on the Lahu Shi language in Chieng Rai province)," Tōnan Ajia Kenkyū (Southeast Asian Studies) 7,1: 2-39.
In Japanese.

Nyunt, Khin Maung

1969 "Little known Kaws," The Guardian (Rangoon) 16,1: 28-32.

Ollone, Henri Marie Gustave, Vicomte d' (See also Maitre 1908, Maitre and d'Ollone 1909.)

1907a "La mission du capitaine d'Ollone. Traversée du pays des Lolos," Société de Géographie de Lyon et de la region lyonnaise, Bulletin 22, 137: 147-48.

1907b "La traversée du pays des Lolos par le Capitaine d'Ollone," Société de géographie de Lyon et de la region lyonnaise, Bulletin 22, 138: 203-04.

Lolo country is divided into rival fiefdoms.

1907c "Mission d'Ollone," La Géographie 16,1: 71-73, 3: 196-97.

Lolo: Progress of the expedition.

1907d "Rapport du Capitaine d'Ollone," La Géographie 16,4: 265-69.

Lolo: First voyage by a European going west to east across Ta Liang Shan (but cf. Bonin 1907).

1907e "Lettre du 1 Octobre 1907 de Yunnan-fou," Ecole française d'Extrême-Orient, Bulletin 7, 3-4: 440-42.

Lolo inscriptions and books found near Wei-ning, Kweichow.

1911 Les derniers barbares: Mission d'Ollone 1906-1909: Chine-Tibet-Mongolie, 3d ed., Paris, Pierre Lafitte. (English translation by Bernard Miall, In forbidden China: The d'Ollone Mission 1906-09: China-Tibet-Mongolia, Boston, Small, Maynard and Company, London and Leipzig, J. Fisher.) 372 pp.

Lolo depend upon Chinese for firearms and cloth. Chinese get wax from Lolo. Lolo may enter towns, leaving weapons at gate and hostages with yamen, but Chinese do not have reciprocal rights of entering Lolo territory unless a Lolo extends his protection.

Chinese who enter are killed or enslaved. Lolo raid Chinese. Long-tiu-shan (Lolo: Chonolevo) is the cradle of Lolo ancestors. In past 200 years, Lolo have moved west. Seigneur-warriors, serfs, and slaves each of whom has several subclasses. Seigneurs are divided into clans with council or ruler. In 1868, General Chao was defeated by the Lolo. Since then, Chinese have made a score of attempts to regain the country, the latest in 1905 under commissary Chang and the Lolo prince, Chaowu. Eldest son inherits political power, but youngest is given advantage in herds, houses, and land. Women receive dowry. For three years after death, the soul roams; an effigy of wood, hemp, or orchid root, in which magical formulas have fixed the soul, is kept in a box or under the roof. At the end of three years, the effigy is thrown away, the body is exhumed and burned, and the ashes are put in an urn and buried in a new location. Sinicized Lolo.

Lissou are said to intermarry only with Mitcha or Minkia. Lissou vocabulary from Mitala, near Woutingtcheou, just north of Kunming. Maps, photos.

1912a Langues des peuples non chinois de la Chine, Mission d'Ollone, vol. 6, Paris, E. Leroux. 244 pp.

Lolo vocabularies, nos. 14 (by Liétard), 15 (Maire), 16 (Tapponier), 17 (Lepage), 18 to 22 (d'Ollone), 23 (the Mitcha who intermarry with Lissou and Minkia), 24 (Lipou or Lissou), 25 (Lissou west of Wutingchow, by Charria and Monbeig), 26 (Lolopo, by Liétard), 27, 28 (the Née), 29 (the Chouitien,

	Sinicized Lolo, by de Fleurelle), 30, 31 and 32 (d'Ollone).
1912b	Ecritures des peuples non chinois de la Chine; quatre dictionnaires lolo et miao tseu, Mission d'Ollone 1906-09, vol. 7, Paris, Ernest Leroux. 301 pp.

Lolo writing used for family books and for legends (deluge, dispersion of races, description of animals, rivers, and mountains). Four Lolo inscriptions. Dictionaries of characters used near Kang siang ying (250 characters), Kiao kio (480), Wei ning tcheou (1030). Map.

Reviews: by A. Vissière, 1913, Asie Française: 46-48; 1913, Missions Catholiques 45: 144; by E.H. Parker, 1914, Asiatic Review: 261-63. |

Orléans, Henri Philippe Marie, Prince d' (See also Scott and Hardiman 1900.)

1896	"From Yun-nan to British India," Geographical Journal 7: 300-09.

Lissu: The wild Lissu constantly raid and kidnap the Lissu and Lamajen of the Mekong for slavery or ransom. Map. |
| 1898 | Du Tonkin aux Indes, Paris, C. Lévy. (English translation by Hamley Bent, 1898, From Tonkin to India by the source of the Irawadi, January '95-January '96, London, Methuen.) 467 pp.

Lissou: Orléans passed east and north of the main Lissou area in 1895, but he collected two vocabularies (Nos. 20,23). Their language resembles Lochai and Lolo. The Lissou collect tribute from Kioutses, whom they have driven west; perhaps they |

came from the south, because of legends about elephants.

    Akha of Pichu, vocabulary No. 9. (No. 10 is possibly Akha.)

    Lolo vocabularies (Nos. 7, 12). Pula (not Liétard's Phupha) (No. 1). Map, illustrations.

Oughton, Gary
  1969   Hill-tribe agriculture in northern Thailand (manuscript), Chiang Mai, Tribal Research Centre-Agricultural Research Office.

Oxibar, Jean-Pierre
  1959   "A la recherche des Lahous," Feuilles Missionaires 16: 1-5.

    Lahu spirit possession in a village in Chiangdao district, Thailand. Photos. See Saint-Guily 1964, Mieyaa 1973.

Palangtirasin, Ome
  1970   "Hill tribes: The hidden minority," Bangkok Post, Sep.

    Akha, Lahu, Lisu: Efforts to win their loyalty. Unsuccessful approach of government's mobile contact teams. Related articles in same issue on "Terrorism in Thailand" and "Rehabilitation is the CSOC's aim."

Parker, E. H.
  1895   "The Lolo written character," Indian Antiquary 24: 172.

Parsons, Hy
  1931   "Aborigines in West China," Missionary Review of the World 54,2: 87-90.

    Ko-pu, a branch of the No-su, were probably former serfs of the No-su. Located north of Tong-Chuan in villages of 5 to 60 families. They recognize their inability to withstand the Chinese, who are encroaching on their land, and this has been a factor in their movement toward Christianity. In litigations, the Chinese bleed both parties. The Ko-pu worship Ya-so-mu, the all-powerful, and keep ancestral tablets. They have copied the Chinese in smoking opium and now grow their own. Photo.

Paw U, Richard
1961   <u>Report by Mr. Richard Paw U on a field trip undertaken in connexion with the project on a socioeconomic survey of the hill tribes of northern Thailand</u>, Bangkok ECAFE Division of Social Affairs (mimeographed). 46 pp.
Lisu and Lahu of Tak nikhom (reservation). Maps.

Peet, Lawrence J.
1961   <u>Lahu language lessons-Looking for a loquacious Lahu</u>, Tak, n.p. (mimeographed). (Reissued 1964, Chiang Mai, <u>Towards a more loquacious Lahu</u>.)
Lahu language of Tak, Thailand.

Peking Review.
1975   "A national minority area in Yunnan Province," <u>Peking Review</u> 18,5: 22-23.
Lisu of Nuchiang Autonomous Chou: 90% of cadres at prefecture, county, commune, and brigade level are minority members. 7,700 theoretical workers and 210 schools for criticizing Lin Piao and Confucius. Of the 2,700 Tulung, 58 are Party members and 110 cadres.

Pelliot, Paul
1904   "Deux itinéraires de Chine en Inde à la fin du VIIIe siècle," <u>Ecole Française d'Extrême-Orient, Bulletin</u>

-230-

4,1-2: 131-413.

 Based on <u>Sin t'ang chou</u> (New History of the T'ang) by Kia Tan, written about 785-805 A.D. The eastern Ts'ouan (Wou-man, Black Man) include the Lou-lou (k 222, p. 8) which Yuan historians identified with Lolo (<u>Yuan che lei pien</u> k 42, p. 65). They were located southeast of Yunnansen, as far as Pou-t'eou, or Linngan (pp. 137-38). Lolo writing and inscriptions (pp. 154-55, 159).

People's Republic of China
1954 Xīn Zhōng-guó shǎo shù mínzú di sheng huo (Hsin Chung-kuo shao shu mintsu ti sheng huo) (National minorities in the New China), Peking, People's Republic of China Foreign Language Press. 24 pp.
  Yi: A large color photo of Yi celebrating the Torch festival in Milo County. (Captions in Chinese, Russian, French, Indonesian, and Arabic.)

Perazic, Elizabeth
1960 "Little Laos next door to Red China," <u>National Geographic</u> 117,1: 46-69.
  Akha of Muong Sing: photos.

Percheron: see Teston and Percheron 1932.

Phanphayap, Nopphaburi
1967 Chaaw Khǎw (Hill peoples), Chiang Mai, n.p.
  Akha, Lahu, Lisu: Short cultural summaries. In Thai.

Phillips, J.F.V., W.R. Geddes, F.T. Merrill, and A. Messingzejewski: see United Nations 1967.

Playfair, George Macdonald Home
1876 "The Miaotzu of Kweichow and Yunnan from Chinese

descriptions," China Review 5: 92-108.

Kouo-lo (originally Lou-lou) located in Ta-ting prefecture of Kweichow and most prefectures of Yunnan. They are divided into Black and White. Their clothes of grass (hemp?), their hair in knots similar to those of the Li Sou. In the little Han period (ca. 221 A.D.), Tchou-ko-liang (Wou Hou) fought Meng Houo and was made prince of Lo-tien; he also brought fire to the Kouo-lo. See Clarke in Colquhoun 1883; Cordier 1907: 6-7.

Pollard, Samuel (See also Hammerton 1922-24.)

1911 Tight corners in China, London, Andrew Crombie. 2d ed. 167 pp.

Nosu nearly kidnapped Pollard, then nearly had him marry a Nosu. A missionary's anecdotal adventures. Photos.

1921 In unknown China, Philadelphia, J.B. Lippincott Company; London, Seeley, Service & Co. Ltd. 324 pp.

Nosu dish of sheep liver, stomach, and heart, which are minced, spiced, and eaten with porcupine quill. Nosu use white towers as refuge. Nosu have Chinese tenants (pp. 63, 84, 93, 98, 103, 106). Va-sa-neh, the flying pony. Nosu send 48 horses to Peking as tribute (pp. 134-35). Ranked groups: Earth Eyes (landowners registered with Chinese), Black, White, Lama Tibetans (?), slaves. Three souls; at death, one goes to heaven, one to grave, and one to Hades (but kept in basket in corner of house). Chinese hire Nosu mercenaries in Mohammedan revolt; Nosu ambush Taiping rebels. Opium growing. Spririt mediums.

    Manuscripts. (Pages 178, 180, 234-35, 238-39, 246-66, 288, 311-12.) Maps, photos.
    Review: 1921, Geographical Journal, 58: 387-89.

Pritchard, B.E.A.
 1914 "A journey from Myitkyina to Sadiya via the N'Mai Hka and Hkamti Long," Geographical Journal 43: 521-35.
    Lissu came to dig for gold at A'mekh River junction in previous few years, driving out the Naingvaws from the N'Mai area. Lissu trade metal pots and blue Chinese coats for the rice, eggs, and salt of the Naingvaws.

Pu, Kuei-chung
 1958 "Yi slaves of Xiaoliangshan head for socialism," Guāng-míng rì-bào Sep. 9 (English translation: Survey of China Mainland Press 1928: 19-21.)
    Yi autonomous xian, Ninglang, Yunnan, has 94,000 inhabitants of 12 nationalities. Slavery was abolished in 1956-58, and the 10,000 freed slaves were first in agricultural cooperatives and industry during the Great Leap Forward. 4,000 were labeled slave-owners, and saboteurs of the Leap were dealt with. The author is secretary of the Communist Party Working Committee, Yi Autonomous Xian, Ninglang.

Puttawatana, Pichai
 1963 "Hill tribes of the north," Journal of Social Science Research.
    Akha, Lahu, and Lisu: short cultural descriptions. In Thai.

Qǔ, Běn-zàng-yáo, and Gāo Bó-shēn
 1934 "Xī-nán guo fáng yǔ luó-yí mín-zú (Southwestern

national defense and the Lolo tribes)," Fang-zhi yue-kan (Fangshi Monthly) 7,5.

Rachanee, M. C. Bhisatej
1972 "News from the poppy fields," The Nation, Sep. 3: 3.
Lisu from Burma attempt to sell opium in Thailand, but government enforcement of law scares buyers.

Rajan, Bhistej
1970 His Majesty's assistance to the hill tribes, Bangkok, Royal Thai Government. 5 pp.
Akha, Lahu, Lisu receive medical help, advice on sericulture and vegetable growing.

Raquez, A.
1902 Pages laotiennes, Le Haut-Laos Le Moyen-Laos Le Bas-Laos, Hanoi, F.-H. Schneider, Imprimeur-Editeur. 537 pp.
Mouceu (Lahu?) near Xieng Kok offer to the spirit of the household during fourth month (pp. 301-04).

Rashid, Mohammed Razha: see Walker, ed., 1975.

Ratzel, Friedrich
1888 Völkerkunde, 3 vols., Leipzig, Verlag des Bibliographischen Instituts. 778 pp.
Lissu (3: 340), Lolo (3: 509-10) mentioned.

Reclus, Elisée, and Onésime Reclus
1902 L'Empire du milieu, Paris, Librairie Hachette et Cie. 667 pp.
Lolo may mean someone who cannot speak properly. Also called Laka. Came from Chensi. In Ningyuen, they have become Chinese, even passing the examinations to become mandarins. Black Lolo only slightly darker

than White. Physical description by Thorel (pp. 319-21).

Reinhard, Kurt
1955 "Die Musik der Lolo," Baessler Archiv 28, n.s. 3: 195-216.
    Lolo music in Western notation.
1956 "Acht Lieder sinisierter Lolo," Baessler Archiv 29, n.s. 4,1: 105-16.
    Lolo songs.

Ren, Chen-tong
n.d. "A study of the rural economy of the Lolo," Reconstruction Weekly 7, 13.
    Black Lolo families average 5.30 plus 10 slaves; White Lolo families average 6.34 members. Average income for Black family is $485.66, for White $60.21. Author is an agricultural economist, who worked among the Lolo about 1918.

Rén-mín rì-bào [People's Daily], Peking
1959a "Social reforms in minority areas in China," Aug. 15: 7. (English translation: Joint Publications Research Service DC 984.)
    Lisu area, once known as "poor hills, bad water," has made great progress between 1954 and 1958.
1959b "Liangshan Yi nationality autonomous zhou heads toward happiness," Nov. 8 (English translation: Survey of China Mainland Press 2150: 32-34.)
    Yi feuds with Han forgotten. Some 3,000 Han have come to work in industrial enterprises and to teach the Yi.
1959c "New cities and towns spring up in Liangshan Yi

nationality autonomous zhou," Nov. 8.(English translation: Survey of China Mainland Press 2150: 34-35.)

Yi have one city over 10,000 (Chaochueh, the capital), and five others over 1,000 (Meiku, Put'o, Kanlo, Wakang, and Puhsiung).

1962 "Over one hundred work teams and work groups of the People's Liberation Army in Yunnan....," Sep. 3. (English translation: Survey of China Mainland Press 2828: 1-2.)

Lisu are guided by Chinese soldiers in agriculture and education. Many Lisu had never eaten rice before, now they have paddy fields, and often place a bowl of cooked rice before the portrait of Mao.

1963 "Education develops rapidly in areas of national minorities in Yunnan," Nov. 6.(English translation: Survey of China Mainland Press 3107: 15.)

Lisu: The first Lisu teacher graduated from Kunming Normal College in 1962.

1970 "People of various nationalities in Nuchiang autonomous region, Yunnan, creatively study and apply Mao Tse-tung's thought by integrating it with the struggle-criticism-transformation movement," Jan. 9. (English translation: Survey of China Mainland Press 4578: 133-36.)

Mao thought study classes inspire the Lisu toward new progress in the direction of socialism.

1972a "Under the guidance of Chairman Mao's revolutionary line, minority nationalities cadres are growing up and maturing," Jan. 13. (English translation: Survey of China Mainland Press 72-4: 137-38.)

Liangshan Yi: Liu Shao-chih and his agents allowed former slaveowners to take important posts; now the emphasis is on ideology. Over 50 "May 7" schools. At xian level, 51% cadres are Yi; at zhou, commune, and village levels, 80% are Yi, mostly of serf background. In 1970, a "learn from Tachai" campaign was begun in the zhou. Wang Hai-min, former serf who joined the Red Army in 1935 and is now the zhou Party secretary, talked to cadres of the struggle between two lines, and led a visit to Walikou commune, an advanced example of learning from Tachai. Pan p'o commune is another advanced unit, partly due to the efforts of He-i-po, former serf who is now political instructor of the local militia company.

1972b "Seriously carry out the party's nationality policy and cadre policy on a solid basis," June 11. (English translation: Survey of China Mainland Press 72-25: 187-89.)

Lisu: Party committees of Nuchiang Lisu autonomous zhou stress re-education of old minority cadres, and training and promotion of new minority cadres. For example a Lisu ex slave had become a cadre, but erred. He was criticized, exposed to Mao thought, and now he is active once again.

1973 "Minority nationality cadres in Ssumao district grow up rapidly following tempering in the Great Proletarian Cultural Revolution," Mar. 30. (English translation: Survey of China Mainland Press 73-15: 136-37.)

Laku, Hani, Yi, Pulang, K'uts'ung: 36% of all cadres in Ssumao district are minority peoples.

Rheinwald, Otto
1942 "Die nicht chinesischen Stämme Südchinas, Ein Überblick," Mitteilungen Deutsche Gesellschaft für Natur- und Völkerkunde Ostasiens 33, part A.

Richtohofen, Ferdinand, Baron de (See also Tiessen 1907.)
1903 Baron Richthofen's letters 1870-1872, 2d ed., Shanghai, North China Herald. 211 pp.
    Lolo raid Chinese (pp. 67-68), raid for salt in Szechwan (pp. 186-87), opium growing.
    See Cordier 1907: 56-57.

Roberts, T. D. : see Henderson 1971a, Whitaker et al. 1972.

Robinson, Joan
1975 "National minorities in Yunnan," Eastern Horizon 14,4: 32-43.
    Hani underwent land reform, 1953-54. Nu had common forest parceled out by chief.

Rocher, Emile
1879-80 La province chinoise du Yün-nan, 2 parts, Paris, Ernest Leroux. 286 pp.
    Lissou live along both sides of the Salween, north of 27°. Lolo (I-jên) of Liang shan have been peaceful for the past 17 years. In K'un-yang, much of the valley population has fled, and I-jên have replaced them. I-jên of Hsin-kai have been decimated by the plague. I-jên work iron industry in Hsi-o-hsien (pp. 68, 115, 117, 130-34). Revolts in 60 B.C., 58 A.D., 1294, 1330, and 1775 (pp. 153, 172, 174, 193). I-jên live alongside Pa-i and Chinese (pp. 139, 250, 274). Map.

Rock, Joseph Francis Charles
1947 The ancient Na-khi kingdom of Southwest China, 2 vols., Cambridge, Harvard University Press. 554 pp.

Lisu rebellions from 1592 on. Rock visited several Lisu villages, including Ba-ssu-ko, with 130 families. Some Lisu speak Nakhi and Chinese. High incidence of cretinism and interbreeding, many afflicted with goiter.

Lo-lo forced to migrate by clan feuds from Ta liang Shan to Yunnan have cut down pine forests for fields. Near Shih-ku, Lo-lo live alongside Na-khi and Li-su. In 1796, Chinese killed many Lo-lo rebels. Constant Lo-lo plundering and raids have given them the upper hand, and the other tribes and the Chinese of the area live in fear of them. Tso-so T'ussu lives in constant fear of his Lo-lo "subjects." Kua-pieh T'ussu, a Mo-so, was killed by Lo-lo in 1924. Yung pei t'ing records mention Lo-lo as original inhabitants of Yung-ning Lake.

Nu-tzu (Nu or A-nu) live along Salween, from Lyu ra-gang north to Sang-tha (north of the Black Li-su). Also called Lu-tzu at Bahang. Staple is maize. Mentioned in Yun-nan T'ung-chih and Li-chiang fu chih lüeh. Village locations and populations. Superb maps and photos. See Sutton 1974.

Rockhill, William Woodville
1891 The land of the Lamas, New York, Century Company. 399 pp.

Lissu, Lolo, and Moso rites resemble those of the

<dl>
<dt></dt>
<dd>Bonpo. Many Tsarong Tibetans have Lissu debt-slaves. Lichiang fu traders buy pine tree coffins from the Lissu, and therefore opposed missionaries, who might disrupt this trade (pp. 218, 284-86).</dd>
<dt>1895</dt>
<dd>"Notes on the ethnology of Tibet. Based on the collections in the U.S. National Museum," <u>Report of the U.S. National Museum for 1893</u>: 665-747, with plates 1-52.

Lolo dress.</dd>
</dl>

Roop, DeLagnel Haigh
1969   "The problem of linguistic diversity in Thailand," in Peter Hinton, ed., <u>Tribesmen and Peasants in North Thailand</u>, Chiang Mai, Tribal Research Centre: 100-07.

    Lisu: Problems in teaching Thai to them.

1970   <u>A grammar of the Lisu language</u>, doctoral dissertation, New Haven, Yale University. (<u>Dissertation Abstracts</u> <u>31</u>: 3535A, University Microfilms order no. 71-51.) 334 pp.

    Lisu of Tak nikhom (reservation) in Thailand. Phonemics and systematic grammar. See Nishida 1967a.

Rorak, Gloria
1969   "Life among the Lahu," <u>Catholic Life</u>, Nov.: 20-22.

    Lahu of Thailand: Anecdotes of a missionary.

Rose, Archibald
1909   "The reaches of the upper Salween" <u>Geographical Journal</u> <u>34</u>,6: 608-13.

    Lisu villages have buried stockades of sharpened bamboo. Story of Brunhuber and Carl Schmitz, who traveled along the Salween, among tame and Black Lisu,

	and were killed by Lutzu between 27°15' and 27°30'N. Chinese punitive force was sent. Map. See Brunhuber 1912: Geographical Journal 32: 529 and 34: 341.
1912	"Chinese frontiers of India," Geographical Journal 39: 193-223.
	Lisu village with 85 houses, 5 of which were Chinese. Photos.
Rose, Archibald, and J. Coggin Brown	
1911	"Lisu (Yawyin) tribes of the Burma-China frontier," Royal Asiatic Society of Bengal, Memoirs 3: 249-76.
	Lisu distribution, legends, dress, housing, life cycle, crops, religion, word list, anthropometric measurements. Previous European visitors. The most useful of the early descriptions. Rose was British consul at Tengyueh, and Coggin Brown was a geologist. Map, photos.
Roux, Emile	
1897	"Aux sources de l'Irraouaddi," Le Tour du Monde, n.s. 3: 193-276.
	Lissou as far as 95°30'E. They are hunters, drinkers, and bandits. An interesting description of a curing ceremony. Roux accompanied Orléans, following the Salween from 26°to 26°10'N. and the Mekong to 28°30'N. Map, sketches.
Roux, Henri	
1924	"Deux tribus de la région de Phongsaly (Laos septentrional)," Ecole française d'Extrême-Orient, Bulletin 24: 373-500. (Reprinted with minor changes made by Tran Van Chu, 1954, "Quelques minorités ethniques du

Nord-Indochine," France-Asie 10,92-93: 135-419.)

"A-Kha" means intermediary. 4,500 A-Khas in the Fifth military territory, in 7 groups. They claim that they didn't know about opium smoking 20 years ago, but now they overdo it. Physical traits. Costume. Legends: 700 years ago they lived on Cha Ten Plateau, between the Shan States and China. Wasps were devastating the country, and the Akha and Ho agreed that whoever could destroy them would rule the land. Ho tricked the Akha into submission. 200 years ago, the Akha tired of Ho sovereignty, and moved to the Lu territory of Muong U Nua. Akha ate buffalo hides, on which writing had been given them. Villages more every 3 or 4 years. Houses. Illness, sorcerers. They have 3 souls. The spirits of the ancestors are kept in a special basket, along with 2 bowls, black or blue cloth, small bamboo basket, and 9 cowries. The sorcerer has a larger basket to worship his protective spirit. Marriage, marriage payments, and songs. Birth, names; twins, who are considered unlucky, are killed. Funerals, buffalo sacrifices. Dreams. Taboos. Festivals. Omens. Spirits. Vocabulary, Texts. Map, photos.
Review: by E. Seidenfaden, 1956. Siam Society Journal 43: 143-61.

1952 "Quelques souvenirs du Nord-Indochine," France-Asie 8,79: 1049-58.

A-Kho never place pot with handle perpendicular to main beam of the house, and never enter a house by the back door.

Roy, Claude

1953   Clefs pour la Chine, Paris, Gallimard. (English translation by Mervyn Savill, 1955, London, Sidgwich and Jackson; 1956, New York, Robert M. McBride.) 353 pp.

Yi stripped advance detachment of Red Army on Long March in 1934, but were won over by Mao, who helped them revolt in 1935 (pp. 45-46). By 1938, two Yi were generals in Red Army. Commission of National Affairs, Peking, has Chairs of Yi and Liso. Mentions Lolo, Yassi, and Nosu as if distinct from Yi.

Ruenyote, Suwan

1967   The development and welfare scheme for the hill tribes in Thailand, Bangkok, Department of Public Welfare, Ministry of Interior. 24 pp.

Akha, Lahu, Lisu relations with Thai government. In Thai and English.

Ruey, Yih-fu (Jui I-fu) (Pinyin: Ruì, Yi-fū)

1948a   "Jì lì-sù yīn jiān lùn lì-sù wén (On the sounds of the Lisu language with remarks on the 'Lisu script')," Lì shǐ yǔ yán yán jiu suǒ, Zhōng yāng yán jiu yuàn (Bulletin of the Institute of History and Philology, Academia Sinica) 17: 303-26.

Hwa (Flowery) Lisu of western Yunnan: Phonemes. (In Chinese, with English summary.)

1948b   "Yún-nán xī-nán biān-jiāng di ló-hēi-rén (The Lahu people of the southwest border of Yunnan)," Gúo-jì wén-hùa (International Culture (Nanking)) 1,3: 1-2.

Lahu, Lo-hei, Black Lolo or Muhso number 100,000 in Yunnan and Lantsang, Chuang chiang, Tsangyuan, etc., 20,000 in Burma, and 10,000 in Thailand. A few in

	Vietnam. Distinction between Big and Small Lo-hei, as well as Red, Black, and Yellow. Clothing. Houses. Forbidden to eat sheep. Marriage is by love match and negotiated through groom's father or elder brother. Cremate the dead. Hunt with crossbow; mash roots to make poison, which can be counteracted by pregnant women. In 1723-35, a Buddhist monk acquired many Lo hei followers; monks became village officials; and temples became courthouses. In the eighteenth and nineteenth centuries, monks led rebellions and were persecuted by the Chinese. Especially in the last quarter of the nineteenth century, there were many rebellions in league with neighboring highlanders. In the twentieth century, American missionaries spread Christianity, using children they had educated in Burma. Priests are leaders.
1950	"Rui ai tai yĕ lu zú de gin zi lian ming zhi yŭ luo-lŏ mō xie (The patronymic linkage systems of the Rui Ai Tai Ye Lu tribe and that of the Lolo Mo Xie)," Tái-wān wén-huà (Taiwan Culture) 6,1.
	See Lo 1944a, 1944b, 1945a, 1945b; Mă 1942-44; Shiratori 1957.
Saihoo, Patya	
1963a	"The hill tribes of northern Thailand and the opium problem," Bulletin on Narcotics 15,2: 35-45.
	Akha, Lahu, Lisu opium cultivation. A family of 6 or 7 is estimated to cultivate 2 to 4 rai (one rai is 0.16 hectare), yielding about 4 kilograms of raw opium. Lisu and Black Lahu consume about 5% of the

opium they grow; while the Red Lahu consume 30-40%.
Photos.

1963b   The hill tribes of northern Thailand, Bangkok, Faculty
of Political Science, Chulalongkorn University. 72 pp.

Akha, Lahu, Lisu: Cultural summaries and information contained in 1963a, above.

Sainson, Camille
1904   Nan-tchao Ye-che, Paris, Ernest Leroux.

Kouo-lo are mentioned in the Nan-tchao chronicles as Ts'ouan and descendants of Lou-lou. Their great sorcerer is H'i-p'ouo. They hold a festival of the torches on the 24th day of the 7th moon. They have a cult of the white horse. They divine, using cock's femurs. Subgroups include White, Black, Dry, Water (who cultivate irrigated fields), Miao, Ko, A-tcho, A-wou, Lou-wou, Sa-mi, and Lao-wou. See Cordier 1907: 13-16.

Saint-Guily, Jean
1964   "Le Père Jean-Pierre Oxibar (1898-1964)," Feuilles Missionnaires 36: 1-6.

Lahou of Yunnan were missionized by Oxibar.
Photos. See Mieyaa 1973.

Savina, F. M.
1930   Histoire des Miao, 2d ed., Hongkong, Imprimerie de la Société des missions-étrangères. (First edition, 1924.) 303 pp.

Lolo legends of creation, ancestors, and deluge, and a 250-word list from Vial (pp. 42-69, 77-78, 109-12).

Saw Aung Din and E. E. Sowards
1963   "Work among Lahus, Was, Akhas," in Maung Shwe Wa,
             Genevieve Sowards, and Erville Sowards, eds., Burma
             Baptist Chronicles, Book 2: 407-19, Rangoon, Board of
             Publications, Burma Baptist Convention.
                  Lahu prophet A Teh Pu Cu predicted the coming of
             God when white people arrived on white horses bringing
             Scriptures. These were the missionaries: Cushing in
             1870 and William M. Young in 1901. First Lahu was
             baptized in 1904. Drawings. See Crider 1963, Maung
             Shwe Wa 1963, Walker 1974-75.

Sayamnotr, Chidpong
1966   The administration of hill tribe development and
             welfare programs of the Department of Public Welfare,
             Bangkok, Ministry of Interior. 132 pp.
                  Akha, Lahu, Lisu: Describes objective, organiza-
             tion and administrative problems of government programs,
             including the structure of the projects, coordination,
             personnel, and funding. In Thai, with English abstract.

Scherman, L.
1915   "Wohnhaustypen in Burma und Assam," Archiv für
             Anthropologie 14,3: 203-34. (French translation by
             Barbara Wall, 1975, Asie du Sud-est et Monde Insulindien
             6,2-3: 159-99.)
                  Lishaw village of Pangsapyi near Hsipaw forced by
             government to move there 6 months before Scherman's
             visit in June 1911. They now work on Palaung tea
             plantations. Description of bamboo house is same as
             houses used by Lisu in Thailand today. Photo (plate

VI, number 4), map.

Scholz, Friedhelm

1967   Preliminary report on the results of ethnological field research in the Akha village Ban Alom, May 1966-December 1966, Heidelberg, South Asian Institute, University of Heidelberg.

  Akha of Mae Chan district, Chiangrai Province, Thailand. Sociopolitical organization, religion, types of households, surname groups, kin terms.

Schrock, Joann L., Irene Crowe, Marilou Fromme, Dennis E. Gosier, Virginia S. McKenzie, Raymond W. Myers, and Patricia L. Stegemen

1970   Minority groups in Thailand, Pamphlet No. 550-107, Washington, D.C., Department of the Army. 1,135 pp.

  Akha (chap. 14), Lahu (chap. 6), and Lisu (chap. 5). A superficial synthesis of published works, repeating most of the misinformation possible. Emphasis is on communications, civic action, paramilitary capabilities, and advice for personnel working with these groups. No attempt is made to see them as cultural systems or social structures. The 25,000-28,000 Akha in Thailand are said to be patriarchal, and their villages are said to be much larger than those of the Lisu. The 16,000-17,000 Lahu are said to be matrilineal (sic), and poorer Lahu are said to be hired by Karen to work in their opium fields (sic: it is the other way around). The 19,000 Lisu in Thailand (an inaccurate estimate, see Dessaint 1972a) are said to have the largest villages of any of the hill tribes (p. 316 difficult to reconcile with the estimate of Akha village size above, pp. 879-80). Sketches. Maps.

Schrock, Joann L., Dennis E. Gosier, Diane S. Marton, Virginia S. McKenzie, and Gary D. Murfin

1972   Minority groups in North Vietnam, Pamphlet No. 550-110, Washington, D. C., Department of the Army. 653 pp.

    Lolo of North Vietnam, ethnographic sketch (pp. 102-42). Several errors in references. Map.

Schweinfurth, Ulrich

1969   Problems of land use in South Asia, Heidelberg, University of Heidelberg. 11 pp.

    Akha village in Chiangrai Province, Thailand. Demand for land, agricultural activities, tools, crops. Rice is now the only cash crop. The village economy is upset by the need to buy opium, formerly grown by the villagers. In German, with English abstract.

Scott, Sir James George (See also Grierson 1903-28, Hammerton 1922-24, Mitton 1936.)

1921   Burma, 3d ed., London, Daniel O'Connor. (1st ed., 1906.) 520 pp.

    Li-hsaw (or Yao-yen) speak Chinese and resemble the Chinese, but they are related to the Lahu. Photo.

1932   Burma and beyond, London, Grayson and Grayson. 349 pp.

Scott, Sir James George, and John Thomas Percy Hardiman

1900   Gazetteer of Upper Burma and the Shan States, Pt. I, vol. 1, Rangoon, Superintendent of Government Printing.

    Word lists: Akha (by G. C. B. Stirling, pp. 692-94), Lahu (670-80), Lahu-hsi (by Stirling, pp. 699-702), Lahu-na (by Stirling, pp. 697-99), Lishaw (by Stirling, pp. 661-69, 681, 702-04), and Lisu (by Orléans, pp. 671-81).

Seidenfaden, Erik
1930 "The Gospel of St. Marc in Mussö," Siam Society, Journal 24,1: 84-87.

Mussö are identical to Moso (sic). Chronicles mention that in 796 the Mussö were subdued by the king of Nan-Chao. Later, the Mussö had a confederation of 36 Fu. Part of it was overrun by the Burmese, and placed under the rule of the governor of Mulang Laem, but the confederation continued in China until 1887. Since then, there has been a continuous migration to the Shan States and Siam, where they were first contacted near Doi Pha Hum (northwest of Fang, in Chiang Mai Province). There they were govened by Phraya Kili, who wielded great power. The American Presbyterian Mission has started work east (west?) of Chiangrai, and has 60 to 70 converts. The American Baptist Mission in Chieng Tung has baptized 17,000 Mussö.

1958 The Thai peoples, Bangkok, Siam Society.

Lisu of Fang district, Chiang Mai Province, are said to reside for 40 to 50 years in the same locality and to have hereditary chiefs (neither of these statements is true of the Lisu in Thailand today).

Shabad, Theodore
1965 "China, People," Encyclopedia Britannica 5: 566-69.
1972 China's changing map, National and regional development, 1949-71, revised ed., New York and Washington, D.C., Praeger Publishers. (Original ed., 1956.) 370 pp.

Minorities, their locations and autonomous areas,

and 1953 populations.

Shafer, Robert

1938a "Phunoi and Akha tones," Sino-Tibetica 4: 29-38.
Akha tonal and phonetic correspondences with Burmese.

1938b "The link between Burmese and Lolo," Sino-Tibetica 2: 8-10.
Review: Henri Maspero, 1938, Société Linguistique de Paris, Bulletin 39: 206-07.

1952 "Phonétique historique des langues lolo," T'oung Pao 41,1-3: 191-229.
Comparative lexical items from Akha, Ahi, Gni, Lolopho, Oulou, Phunoi, and Phupha.

1955 "Classification of the Sino-Tibetan languages," Word 11: 94-111.
Lolo branch includes: (1) Phunoi (Akha, Lahu; Woni); (2) Lisu (Kesopho, Kosopho; Lisu, Lishaw, Lipha, Lipho), Nyi Tsŏkŏ, Weining, Ahi, Lolopho; (3) Thongho; (4) Mung; (5) Unclassified, including Mossŏ.

1957 Bibliography of Sino-Tibetan languages, Weisbaden, Otto Harrassowitz. 211 pp.
Comprehensive. See 1963, below.

1963 Bibliography of Sino-Tibetan languages II, Weisbaden, Otto Harrassowitz. 141 pp.

Sharp, Lauriston: see Hanks, Hanks, and Sharp.

Shī, Huaí-rén: see Cháng, Lúng-ching et al.

Shǐ-liào-xún-kān (Historical Material Quarterly)

1930 "Yún-nán yĕ yí li-sù shā hún qiàng lù àn (The case of the killing, burning and pillaging of the wild Yi Lisu

                           of Yunnan)," Shi-liao-xun-kan 17-18.
Shi-shi shou-ce (Current Affairs)
1956a   "The existing national autonomy areas in China,"
                Shi-shi shou-ce 17 (Sep. 10). (English translation:
                Current Background 430: 4-5.)
                     Nukiang Lisu autonomous area, which was established
                prior to the promulgation of the Constitution, will
                soon be reorganized into a zhou.
1956b   "The minority nationalities of China," Shi-shi shou-ce
                18 (Sep. 17). (English translation: Current Background
                430: 6-10.)
                     Lisu are mostly Christians.
Shiratori, Yoshiro
1957   "Fushi renmeisei to Sanshi no keifu (The particular
                form of genealogical kinship terminology and the
                lineage of Ts'uan family)," Minzokugaku Kenkyū
                (Japanese Society of Ethnology) 21,4: 33-42.
                     Lolo: Before the rise of the Lolo kingdom of
                Nan Chao, the Ts'uan family belonged to a Tai tribe.
                When the Lolo arrived in the area, they, too, were
                called Ts'uan. Therefore, the Ts'uan of the Sung, Yuan,
                and Ming dynasties are Lolo, but those before are Tai.
                Dŏng (1940) does not realize the break in the genealogy.
                Ling (1953) claims that this system is general through-
                out Southeast Asia, but the evidence for this is very
                dubious. In Japanese, with English abstract. See
                Chén 1948a, Dīng 1936, Dŏng 1940, Fang 1945a and 1945b,
                Lǐng 1953, Lo 1944a and 1944b, 1945b, Ma 1942-44, 1946.
1962   Beiträge zur Ethnogenese der Minoritatenvölker Sudwest

Chinas (Contributions to the ethnogenesis of minority groups in Southwest China), Wien, doctoral dissertation, Universität Wien. 122 pp.

Cited in Leonard H. D. Gordon and Frank J. Shulman, eds., Doctoral Dissertations on China, A Bibliography of Studies in Western Languages, 1945-70 (Seattle and London, University of Washington Press, 1972).

Shirokogoroff, Sergei Mikhailovich

1930 "Phonetic notes on a Lolo dialect and consonant 1," Li shi yu yan yan jiu suo zhong yang yan jiu yuan (Bulletin of the Institute of History and Philology, Academia Sinica) 1: 183-225.

Review: Paul Pelliot, 1931, T'oung Pao série 2, 28: 207.

Shwe Boh: See Boh, Shwe

Siguret, J., ed. and trans.

1937 Territoires et populations des confins du Yunnan, Peiping, Editions Henri Vetch. (A translation of Yun-nan pien ti wen t'i yen chiu.)

Li-sou: Li Cheng-tchoang claims that there is no social stratification and that there are no chiefs, except among the sinicized groups, whose elected headmen may eventually act like mandarins. Each nuclear family lives separately, although in some districts a man may adopt a son to live with him. Differences in customs between northern and southern Yunnan Li-Sou. Marriage, death customs, religion, songs. Briefer notes on the Li-Sou of the Salween Valley by Miao Hoei-i.

Simonnet, Christian

1949   Thibet, voyage au bout de la Chrétienté, Paris, Editions
                 du Monde Nouveau. 186 pp.
                         Lisu revolt against Chinese (pp. 161-62). Lisu
                 fire crossbows at first planes in World War II (p. 126).
                 Missionaries from the Grand St. Bernard order began
                 residence at Latsa pass (near Weisi) in 1931.
Skipton, R. Kennedy
1973   "Hill peoples of Yunnan-China," in Sir Edward Evans-
                 Pritchard, ed., Peoples of the Earth, vol. 13, China
                 (including Tibet), Japan and Korea, London, Tom Stacey
                 Ltd., n.p., The Danbury Press; 68-73.
                         Akha and Lahu ethnographic sketches. Lisu, Lolo,
                 and Lu-tzu mentioned in glossary (pp. 139-40), although
                 no mention is made of those living outside China.
                 Photographs were probably taken in Thailand.
Smalley, William A.
1964   Notes on some phonological problems in Akha (manuscript).
Smith, A. W.
1930   "Working teak in the Burma forests," National Geographic
                 58,2: 239-56.
                         Kaw (Akha), Lahu Na, and Lahu Shi. Photos.
Smith, Harvey Henry (see also Henderson 1971b), Donald W. Bernier,
                 Frederica M. Bunge, Frances Chadwick Rintz, Rinn-Sup
                 Shinn, and Suzanne Teleki
1967   Area handbook for North Vietnam, DA Pam 550-57,
                 Washington, D.C., Foreign Area Studies, American
                 University and Department of the Army. 493 pp.
                         Lolo in Vietnam number less than 25,000 (p. 77).
Smythe, Hugh H.

1964 "Inside Thailand (I)," Eastern World 18,4: 7-9.

Lahu, Lisu, and other highlanders have no attachment to Thailand.

Snow, Edgar

1937 Red star over China, London V. Gollancz. (Various reprints, including 1938, New York, Random House. Revised ed., 1968, New York, Grove Press; 1969, London, Gollancz.) 464 pp.

The Long March went through Lolo country in 1935.

1962 The other side of the river, New York, Random House. (Various reprints, including 1963, London, Gollancz. Revised ed., 1970, Red China Today, Hammondsworth, Penguin.) 810 pp.

Mixed Lolo-Minchia-Han commune in Kuan-tu district, Yunnan. Reluctance to leave individual huts for new apartments.

Soulié, G., and Tchang Yi-tch'ou (with notes by A. L. Bonifacy)

1908 "Les barbares soumis du Yunnan," Ecole française d' Extrême-Orient, Bulletin 8: 149-76, 333-79. (Based on Tien hi, by Che Fan, 1807.)

Li-so are located only in Yu-long tcheou. Dress. Li-sou are found in districts of Kin-tch'eng (Szechwan), K'ang-p'ou, Kong-long, and Pen-tseu-lan (Yunnan). Dress. Houses. Food. Bride-price consists of cattle. Abandon dead. Spirits. Debts recorded by marks on wood. If contract is violated, they call a sorcerer. Ordeals include two parties placing their hands in boiling oil. Quick to use bow and knife, but they are held in check by Moso and Lolo chiefs. Each year they offer the chief 5 bushels (13 liters?) of wheat and 5 of millet, and swear allegiance (pp. 377-78)

Woni (pp. 353-54).

Sowards, Genevieve, and Erville Sowards: see Crider 1963, Maung Shwe Wa 1963, and Saw Aung Din and E. E. Sowards 1963.

Spielmann, Hans J.

1967 <u>Lahu</u> <u>Shehleh</u> <u>and</u> <u>Lahu</u> <u>Na</u> <u>of</u> <u>northern</u> <u>Thailand</u>, Report to the National Research Council, Bangkok.

1968a "Religious attitudes and economic activities of the Lahu (Northern Thailand)," Tokyo, <u>VIIIth</u> <u>Congress</u> <u>of</u> <u>Anthropological</u> <u>and</u> <u>Ethnological</u> <u>Sciences</u>.

Lahu Na and Lahu Shehleh: Nonworking days. Gearing of agricultural activities to moon phases (rather than seasons) among the Lahu Na.

1968b <u>The</u> <u>Guisha</u> <u>problem-Monotheism</u> <u>among</u> <u>the</u> <u>Lahu</u> (manuscript). Not seen.

1969 "A note on the literature on Lahu Shehleh and Lahu Na of northern Thailand," <u>Siam</u> <u>Society</u>, <u>Journal</u> <u>57</u>,<u>2</u>: 321-32.

Srisawat, Bunchuai (also spelled Boon Chuey Srisavasdi or Sisawat)

1952 Sǎamsip châad naj Chiangrai (Thirty peoples of Chiangrai), Bangkok, Outhai Press. (Revised ed., 1963, Chaaw khǎw naj Thai (Hill peoples of Thailand), Bangkok, Outhai Press.)

Akha, Lahu, Lisu: A member of parliament who has traveled mainly in the Mae Chan and Mae Suaj districts of Chiangrai Province, Srisawat tends to generalize on the basis of limited knowledge or observation. He states, for example, that all Lisu build their houses on the ground without posts, eat with chopsticks, speak Lahu and Chinese, and chew betel all of which is true for only some Lisu, even in Thailand. He erroneously describes women as slaves and as felling trees. He also states (erroneously) that a man takes his prospective bride to his house, and that his parents negotiate directly with her parents. He uses Thai terms, implying that they are Lisu, and describes Lisu spirits and ceremonies in terms of Thai religion. Nevertheless, this was the first substantial description of the Lisu, Lahu, and Akha of Thailand, including data on distribution, clans, housing, names, dress, food, fields and livestock, spirits and ceremonies, courting and marriage customs, birth and death customs, New Year festivals, beliefs, and the role and status of women. Photos. In Thai.

1954 Thai sìp sǒng panna, Bangkok, Outhai Press. 626 pp.
Akha and Lahu mentioned, but most of the book is about the Lue of Yunnan. In Thai.

1963 The hill tribes of Siam, Bangkok, Khun Aroon. 203 pp.
Akha, Lahu, Lisu: Photographs with captions. The distribution maps are incorrect.

Starr, Frederick
1911 "Lolo objects in the Public Museum, Milwaukee," Public Museum of the City of Milwaukee, Bulletin 1,2: 209-20, with 8 plates.
Lolo cape, skirt, jacket, trousers, cap neckband, pipe, bow and arrows, quiver, bowstring wrist guard, sword, Jew's harp, musical pipes, and other objects

-256-

obtained in 1899 by Owen L. Stratton in Opien-ting, northwestern Szechuen. Account of the Lolo killing of Mr. Brooke from the North China Herald, April 17, 1909. See Meares 1909a and 1909b.

Start, Laura E., and Mabel C. Wright
1936   "Decorated textiles from Yunnan collected by Augustine Henry, 1896-1898," Manchester Memoirs 53,8: 59-84.

The collection is probably from Miao tenants of Nosu lords. Sketches.

Steele, R. J. : see Hammerton 1922-24.

Stevenson, Henry Noel Cochrane
1944   The hill peoples of Burma, Burma Pamphlets, No. 6, London and Calcutta, Longmans, Green & Co. Ltd. (HRAF AP1-8) 50 pp.

Lisu (Yawyin, Lishaw) included with Kachin. Lahu and Kaw mentioned. Maps, photos.

Stevenson, Paul Huston
1927   "The Chinese-Tibetan borderland and its peoples," China Journal 6: 180-88, 234-42, 297-312.

White and Black Lolo country near Tzu-ta-ti (area ruled by Hsifan chief) and Fulin (southwestern Szechuan). The frigid, unbending attitude of the Black Lolo. Physical features. Dress. Battles with Chinese.

1932   "Notes on the human geography of the Chinese-Tibetan borderland," Geographical Review 22: 599-616.

White Lolo and Hsifan inhabit slopes of the Ching Chi Valley, and Chinese live on valley floor. Visited in 1926. Black Lolo, who are free and easy among themselves, are unapproachable by strangers. Physical description of Black Lolo, who are somatically Indo-Afghan rather than Mongoloid. Jamieson and Buxton believe they came from Burma. Use of felt and horses suggests their origins to be in the Pamir.

Stevenson, William

1959   The yellow wind, An excursion in and around Red China with a traveler in the Yellow Wind, Boston, Houghton Mifflin Company; London, Cassell. 424 pp.

    Lahu (p. 57). Lisu said to have ambushed and killed a Japanese patrol in late 1941 after they had gotten drunk, quarreled, and taken Lisu women. Survivors claimed that the Lisu ate some of the corpses (p. 73). Li Su of Peng-lung, Yunnan, live with Kachin and Chinese, and their land was formerly communally-owned (p. 81). Yi, once called "tottering weaklings," attacked advance party of Long March (pp. 61, 64, 129).

Stirling, G. C. B.: see Scott and Hardiman 1900.

Story, Joan H., and John H. Story

1969   "Hill tribes," the Target Audience, Bangkok, United States Information Service Research Office. 16 pp.

    Akha, Lahu, Lisu: Radios owned and favored programs. Their relations with the Thai.

Stratton, Owen L.: see Starr 1911.

Stübel, Hans

1952   "Die nichtchinesischen Völker Chinas," Sociologus 2,2: 84-117.

    Lolo: Two different groups reflect different phases of adaptation to Chinese culture.

Studia Serica

1940-41 "On Lolo I Yu Lolo-Chinese vocabularies. A comparison of the four varieties of the Lolo script in Yunnan," *Studia Serica* 1.

Sun, Kee-wong
1942 "When Lolos meet Chinese," *Asia* 42: 95-99.

    Lolo spread west of the Great Cool Mountains (Taliang Shan), driving out the Sifan two centuries ago. Early in the last century, they pushed west of the Yalung River, driving out the Mohsis. However, the Lolo are divided, and General Teng Hsiu-ting uses old feuds to fight Lolo with Lolo. He commands the Sikang Border Pacification Army, whose Chinese and Lolo soldiers are not paid, but share the spoils. Lolo use wooden tablets with notches, and bonfires to communicate. They buy salt, cloth, and wine from the Chinese. In 1914, they revolted so that even Sichang kept its gates closed. This article is a good illustration of the superior Chinese attitudes toward the Lolo. See *China at War* 1941.

Súo, Wén-jīng (or Swo, Wen-ching)
1962 "Hā-ní zú," *Minzu Huabao* (Nationalities Pictorial) 11: 13-14.

    Hani (Akha) number 540,000 in Hung He, Yuan Yang, Lyu Chwun, and Jin Ping counties, south of the Red River in Yunnan. After Liberation, several other ethnic groups were grouped with them: Ai Ni, Bu Dou, Bi, Ywe, and Ka Dwo. According to Wen Syan, predecessors of the Hani lived 2,000 years ago, with the Sou along the Lu Jyang Basin. They established relations with the Han dynasty, and the headman system was established after the Yuan and lasted until the Ching dynasty. In the last few decades, the Hani rose against their oppressive headmen. The Hani who live in the Ai Lou Shan cultivate rice on terraces, maize, cotton, beans, bananas, pineapples, and mangoes. The Hani of Pu Er cultivate tea. After communes were established in 1958, production increased and motor transport, education, and health conditions improved. A written language was adopted in 1958. Major festivals include the Dragon Tree festival in the first month and two New Year festivals in the sixth and tenth moons. Photos.

Suraphong: see Bunnâag, Suraphong, 1963.

Sutton, Stephanne Barry

1974 *In China's border provinces, The turbulent career of Joseph Rock, botanist-explorer*, New York, Hastings House. 334 pp.

      Lisu and Lolo mentioned. Rock (1884-1962) used Lolo as carriers, although he thought them filthy, afflicted with goiter, and prone to congenital idiocy. He intervened on the behalf of two Lolo prisoners being held in horrible conditions by the Prince of Muli. Information on Lung Yun, the warlord of Yunnan and a Lolo. Photos.

Széchwān ri-bào (Pinyin: Sichūan)

1956 "Yi and Tibetan areas in Széchwān prepare welcome for central comfort mission," *Széchwān ri-bào* (Chengtu) Oct. 28. (English translation: *Survey of the China Mainland Press* 1427: 13-14.)

                  Yi receive representatives sent by the Central Committee of the Communist Party, the Central government, and Chairman Mao.

Takemura, Takuji
    1957-58   "Bibliography of ethnographies by Chinese ethnologists on the non-Han-Chinese people in south and south-west China, 1-3," <u>Shakai Jinruigaku</u> <u>1</u>: 62-74, <u>2</u>: 68-75, <u>3</u>: 54-61.

                  Lisu, Lolo includes 110 entries (<u>3</u>: 54-58).

Tan Chee Beng: see Walker, ed., 1975.

Tang, Zhen-zong (or Chen-tsung)
    1953   <u>Zhōng-guó shǎo-shù mín-zú di xīn miàn-mào</u> (The new appearance of China's national minorities), Peking, n.p. 53 pp.

T'ang, Tsai-fou: see Chen, Ding 1905.

Táo, Yún-kuí (or Yǔn-k'uéi)
    1945   "Jǐ-ge yún-nán zàng-miǎn yǔ-xì tǔ-zú di jūang-shi gu-shi (Chi-ko Yun-nan Tsang-mien yü-hsi t'u-tsu ti Ch'uang-shih ku-shih) (Some creation stories told by the native peoples of the Tibetan-Burmese group in Yunnan)," <u>Biān-jiāng yén-jiū lùn-cóng</u> (Frontier Studies) <u>45</u>: 1-12. (English translation: HRAF AE3-2.)

                  Lisu legend from Kung-shan and two legends from Weisi.

    1948   "Bì ló xuē shān zhī lì-sū zú (Pi luo shui shan zee Li su zu) (The Lisu tribes of Pi-luo Mountains)," <u>Lì shǐ yǔ yán yán jiū sǔo, Zhōng-yāng yán jiū yuàn</u>) (Bulletin of the Institute of History and Philology, Academia Sinica) <u>17</u>: 327-408.

Lisu: In August and September 1935, Táo visited the Pi-luo Mountains, between the Mekong and the Salween. This article consists of notes on Lisu food, housing, clothing, transport, hunting, life cycle, clans, warfare (including an eyewitness account of a rebellion against the Chinese), religion, and legends. He discusses the ethnic and linguistic affiliations of the Lisu, and quotes from local Chinese records. Map, drawings, photos.

Tatu, Marian, and Darlene Montgomery
1969   <u>Hill</u> <u>tribes</u>: <u>Population</u>, <u>problems</u> <u>and</u> <u>RTG</u> <u>involvement</u>, Bangkok, Thailand Information Center, Batelle Memorial Institute.

         Akha, Lahu, Lisu: A list of Thai agencies dealing with "hill tribes."

Taw, Sein Ko, and A. E. Eastes
1915   "The linguistic affinities of the Pyu language," <u>Burma</u> <u>Research</u> <u>Society</u>, <u>Journal</u> <u>5</u>.

         Pyu affinity with Lolo-Lisu. Vocabularies of Yung-ning Lisu and Pa-U-Rong Lolo.

Taylor, L. F. (See also Grierson 1903-28.)
1956   "The general structure of languages spoken in Burma," <u>Burma</u> <u>Research</u> <u>Society</u>, <u>Journal</u> <u>39</u>: 101-20.

         Lisaw, Lolo, and Muhso are classified in the Assam-Burmese branch of the Tibeto-Burman subfamily (which, with Chinese but not Tai, forms the Tibeto Chinese family) on the basis of syntactic features.

Taylor, Mary Geraldine
1944   <u>Behind</u> <u>the</u> <u>ranges</u>, <u>Fraser</u> <u>of</u> <u>Lisuland</u>, <u>S.W.</u> <u>China</u>,

London & Redhill, Lutterworth Press, China Inland
Mission. 255 pp.
Lisu: Biography of missionary J. O. Fraser.
Tch'en: see Chen, Ding.
Telford, J. H.
1937 "Animism in Kengtung State," Burma Research Society,
Journal 27,2: 86-238.
Lahu Na includes Na Penh, Huli, Kulough, La Law,
Veya, Laba, Hpu, and Keleh. Lahu Shi includes Balang,
Banceu, Namkyo, and Meukeu. History and legends.
Centuries ago, a large Lahu village between Mung Lem
and Meng Meng in Yunnan was invaded by Burmese and
later by Shan. In 1887, Lahu and Wa fought the
Chinese. Lahu have been in Burma at least a century,
coming from Meng Meng and Mung Lem. Animism as revealed
in birth, naming, eating, working, mating, playing,
dancing, travel, trade, hunting, fighting, judging,
divination, ailing, sacrifices, praying (prayers in
Lahu and translation), healing, burial, and afterward.
Spirits include ancestors, nature, independent, and
demonical possession. G'uisha as the omnipotent creator,
able to punish both bumans and spirits; he is humanlike.
Kaw (Aka) divisions include Lehleubo, Jeu G'we,
Jeujaw, Jo Byawn, Leh Nyi, Che Mui, Hpyo Hso, Zeu Zi,
and Hteu La. Animism among the Kaw.
Lisu mentioned. Telford was a missionary who
lived in Kengtung from 1924 on and came to speak fluent
Lahu.
Telford, J. H. (assisted by Saya David)

1938 Handbook of the Lahu (Muhso) language and English-Lahu dictionary, Rangoon, Superintendent, Government Printing and Stationery, Burma. 100 pp.

Lahu probably originated near the headwaters of the Salween, Mekong, and Yang Tze. Now found from north of Meng Meng to Mung Lem and west, Mung Lun, Kengtung, Haut-Laos, and as far south as Chiangrai. Dress. Houses. Headman and blacksmith receive choice meat. In non-Christian villages, there is a temple-hut for G'uisha, but no blood sacrifices. Bride service of one to three years, but for seven among Lahu Shi, who must also pay a bride-price of Rs42 to 48. Unlike the Kaw, the Lahu do not kill twins. Language is similar to Burmese, Lolo, Lisu, Kaw, and K'a To. Lahu Na sounds, grammar, idioms, time, names, weights, measures, and money. About 2,000 words. Names are given according to the time or animal day born, birth order, physical circumstances, or teknonymic.

Telford, J. H., translator
1949 G'ui sha hkaw li awsuh (New Testament in Lahu), Rangoon, Bible Society of Burma.

Telford, J. H. (assisted by Sala David and Sala Ai Pun), translator
1953 Chi Mvuh ve Li (The book of Psalms), Rangoon, The British and Foreign Bible Society.

Telford, J. H., and Saya Ai Pun
1939 Lahu ka pui ka lao (Lahu reader), Pang Wai, Loimwe (Burma).

Temple, Richard C.
1910 "The people of Burma," Royal Society of Arts, Journal

58,3003: 695-711.

    Lihsaw subgroup (including Lihsaw, Lahu, Akha, and Akho) is part of the Burmese group. Wife is salable chattel among Lihsaws (sic). Polygamy is unrestricted among Akha. Discussion of the common mental and religious traits among all peoples of Burma. Map, showing distribution of ethnic groups.

Terrien de Lacouperie, Albert Etienne Jean Baptiste

1882a   "Lolo not connected with Vei characters," <u>Athenaeum</u> Sep. 23.

    An answer to Clarke 1882, 1883.

1882b   "On a Lolo Ms. written on satin," <u>Royal Asiatic Society, Journal, n.s. 14</u>: 119-23.

1882c   "The Lolo and Mosso writings," <u>Royal Geographic Society, Proceedings, Supplemntary Papers 1,1</u>: 142-43.

    A discussion of Baber 1882.

1894a   <u>Beginnings of writing in central and eastern Asia</u>, London, S. Austin & Sons.

    Lissou language is related to Lou-tze and Moso.

1894b   <u>Western origin of the early Chinese civilisation from 2,300 B.C. to 200 A.D.</u>, London, Asher & Co. 418 pp.

    Lolo: Terrien has identified 450 different signs on Lolo manuscripts (p. 201).

Teston, Eugene, and Maurice Percheron

1932   <u>L'Indochine moderne, Encyclopedie administrative, touristique, artistique et économique</u>, Paris, Librairie de France. 1028 pp.

    Lolo of Bao-Lâc, Hoang-su-phi, and Phong-Tho include A-Ni (Houo Ni) of Phong-Tho and A-Kha (Ko) of

Muong-sin and Phong-sali. The Ko eat clay at some rites. A few families of Lisu live in Muong-Hou, Laos (pp. 307, 309, 387-89). Photos.

Thailand Information Center

1970 North Thailand: Distribution of hill tribes, Bangkok, Battelle Memorial Institute. 4 pp.

Lahu, Lisu migrations. Map.

Thamsukati, Thanit

1973 "Musers blame fighting on Burmese mistreatment," Bangkok Post, June 16: 3.

Muser (Lahu) leader Pu Chong Luang claims Burmese officials confiscate Muser weapons, refuse to allow them to sell livestock. There are several thousand Muser rebels in Burma. He and about a hundred followers have taken refuge in Fang District, Chiang Mai Province, Thailand. Photo.

See Kasemsri 1973, Thavisin 1973.

Thatnaasuwan, Pramootya

1968 "Kwaamlang thi Dooj Mâe Salong (The past at Doi Mae Salong)," O.S.T. 8,2: 36-40, 45-50.

Akha: A visit to villages near the headquarters of Mae Chan nikhom (reservation), Chiangrai Province, Thailand. Photos. Map. In Thai.

Thavisin, Anussorn

1973 "Four towns fall, hundreds killed," Bangkok Post, Jan. 23: 3.

Muser (Lahu) reported to have killed hundreds of Burmese troops in uprising sparked by heavy taxes and attempts to disarm them. Photos. See Kasemsri 1973,

Thamsukati 1973.

Thomas, Lowell (aided by Hugh Gibb)

1965   Land of the Yao, Film, BBC-TV. 25 minutes.

         Lisu: Among the errors in the soundtrack: Thomas speaks of pigs as making up dowries, that a new house may be built in a week, that houses are flimsy, that houses are built with only the use of a machete. He identifies a slingshot as a bow. He says that the Lisu have grown opium for centuries. He says that there is only one blacksmith per village. He maintains that they wear embroidered petticoats. He says that they build a water bridge annually. He uses "maw phii" as a Lisu phrase (it is Thai). He says that red berets were left behind by British paratroopers (they are used by Lao troops). He says that the Yao despise the Chinese, and that the area has been exposed to waves of Chinese invaders. Without the sound track, the film is a colorful introduction to the Lisu of Thailand.

Thompson, H. Gordon

1926   "From Yunnan-fu to Peking along the Tibetan and Mongolian borders," Geographical Journal 67: 2-27.

         Lisu mentioned as using cowrie shells. Map, photos.

Thompson, Phyllis

1956   King of the Lisu, London, China Inland Mission. 63 pp.

         Lisu: Thompson claims that there was a Lisu legend that a white man would come, and that this came true when missionary J. O. Fraser arrived in Yunnan.

Thompson, Virginia McLean
   1937   French Indochina, New York, The Macmillan Company
                 517 pp.
                     Lolo mentioned (p. 383).

Thomson, John R.
   1968   "Mountains to climb," Far Eastern Economic Review 59,10: 420-22.
                    Lahu of Burma have been exposed to Communist influences, and 20,000 of them are ready to attack along the Thai-Burma border. Photos.

Thorel: see Reclus and Reclus 1902.

Tian, Liang-geng (or T'ien, Liang-keng)
   1959   "Yi peoples of the lesser Liang-shan make rapid transition to socialism," Rén-mín rì-bào, June 14. (English translation: Survey of the China Mainland Press 2043: 26-28.)
                    Yi of Xiao Liang Shan number 56,000, including 26,000 former slaves and 15,000 former serfs. Freed slaves have cooperated to build new farms, and now reap yields of 800 to 1,000 catties of grain per mou. A new song on the progress.

Tián, Mù
   1910   "Liáng-shān píng yí (Subjugation of the Yi of Liang-shan)," Jiào-yù zá-zhì (Educational Magazine) 2,4.

Tie, Zhun (or T'ieh, Chun)
   1959   "Family branch system gives way to general cooperation in Liang-shan Yi Nationality Autonomous Zhou in Szechwan," Mínzú Tuánjié. (English translation:

Joint Publications Research Service DC 860: 36.)
  Yi clan feuds give way to cooperation in Nan p'ing Peoples Commune. Formerly, slaves fought their masters' battles, and even after the abolition of slavery, the family system caused conflict. Hence it was done away with, and great economic progress has been made.

Tiessen, Ernst, ed.
1907 Ferdinand von Richthofen's Tagebücher aus China, 2 vols., Berlin, Dietrich Reimer.
  Lolo mentioned (2: 241-324). See Richthofen 1903.

Tilke, Max
1945 Kostümschnitte und Gewandformen, Tübingen, Verlag Ernst Wasmuth. 60 pp. + 128 plates.
  Lolo costume (color plate 89).

Ting, Wen-chiang: see Dīng, Wén-jīang.

Tinker, Hugh
1956 "Burma's northeast borderland problems," Pacific Affairs 29: 324-46.
  Akha, Lahu, and Lisu mentioned.

Tirrell, Raymond F.
1972 An analysis of factors that are assumed to influence acculturation and assimilation of tribal minorities in northern Thailand, doctoral dissertation, Syracuse University (Dissertation Abstracts International 33,11: 5109B, University Microfilms order no. 73-9569). 509 pp.
  Akha, Lahu, Lisu: A comparison of 15 villages (plus 20 of other minority groups) on which there is published or unpublished information available.

Acculturation and assimilation of minorities into Thai society are strongly influenced by the degree of access to Thai settlements, by direct cultural contacts, by available transportation, the duration of contact, urbanization, Thai welfare and development activities, Thai public schools, wet-rice agriculture, large-scale wage labor, and related cultural changes. Christian mission contacts and Border Patrol Police schools have no consistent influence upon acculturation and assimilation. Cultural summaries of each ethnic group and village are appended. This dissertation is not based on first hand research and therefore contains many minor errors. It is not clear which factors are causal, rather than concomitant, and it is not tied into theories of social and cultural change. However, this type of comparative study is very much needed to synthesize the data that are already available. Maps.

Toa Kenkyujo (East Asia Institute)

1940　　Taikoku (Kyumei shamukoku) no minzoku (The peoples of Thailand), Tokyo, Toa Kenkyujo.

　　　　Lahu or Musso are incorrectly grouped with the Lawa of Kanburi. Akha and Lisu not mentioned. Map.

Tóng, Zhèng-zāo

1936　　"Yě-rén shān kǎo (A study of Lisu Mountain)", Yǔ-gòng 6,2.

Torrance, Thomas

1932　　"Notes on the west China aboriginal tribes," West China Border Research Society, Journal 5: 10-24.

　　　　Lolo, Kolo, or Nosu. The Yueh Hsi history is

quoted. The Chinese say: "Cut off a Lolo's head in battle, and he will turn round and fight you with his tail." Ih Chia are of Lolo stock, they are landlords of Miao serfs. Bolotsze of small Heh-Shui (near Songpan) are mixed Lolo and Tibetan, renowned for their plundering.

Tribal Data Project

1971-72 *Directory of tribal villages in northern administrative divisions*, Chiang Mai, Tribal Data Project.

Akha, Lahu, and Lisu included in the volumes on the following changwad (provinces): Chiang Mai; Phrae, Lampang, and Lamphun; Mae Hong Son; Nan; Kamphaeng Phet and Tak; Chiangrai. Includes village names, location by administrative divisions and map coordinates, number of households and population, ethnic identity. In Thai and English.

Tribal Research Centre

1967-73 *Tribal Research Centre, Bulletin nos. 1 and 2*. Chiang Mai.

Akha, Lahu, and Lisu of Thailand: Summary of research activities.

Trumbull, Robert

1963 "U.S. trains Thais to guard border," *New York Times*, May 19: 21.

Lahu: The Chinese are said to have presented a Communist wife to the Lahu "man-god." U.S. Special Forces have equipped and trained the Thai Border Police Patrol to stem Communist influence among the "hill tribes."

Ts'ai, Yung-ch'un (Pinyin: Cai, Yong-chun)
   1941   "The call of the border tribes," <u>Chinese Recorder and Educational Review</u> (Shanghai) <u>72</u>,4: 183-89.
> Lisu seem to be ready for mass conversions. Nosu doctor and educator employed by missionaries.

Tseng, Chao-lun: see Zēng, Zhāo-lún.

Tsung, Yun (Pinyin: Zong, Yun)
   1954   "China's national minorities," <u>People's China</u> <u>11</u>: 17-23.
> Yi number 3.3 million. The Yi epic "Asma" has been written down. See Yang, Gladys, 1955a and 1955b.

Tu, Pin: see Du, Bin.

Tŭng Tsŏ-pīng: see Dŏng, Zuò-bīn.

Tung, T'ung-ho (Pinyin: Dong, Tung-he)
   1953   "China's spoken languages," <u>Chinese Culture</u>, Mar.: 33-41.
> Lolo-Moso group includes Lolo (and Lisu) and Moso (and Lahu and Nashi).

Tung, Ying: see Dŏng, Yĭng, and Xúe Jiàn-huā.

Tuyen, Vuong Hoang
   1973   "De quelques groupes ethniques arrachés de justesse à l'extinction aux confins de la zone du Nord-Ouest," <u>Etudes Vietnamiennes</u> <u>36</u>: 149-200.
> The Ha Nhi (or U Ni, Hua Y, or Hey Yi) were much reduced in number, according to the 1960 census, which gave their population as 5,259. The Co Sung (or La Hu) numbered 2,447. Other groups discussed are the Xá Cööng, Si La, and Bo Kho Pa (Lao or Xa Pho). These groups are now in the process of passing directly from the primitive stage to socialism. Photos.

1975 "Notes sur les Lô Lô, les Cao Lan et les Giay," *Etudes Vietnamiennes* 41: 102-61.

Lô Lô (La La, Qua La, or Zi) numbered 6,898; Cao Lan (or San Choi) numbered 22,543; and the Giay were 16,429 "before the census of 1974" in the northernmost part of Vietnam. Photos.

United Nations

1967 *Report of the United Nations Survey Team on the economic and social needs of the opium-producing areas in Thailand*, Bangkok, Department of Public Welfare, Ministry of Interior. (Excerpts reprinted in: 1968-69, *Bulletin on Narcotics* 20,3: 7-17; 21,1: 1-29.) 144 pp.

Akha, Lahu, and Lisu mentioned, although most of the report is about the Miao. Ecology, opium production, Thai government legislation dealing with opium, with recommendations. Photos.

United States Army

1961 *Non-Chinese ethnic groups in southern China and contiguous areas*, Washington, U.S. Army Broadcasting and Visual Activity, Pacific, Analysis No. 010461. (Copy located at U.S. Army War College, Carlisle Barracks, Pa.) 33 pp.

A-che (A-hsi), Ah-chang, Ah-ka (Akka), Ai-ni (Hani), Kutsung, La-hu (Lo-hei), Li-su (Lissou), Nu-jen (loutse or Nutzu), Sa-ni, Wo-ni, and Yi (Lolo). Distribution and miscellaneous notes on customs compiled from published sources. (A more complete gazetteer is available in LeBar et al. 1964.) Map.

United States Operations Mission (USOM)
1963 The Civic Action Program of the Border Patrol Police and the USOM Public Safety Division, Bangkok, United States Operations Mission. 49 pp.

Akha, Lahu, and Lisu mentioned. In Thai and English.

Upcraft, W. M.
1892 "The wild men of Szechuan," Chinese Recorder, Oct.: 475-78.

Lolo do not use opium. They have three-storied towers. See Cordier 1907: 76.

Urbani, Arialdo
1968 "Premières impressions," Feuilles Missionnaires 53: 13-15.

Lahou: A missionary in Thailand. Photos.

1970 "Chez les montagnards Lahous," Feuilles Missionnaires 59: 13-15.

Christian Lahou near Muang Ngam, Chiang Mai Province, Thailand. Photos.

1971 "Aï-là, le premier baptisé Ikho," Feuilles Missionnaires 64: 13-14.

Ikho (Akha) man converted to Catholicism two hours before his death in Pa-Kha village, Chiangrai Province, Thailand. Photos.

1974 "Fête de la balancoire chez les Akhas (Ikos)," Feuilles Missionnaires 75: 12-16.

Akha of Pha Mi, Chiangrai Province, Thailand. Mourning customs. Swing ceremony. The swing is an offering to the spirits for a good harvest, and it helps put young women in amiable frame of mind. Shaman swings first, then men, then women. Legend has it that this custom was started by a woman whose fields were poor, and she thought the offering would better the harvest. The ceremony lasts three days, but at one time it lasted 33 days (one Akha month). Photos. See Kacha-ananda 1971.

Vacca, Giovanni
 1934   "Li-su," Enciclopedia Italiana 21: 272.

Valtat, Maurice
 1915   "Dans les derniers recoins de la Chine inconnue. Chez les Lolos noirs De Yüeshi à Tchaokia," Les Missions Catholiques 47,2394: 202-04, 2395: 214-16.
      Black Lolo: Voyage from Yüeshi to Ningyuanfou via Léang-chan in 1914 through the territory of Gougui Lolo. Houses. Mouth organ. Map, photo.

Vannicelli, Fr. Luigi, O.F.M.
 1944   La religione dei Lolo, Contributo allo studio etnologico delle religioni dell'estremo oriente, Milano, Società Editrice "Vita e Pensiero," Publicazioni dell'Università Cattolica del S. Cuore, n.s. 2, xi, 263 pp.
      Lolo religion. Based mostly upon French writings of Vial, Liétard, Legendre, and others. Comparisons with Chinese and other peoples of southwestern China. Suffers from attempts to prove parallels with Christianity. Agrees with Müller that the name of a specific tribe (Lolopho) was applied to all Lolo. Savina says there are 2 million Lolo, but there must

be 3 or 4 million in Yunnan alone, and Chatagnon says there are 300,000 to 400,000 in Szechwan. Vial distinguishes between the u and a dialects, and Liétard recognizes an o dialect. White Lolo include Na-se, Ko, Kotu, Gni, Asci, A-gie. Lolo writing is similar to the Chinese of the Chou, by which time they are said to have had a feudal state. They believe in an omniscient, omnipotent creator and lord known by different names (pp. 17-19). A Gnipha legend says that Ke-ze created man from earth, but the Spirit of the Earth demanded its return; a compromise was reached whereby it would be returned after one cycle of 60 years. Creation stories, including that of Sun and Moon, original sin and redemption, flood. Flood legends have three parts: God wishes to punish man, siblings are ancestors, incestuous union is approved. Four types of flood legends: moral where only the good brother survives (southern Yunnan and Miao), brothers as ancestors (Gnipha), conflict between two brothers causes flood (Yao), animal warns man of flood (Lolo of Szechwan). Traces of totemism. Personal cult involves sacrifices in spring and thanksgiving; family cult at New Year and 8th moon; village cult at 11th moon, 24th day of 6th moon and harvest. Lolo recognize Sifan, Chinese, Tai, Yao-Man as having descended from the couple who survived the flood. Monogamous, strong conjugal and filial devotion. God created good and bad spirits. The dragon is the opponent of bad spirits, protector of villages and houses. Divination by calendar, coin that oscillates when right spirit is called, scapulimancy, grains in water, orientation of a dying chicken. Male and female shamans, working through personal spirits, deal with evil spirits. Spirits and spirit ceremony have names derived from Chinese. Death is the leaving of the soul from the body. Accidental death is impure. Seven grains of rice (9 for a man) are placed in the mouth of the deceased. Death customs, dances, songs, mourning. Independent Lolo cremate, but others bury the dead. There is a cult of the dead, with figurines or tombs as localizations. The protoparent of the sacred grove or village pagoda obscures the idea of the Creator God. Four periods in Lolo history: monotheism, spirit beliefs, cult of the dead, combination of all three. Rest day is Saturday. Possible origins. Map.

Review: Wolfram Eberhard, 1945, Anthropos, 37: 976-77.

Van Roy, Edward
1965   Economic frontiers: A study of economies in the hills of northern Thailand, doctoral dissertation, Austin, University of Texas. (Available from University of Texas Library.) See his 1971, below.

1971   Economic systems of northern Thailand, Ithaca, Cornell University Press. 289 pp.

Lahu villages of nikhom Chiangdao, Chiang Mai Province, Thailand. They are Christians who no longer grow opium, but engage in labor on the nearby tea plantation and sell handicrafts via missionaries.

Akha, Lahu mentioned.

Reviews: Dessaint and Chia Lin Sien, 1972, <u>Journal</u> <u>of</u> <u>Southeast</u> <u>Asian</u> <u>Studies</u> <u>3</u>,<u>2</u>: 325-29; Pitt, 1972, <u>American</u> <u>Anthropologist</u> <u>74</u>: 881.

Vaulserre, Comte de

1907 "Traversée du pays des Lolos independants," <u>La</u> <u>Géographie</u>, Jul. 15: 71-73.

    Lolo visited by Mission d'Ollone. See Cordier 1907.

Vial, Paul

1888 "Yun-nan (Chine), Un tournoi chez les sauvages Lolos," <u>Les</u> <u>Missions</u> <u>Catholiques</u> <u>20</u>,<u>1007</u>: 445-48.

    Lolo in Yunnan call themselves Pou: in Kouy-tcheou (Kweichow) they are called Miao-tsé. They are dominated but not conquered. Description of wrestling matches.

1890a <u>De</u> <u>la</u> <u>langue</u> <u>et</u> <u>de</u> <u>l'écriture</u> <u>indigène</u> <u>au</u> <u>Yûn-nân</u>, Paris, Ernest Leroux. 23 pp.

    Lolo has no meaning. Man are independent Lolo. Includes many dialects. Examples of writing (pp. 16-18); story of the deluge, with translation (pp. 20-23): three brothers and their sister are told by an elder of the impending flood; the oldest brother hides in an iron box, the next in a copper box, and the youngest in a wooden box with his sister; they wind up on a mountain and are saved by "bamboo." See Devéria 1891.

1890b "Etude sur l'écriture des Lolos de Yün-nan," <u>Le</u> <u>Lotus</u> <u>9</u>: 30-49.

1893-94 "Les Gni ou Gni-Pa. Tribu lolote du Yûn-Nân," <u>Les</u>

Missions Catholiques 25,1244: 160-61, 1245: 178-80, 1246: 189-90, 1247: 200-02, 1248: 208-09, 1249: 222-25, 1250: 236-38, 1251: 244-46, 1252: 258-60, 1253: 268-70, 1254: 281-83, 1255: 293-94, 1256: 308-10; 26,1307: 300-02, 1308: 308-10.

    Gni Lolo: Vial lived first at Tien-sên-koân in 1886, and missionized the Lolo of Lòu-mèiy. Lolo marry by free choice; divorce frequent. Opium smoking unknown. Named after the name-day or some physical peculiarity (pp. 268-70). Literature and poetry (including translations), music, dance, costume (pp. 300-02, 308-10). Photos appear on other pages in these issues as well, especially pp. 222, 224, 258, 259, 270, 281, and 295.

1898   Les Lolos, Histoire, Religion, Moeurs, Langue, Ecriture, Chang-hai, Imprimerie de la Mission Catholique. 71 pp.

    Gni Lolo had 12 original patriarchs, one of whom (Pou) they still worship. They came from Mt. Mouto, led by two chiefs: tou (white) and na (black). Later, there were 18 lords. Creation legend, drought legend, deluge. Midje is a protector spirit sacrificed to on horse or rat day of rat (11th) month. Marriage ceremony. Funerals. Ritual combat when harvests are poor. 25 pages of Lolo script and meanings. Language, literature. Man-tse (lolo) vocabulary from Tong-ho in Sze-ch'uan (29°N) (by Martin).

1909   Dictionnaire Français-Lolo, Dialects Gni, Tribu situee dans les sous-préfectures de Lóu nân tchēou, Lŏu leâng tchēou, Kouàng-si tchēou, Province du Yunnan,

Hongkong, Imprimerie de la Société des Missions-Etrangères. 350 pp.

Lolo measures: previously cowrie shells were used as money; a chen of rice is a full measure, but a chen of rent is 8/10th of this; 12-animal cycle for days, months, and years. Grammar. Texts include a genealogy of the ancestors of the Lolo, a dream, why the earth is wrinkled, sacrament of the eucharist, act of repentance. 424 characters of Lolo writing. See Haudricourt 1957-58.

Review: 1909, Les Missions Catholiques 41,2102: 455.

1917 "A travers la Chine inconnue. Chez les Lolos," Les Missions Catholiques 49,2527: 537-38, 2538: 545-47.

Lolo cultivate wheat, buckwheat, maize. Village of Jedjé has 90 families, 542 inhabitants. Photos.

Vissière, A.

1914 "Les désignations ethniques Houei-houei et Lolo," Journal Asiatique série 11,3,1: 175-82.

Lolo, Kou-lo, and other names, their pronunciation and characters. Reduplication in ethnic names is similar to that of kin terms. The Louo mentioned by Lepage (1910, Journal Asiatique série 10,15,5: 236) must be Lolo. Lou means "ravish, take prisoner," and is widely used.

Review by Léonard Aurousseau, 1915, Ecole française d'Extrême-Orient, Bulletin 15,4: 38.

Voegelin, Carl F., and Florence M. Voegelin

1965 "Languages of the world: Sino-Tibetan fascicle five,"

Anthropological Linquistics 7,6: 1-58.

Lisu: List of other names by which they are known. At least two dialects. Two-page phonemic summary, based on data of Robert Morse from 1956 to 1958.

Wa-cha-mu-chi, and Wang Hai-min (See also China Reconstructs 1953.)
1959 "A leaping decade for the people of the Yi nationality of Liangshan, Szechwan," Minzu Tuánjie (Nationalities Unity) 11. (English translation: Excerpts from Communist Chinese Magazines 203: 27-30.)

Yi of Liangshan: Their progress since Liberation. Both authors are secretaries of Liangshan Yi Party Committee, and administrative heads of the zhou.

Walker, Anthony R.
1966-69 Reports of research activities among the La Hu Ni (Red La Hu), Chiang Mai, Tribal Research Centre (mineographed).

Lahu Nyi of Amphoe Phrao. Fourteen reports concerning especially agricultural activities. Some written together with Snit Wongprasert. See Walker 1970b, below.

1969 "Red Lahu village society An introductory survey," in Peter Hinton, ed., Tribesmen and Peasants in North Thailand, Chiang Mai, Tribal Research Centre, pp. 41-52.

Lahu Nyi of Amphoe Phrao: Social and political organization, ritual organization.

1970a "The La Hu-Nyi (Red La Hu) New Year celebrations," Siam Society, Journal 58,1: 1-44.

Lahu Nyi of Amphoe Phrao: Description of their New Year's ceremonies, including texts and translations.

1970b Lahu Nyi (Red Lahu) village society and economy in north Thailand, 2 vols., Chiang Mai, Tribal Research Centre (mimeographed). 580 pp.

Lahu Nyi of Amphoe Phrao, Chiang Mai Province, Thailand. Based on field research between 1966 and 1970. This is the best and most complete source of information on any Lahu group, including distribution, population, history, demography, village and household structure, kinship, political organization, law, religion, prophets, ritual, life cycle, land tenure, agricultural cycle (with detailed statistical information on labor and land inputs, yields, etc.), husbandry, hunting, trade, wealth, etc. Maps. Sketches.

1972a "Blessing feasts and ancestor propitiation among the Lahu Nyi (Red Lahu)," Siam Society, Journal 60,1: 345-73.

1972b "Aw ha hku ve: The Lahu Nyi rite for the recall of a wandering soul," Royal Asiatic Society, Journal 1: 16-29.

1972c The Lahu of the Yunnan-Indochina borderlands: Ethnic group and village community, doctoral dissertation, Oxford, Oxford University. 448 pp.

1973a "Lahu illusions," Far Eastern Economic Review 5, Mar.: 21.

1973b "From poppies to peaches," Far Eastern Economic Review

Aug. 27: 46-47.

Akha, Lahu, Lisu mentioned. Photo.

1974a "Lahu Nyi (Red Lahu) New Year texts," Siam Society, Journal 57,1: 1-26.

1974b "Lahu Nyi (Red Lahu) tests of innocence: Ethnographic notes and Lahu texts," Acta Orientalia 36: 209-24.

Lahu tests of innocence in legal cases include chewing rice grains (if soft and mixed with saliva, innocent; if dry and hard, guilty), drinking water in which a half-burned piece of wood has been dipped (guilty will die), spirit specialist, invoking spirits, faces accused and dribbles ash from the headman's hearth through his fingers and onto the ground (guilty will die). Photo.

1974c "Three Lahu Nyi (Red Lahu) marriage prayers: Lahu texts and ethnographic notes," Royal Asiatic Society, Journal 1: 44-49.

1974d "Messianic movements among the Lahu of the Yunnan Indochina borderlands," Southeast Asia 3,2: 699-711. (Reprinted 1975 in Alain Y. Dessaint and Ernest C. Migliazza, eds., Anthropology and Linguistics, Dubuque, Kendall/Hunt Publishing Company: pp. 187-91.)

1974e "The divisions of the Lahu people," Siam Society, Journal 57,2: 253-68.

1974-75 "The Lahu of the Yunnan-Indochina borderlands: an introduction," Folk 16-17: 329-44.

Lahu: An historical and ethnographic sketch. Photos, map.

1975a "Lahu Nyi (Red Lahu) New Year texts II," Siam Society, Journal 58,2: 161-98.

1975b "Lahu: Burma, China," in Family of Man: Peoples of the World, How and Where They Live, London, Marshall Cavendish, 5,62: 1719-21.

1975c "Lisu: South-east Asia," in Family of Man: Peoples of the World, How and Where They Live, London, Marshall Cavendish, 5,63: 1752-53.

1975d "The renaming and ritual adoption of a Lahu Nyi (Red Lahu) child," Ajia-Afurika Gengo Bunka Kenkyu/Journal of Asian and African Studies (Tokyo) 10: 183-89.

    Lahu Nyi of Thailand, text and notes.

Walker, Anthony R., ed.

1975 Farmers in the hills: Ethnographic notes on the upland peoples of North Thailand, Penang, Penerbit Universiti Sains Malaysia for the School of Comparative Social Science. 211 pp.

    Akha, Lahu, and Lisu of Thailand. Settlement patterns, village communities, daily life, agricultural festivals, Christian converts, social organization, religion, history, and relations with the Thai government. The following chapters are most pertinent: "Northern Thailand: Hills and valleys, hillmen and lowlanders" (pp. 1-17); "The Lahu people:An introduction" (pp. 111-26); "Ban Luang: A Lahu Nyi village" (pp. 127-37); "Sheh-kaw shi-nyi: A Lahu Nyi agricultural festival" (pp. 139-48); "The Lahu Na (Black Lahu) Christian community at Huai Tadt: Some notes" (pp. 149-55)--all by A. R. Walker; "The Lisu people; An introduction (pp. 157-64) by Mohd. Razha Rashid and Pauline H. Walker: "The Lisu village of Mae Pun naweh: Some impressions: (pp. 165-68) by Mohd. Razha Rashid; "The Akha people: An introduction" (pp. 169-81) by Syed Jamal Jaafar and A. R. Walker; "The Akha of Huai San: A note: (pp. 183-86) by P. H. Walker; "Central government and tribal minorities: Thailand and West Malaysia compared" (pp. 189-203) by Tan Chee Beng. Photos.

Wanat Bhruksasri: see Bhruksasri, Wanat.

Wang, Chi (or Ji)

1951   "The Yis may ride in their towns again," <u>People's China</u> <u>4</u>,<u>11</u>: 28-29.

        Yi of Choakioh may now ride horses in town and go about in groups, previously forbidden. Photo.

Wang, Hai-min (See also Wa-cha-mu-chi and Wang Hai-min.)

1959   "People of Yi nationality on the road to socialism," Rén-mín ri-bao, Nov. 8. (English translation: <u>Survey of the China Mainland Press</u> 2150: 30-32.)

        Yi of Liangshan autonomous zhou use an average of 10,000 catties of manure per mou. National calamities this year kept the harvest at only 25% above last year's.

Wáng, Jié-chīng

1937   "Yún-nán zàng shān liǎng zú zhī fēn bù jí chí fēng huà (The distribution of Tibetan and Shan tribes in Yunnan and their morals)," Wén-huà jiàn-shè (Cultural Reconstruction) <u>3</u>,<u>9</u>.

        Lolo mentioned.

Wang, Leh (or Le)

1959   "Cultural growth of minority peoples," <u>Peking Review</u>

<u>3</u>: 18-19.
Lisu, Yi educational advances.

Wang, Mary T.
1946 "A remote tribe in west China," <u>China Magazine</u> <u>16</u>,<u>5</u>: 45-53.
Yi character means "a man with a big bow." Castes. Village is important unit. New Year and Torch festivals. Prefer father sister's daughter marriage. Cremation three days after death. Memorial service is accompanied by horse racing and bridge building. Ancestor worship stops at great-grandfather.

Wang, Shu-tang
1955 <u>China Land of Many Nationalities A sketch</u>, Peking, People's Republic of China. 63 pp.

Wang, Tien
1956 "CCP Yunnan Provincial Committee maps out new plan to foster nationality cadres," <u>New China News Agency</u>, <u>Kunming</u>, July 18. (English translation: <u>Survey of the China Mainland Press</u> <u>1351</u>: 25-27.)
More than 17,000 cadres of minorities were fostered in past few years. Among the Yi and Hani, 0.2% to 0.3% are cadres, among the Lisu, less than 0.1%.

Wang, Wei-xun (or Wei-hsun)
1959 "The Yi nationality of Da Liang shan and Xiao Liang shan autonomous zhou amid speedy progress," <u>Shàng-yōu</u> (Upstream), Feb. 1. (English translation: <u>Excerpts from China Mainland Magazines</u> <u>169</u>: 37-41.)
Yi have ended slavery. 1,400 agricultural cooperatives with 100,000 households (85% of the population) are

proceeding with commune program. A bumper grain harvest of 815 catties per capita in 1958. There are now 4,700 factories and mines, employing 17,000 workers.

Wang, Wen-chao
1894 Yún-nán tōng zhì (Record of an inspection-tour in Yunnan).
  See Hsú Itáng 1932.

Ward, Francis Kingdon (also Francis Kingdon-Ward)
1912 "Through the Lutzu country to Menkong," <u>Geographical Journal</u> <u>39</u>: 582-92.
  Lissu are related the Black Lutzu. Map, photos.

1913 <u>The land of the blue poppy</u>, Cambridge, Cambridge University Press. 283 pp.

  Lissu live on both sides of the Mekong from 27°10' to 28°N. In summer they go to Li-ti-p'ing to tend flocks; collect honey, poison, and wood; and rob travelers. Peas are sometimes planted to camouflage opium poppy fields. Lissu women wear a headdress which looks like a sun bonnet covered with cowries. Mixed Pêtzu-Lissu villages. 200 revolutionaries, including Lissu and Minchia, take La-chi-mi (pp. 215-17). Garrison at Bahang keeps Lissu in check.

  Lutzu have moved down Salween as far as Bahang. Dress, traps, village locations. K'ang-p'u chief rules 15,000 families, including Lissu, Minchia, Moso, and Chinese; these Lissu are dwarfish and negritoid (pp. 194-95).

  Lu-k'ou are of Shan and Lissu orgin, but speak and dress like Chinese (p. 230).

Ch'utzu is a tribe between the Salween and Nmai kha at 28°N.

1918 "The hydrography of the Yunnan-Tibet frontier," Geographical Journal 52: 288-99.

Lissu have moved west from the Salween Valley.

1920 "The valleys of Kham," Geographical Journal 56: 183-95.

Map, photos.

1921 In farthest Burma, London, Seeley, Service. 311 pp.

Altitude reflects relative power: the Lissu, who are settled at the highest altitudes, are claimed to be the weakest. Map, photos.

1923a "From the Yangtze to the Irrawaddy," Geographical Journal 62: 6-20.

Map, photos.

1923b The mystery rivers of Tibet, London, Seeley, Service 316 pp.

Lisu: Kingdon-Ward was a better botanist than he was an ethnologist, but he traveled widely through the Lisu area. Most of what he observed is summarized on pages 201-12 of this book, although he sometimes contradicts himself elsewhere. He writes about dress, housing, crops, graves, and possible orgins (which appear linguistically and physically to be from north or east, although the houses, household goods, and traditions of elephants suggest a southern or western origin). He claims that the Lisu are moving northward and westward.

1924 From China to Hkamti Long, London, Edward Arnold.

317 pp.

>Lisu are the "most picturesque people on the North-East Frontier." They were driven by the Moso from the east. He erroneously classifies them as Siamese Chinese. Map, photos.

1949   Burma's icy mountains, London, Jonathan Cape. 287 pp.

>Lisu mentioned. Superb photos.

1956   Return to the Irrawaddy, London, Andrew Melrose. 224 pp.

>Lisu pan for gold in northern Burma, and dig for medicinal plants (Fritillaria sp.) near the sources of the Irrawaddy (pp. 52, 214, 47). A Lisu family may own a Chinese coffin tree (Taiwania cryptomerioides) (p. 155). Photographs of Lisu crossbowmen (frontispiece, p. 32), girl (p. 61), and grave (p. 33).

Webb, C. Morgan

1912   Census of India 1911,11,1 (Burma, Report).

>Lishaw kinship terms (Appendixes xlvii-xlix,lxii), Lisaw (lxiii), Muhso (lxiii).

Weed, A. C.

1969   Field notes and recommendations, Border Patrol Center Survey, Area V, Bangkok, United States Operations Mission Public Safety Division. 9 pp.

>Lahu, Lisu: Thai Border Patrol Police should make use of available supplies, engage in soap-making projects, civic action, make use of veterinarians and medics, and place less reliance on air support.

Wehrli, Hans J.

1904   "Beitrag zur Ethnologie der Chingpaw (Kachin) von

Ober-Burma," *Internationales Archiv für Ethnographie,* Supplement zu bd. 16, Leiden, E. J. Brill.

    Lisu, Lishaw, Lahu: Various classifications. Map.

Wén, Bīn
1924   "Mán zi (Barbarians)," *Zhōng-gúo chīng-nían* (Chinese Youth) 41.

    Lolo mentioned.

Wén, Cháo
1936   "Hàn zú túng bāo dùi fú xīng lúo-ló yǐng yǒu de tài du (The attitude which the Han ought to have with regards to the renaissance of the Lolo)" *Xīn yí zú* (New Yi Tribe) 1,1.

Wén, Jiāng
1953   "Sì-chūan hùi-lǐ de tǔ zhù rén zhōng (Aboriginal tribes of Huili in Szechwan)," *Dú-lì píng-lùn* (Independent Critic) 36.

    Lolo mentioned.

Wen, Xue-nong (or Hsueh-nung)
1970   "Re-education work must not be relaxed even for a single moment," *Gūang-míng rì-bào,* Dec. 17. (English translation: *Survey of China Mainland Press* 4809: 95-98.)

    Yi. Author is member of the Hungho Hani and Yi autonomous zhou Revolutionary Committee.

Wén, Yōu
1936a   "Zài lùn lúo-ló wén shù zì (A further discussion of Lolo numerals)," *Tien-jīng dà gōng bào, tú shū fù* (Tientsin News, Illustrated Supplement) 115.

1936b "Dú cuàn wén cóng kè - jiǎn lùn ló wén zhī qǐ yuán (A study of the collection of Ts'uan characters - as well as a discourse on the origins of the Lolo language)," <u>Tiēn-jīng dà gōng bào, tú shū fù</u> (Tientsin News, Illustrated Supplement) <u>150-51</u>.

Lolo (or Ts'uan) writing. See Ding 1935 and 1936.

1940a "Yún-nán sì zhǒng ló wén de chū bù bǐ jiào (A comparison of the four varieties of the Lolo script in Yunnan)," <u>Studia Serica</u> (Huá xī xié hé dà xué zhōng guó wén huà yán jiū suǒ) <u>1,2</u>: 119-54.

In Chinese, with English summary.

1940b "Lúo-ló yí yǔ kǎo (On Lolo i yu - Lolo-Chinese vocabularies)," <u>Studia Serica</u> (Huá xī xié hé dà xué zhōng guó wén huà yán jiū suǒ) <u>1,1</u>: 77-97.

In Chinese, with English summary.

Review: Stein, 1941, <u>Ecole française d'Extrême-Orient, Bulletin</u> <u>41</u>: 430-34.

1945 "A study of the Lolo script with special reference to Yunnan varieties," <u>West China Border Research Society, Journal</u> <u>16</u>: 95-103.

1947 "A comparison of three varieties of the Lolo characters in Szechwan, Yünnan, and Kweichow," <u>Zhōng-guó wén-huà yán-jiū huì-kān</u> (Bulletin of Chinese Studies) <u>7</u>: 245-49, 265.

Lolo characters from Liang-shan, Lu-nan, and Ta-ting. They have a common origin, originally ideograms (not phonograms, as Terrien de Lacouperie assumed). Each character has its own particular composition, though they are now always confused with each other.

	In Chinese, with English abstract.
1948	"On the vowel phonemes in a Lolo dialect spoken at Hsi Ch'ang," Zhōng-guó wén-huà yán-jiū huì-kān (Bulletin of Chinese Studies) 8: 131-38.

In Chinese, with English summary.

1950   "Linguistic affinities between Hsi-hsia and Lolo," Studia Serica 9,2: 105-06.

    Lolo: Laufer (in T'oung Pao, 1933) pointed out the close connection between Hsi-hsia, Lolo, and Moso. Wolfenden (in Royal Asiatic Society, Journal, 1931 and 1934, and T'oung Pao, 1936) proposed that Jyarung was a surviving relative of Hsi-hsia. Wang (in Shishiah Studies, 1933) points out the connection with Ch'iang and Minchia. Hsi-hsia is close to Lolo in its labial initials (p-b-v), and it is a tonal language (like Lolo and Moso, but not Ch'iang and Jyarung), because it was written with small circles in the four corners (a Chinese method of distinguishing tones).

Wēn, Yǒu, and Yáng, Hàn-kuāng

1942   "Wū-mán tǒng zhì jiē jí de nèi hūn jí chí me luò (The intermarriage and decline of the ruling class of Wu-man)," Biān-zhèng gōng-lùn (Border Political Commentary) 2,11-12.

    Lolo.

Whitaker, Donald P., with Helen Barth, Sylvan Berman, Judith Hermann, John MacDonald, Kenneth Martindale, and Rinn-Sup Shinn

1972   Area handbook for Laos, DA Pamphlet 550-68, Washington D.C., Foreign Area Studies Program, American University and Department of the Army. (1967 edition was prepared by T. D. Roberts, Mary Carroll, Irving Kaplan, Jan Matthews, David McMorris, and Charles Townsend.) 337 pp.

    Akha, Lahu mentioned.

Whitaker, Donald P., and Rinn-Sup Shinn, with Helen Barth, Judith Hermann, John MacDonald, Kenneth Martindale, and John Weaver

1972   <u>Area handbook for the People's Republic of China</u>, DA Pam 550-60, Washington, D.C., Foreign Area Studies, American University, and Department of the Army. (1967 edition was by Frederic Chaffee, with George Aurell, Helen Barth, John Dombrowski, Neda Walpole, and John Weaver.) 729 pp.

    Achang, Lahu, Lisu, Nasi, Nu, Tulung, and Yi mentioned (pp. 109-11).

White, Peter T.

1967   "Hopes and fears in booming Thailand," <u>National Geographic</u> <u>132</u>,<u>1</u>: 76-125.

    Akha, Lahu, and Lisu mentioned. Photos of Lahu and Lisu (by Dean Conger).

White, Peter T., and W. E. Garrett

1961   "Report on Laos," <u>National Geographic</u> <u>120</u>,<u>2</u>: 240-75.

    Akha: Photos.

    Mousseudam and Mousseudeng (Black and Red Lahu) mentioned.

Wiens, Herold Jacob

1954   <u>China's march towards the tropics</u>, Hamden, Conn., Shoe String Press. (Reprinted 1967, <u>Han Chinese expansion in South China</u>, Hamden, Shoe String Press.)

(HRAF AF17-2)

Lolo An clan was in Ta-ting area as early as the Three Kingdoms in the third to fourth centuries (p. 87). Their origin was in the north; the western Chiang moved south and were renamed Lolo (pp. 93-96, 79). 1628 revolt against T'ien-ch'i (pp. 220-21). Description based on Lin 1947 (pp. 287-93, 280).

1962 "Some of China's thirty-five million non-Chinese," Royal Asiatic Society, Hong Kong Branch, Journal 2: 54-74.

Yi have lived in southwestern China for 2,500 years. Their hair horns date from at least the Later Chou (951-960). Eickstedt says that their legends, economy, language, and customs indicate an origin in the northeastern Tibetan plateau (eastern Chinghai). They comprise 40 subtribes in Yunnan alone: Na-khi, Lisu, Nu, Tu-lung, Ching-po, La-hu, A-ch'ang, Pai (once thought by Wiens to be Tai, but grouped with Yi by Bruk), Han-yi, and T'u-chia of northwestern Hunan. In the 1953 census, the T'u-chia numbered 90,000, but later Fang Jen found that they numbered 300,000, and Bruk gives a figure of 549,000; they are highly acculturated. Summary of Winnington 1959. 1953 census figures by provinces. Map.

1973 "Yi," Encyclopedia Britannica 23: 893.

Wiin-tham

1972 "Khon phǎw Liisaw (The Lisu people)," Wiin-tham 17,803: 2-6, 18, 27-28.

Lisu of Thailand: Popular introduction. Photos.

1973   In Thai.
"Jîam Ikho (Visit to the Akha)," Wiin-tham 17,819: 4-5, 23-24.
         Akha of Thailand: Popular introduction. Photos. In Thai.

Wilcox, Ruth Turner
1965   Folk and festival costumes of the world, New York, Charles Scribner's Sons. Not paginated.
         Lessu woman's dress (plate 91).

Wilson, Dick
1971   The Long March 1935, The epic of Chinese Communism's survival, New York, Viking Press; London, Hamilton. xx, 331 pp.
         Lolo hindrance and help to the Long March (chapter 14). See Chen 1972.

Winnington, Alan
1959   The slaves of the cool mountains, The ancient social conditions and changes now in progress on the remote South-Western borders of China, London, Lawrence and Wishart 223 pp.
         Yi: Based on residence in the Liangshan area as government adviser, 1957-58. Norsu raids took place as late as 1949. In the 1920s, a Chinese landlord officer of Yung Shen led 400 men on a raid of the Norsu: burning, killing, stealing cattle and horses. Shortly after, 1,000 Norsu struck back, taking 1,000 cattle and 300 slaves (p. 17). Home Guard and defensive village wall to prevent former slave-owners from staging a comeback. Slaves included former Han, Nashi, Lisu,

Hsifan, Chungchia, Mosu, Tibetans (pp. 23-27). Dress
(p. 25). Ninglang has county government building, bank,
hospital, state store selling large variety of goods,
and producer cooperative (p. 28). Norsu of the area
say that 30 generations ago they had a common ancestor
named Lapudior, who had four sons: Buyu, Lomhn, Zeku,
Wadja; the latter took a wife of doubtful antecedents,
so that the latter clan was split with a bastard group,
Loho, whom the other clans refused to marry. The five
clans are further divided into 500 families. Norsu
(Black Bones) have dialect differences with Pu Nor
(White Black), who are bondsmen with feudal obligations
to their lords (pp. 29-31). Caste and class (wealth?)
differences do not necessarily coincide. 47% of the
population were slaves: house slaves (those "at the
lower end of the fireplace") were inherited by nobles'
sons (who took the male slaves) and daughters (who took
the females); when nobles married, their slaves were
paired off (therefore slaves sometimes married within
their clan), and they became separate slaves ("people
sleeping on the side"). Slaves could also possess
slaves. They could buy their freedom, and some ran
away to enemy lords. Non-Norsu were kidnapped and
made slaves, while bondsmen could be abducted and
gambled into slavery (pp. 31-34). Nobles were endogamous, with clan exogamy; parallel-cousin marriage was
forbidden, and cross-cousin marriage prescribed. Women
held high positions; a threat of suicide by a woman
(which would lead to clan feuds) was effective in get-

ting her way. Bride-price consisted of a race horse, 10 silver ingots, 10 horses or cattle, 100 sheep, gifts to the middlemen and managers of the wedding, 3 silver ingots to each family of commoners accompanying the bride, an estimated total of 2,670 yuan (400 English pounds), plus presents each time the wife visited the husband until the birth of the first child. Wife lived with her parents until the birth of the first child, during which time she engaged in love affairs with her cousins. Monogamy, except when the wife is childless. Close relations with husband's younger brother, but avoidance of elder (although in levirate, a widow may marry either, and even the dead husband's father). In 1948, Buyu Wani, leader of the largest clan (and now head of the county and member of the National People's Congress), was contacted by a Communist named Hu Tan. Hu Tan convinced him that the Kuomintang should be prevented from using Liangshan as refuge. The Norsu cut up the Kuomintang trops, including 1,000 at Yung Sheng. Hu Tan also warned Buyu Wani of missionaries such as "Pastor An," who had taught some Lisu how to write, and that now there were disputes between Lisu converts and non-Christians. At the time of Liberation, only the wealthy nobles were certain of food year-round, no one could read, and the "piled-up sufferings of their slaves and commoners ended in drunken feasts, opium orgies and buried silver ingots" (p. 58). At first, the Communists made friends and stressed unity; they brought relief supplies; there were problems with runaway slaves who sought refuge with Han work teams. Rumors of a possible mass massacre of slaves caused more runaways; nobles also feared land reform and the indignities of "speak bitterness" meetings. An estimate of the Norsu population revealed: nobles with 10 or more slaves constituted 2.5% of the population, nobles with less than 10 slaves 2.5%, commoners with 10 or more slaves 3%, commoners with 1 to 9 slaves 25%, commoners without slaves 20%, separate slaves 33%, house slaves 14%. Slaves had no incentive to produce more, since everything went to the nobles. Nobles had no incentive, since they had enough. In 1956, peaceful reforms were carried out from above: slavery was abolished, but the nobles retained their houses, personal property, gardens, 2 acres of farmland, prestige and salaries as leaders and members of local committees; land divided, feudal privileges and usurious debts were canceled. All were classified either as "slave owners" (who owned 10 or more slaves, 10 or more acres, and derived over 70% of their income from the labor of others) or "working people." Five steps in abolition: elect District Reform Committee, investigate individual conditions of slaves, classify into categories, form a District Labor Committee, distribute land. Some slave owners sabotaged the plan by slaughtering their own cattle, but later the Reform Committee could force the sale of cattle. Documents pertaining to reform (pp. 88-96). A greater problem than dealing with former slave owners was getting house slaves to be self-dependent.

Slave households were urged to cooperate in groups of 10 or more.

Lahu headman of a Wa group fought Kuomintang (p. 128). Progress among the Wa and Jingpaw. Changes were not imposed upon the minorities, but they were urged to discuss possible reforms. Three methods of transition to socialism: reform by open class struggle; reform by peaceful negotiation, as among the Norsu (both these methods have an intervening stage of private land ownership); direct transition from communal work to cooperative collective, as among the Wa and Jingpaw (where class differences were unclear).

Wissmann, Hermann von
1943   Süd-Yünnan als Teilraum Südostasiens, Schriften zur Geopolitik Heft 22, Heidelberg, Berlin und Madgeburg, Vowinckel Verlag. 30 pp.

Aka, Buli Aka, Lohei, Lolo, and Yolo mentioned. Elevation cross-sections, showing habitats of different ethnic groups. Maps.

Wohnus, William H.: see Hanks, Hanks, and Sharp 1965.
Wongprasert, Sanit (See also Walker 1966-69.)
1975   "Lahu trade and commerce," Siam Society, Journal 58,2: 199-218.

Lahu Nyi of Phrao district, Thailand. Photos.

Wood, William Alfred Roe
1965   Consul in paradise, London, Souvenir Press. (A revision of 1935, Land of smiles, Bangkok, Krungdebarnargar Press.) 175 pp.

Akha, Lahu, and Lisu mentioned (pp. 151-52).

Photos (mostly by Gordon Young).

Woods, James L.
1969   <u>Hill</u> <u>tribe</u> <u>names</u>, Bangkok, Advanced Research Projects Agency, U.S. Department of the Army. 24 pp.

    List of names.

Woodthorpe, R.G.
1897   "Some account of the Shans and hill tribes of the states on the Mekong," <u>Anthropological</u> <u>Institute</u>, <u>Journal</u> 26,1: 13-28.

    Muhsos located west of Keng Tung and in northern Siam. Include 16 tribes. New Year festival. Drawing of Muhso weaving.

    Kaw located east of Keng Tung and Keng Cheng.

Wú, Shān-chóu
1922   "Sì chūan é biān yí rén xiàn zhòng zhī diào chá (A survey of the condition of the Yi people in the E or O-pien border areas of Szechuan)," <u>Dì-xué</u> <u>zá-zhì</u> (Geographical Magazine) 13,2.

1935   "Sì-chūan jìng nèi zhī ló-lo (The Lolo within the territory of Szechuan)," <u>Chūan</u> <u>biān</u> <u>jì-kan</u> (Szechuan) Border Quarterly) 1,1.

    See Zhōng-guó yín-háng diào chā zǔ, chǔng chīng 1935.

Wu, Wen-tsao (Pinyin: Wu, Wen-zao)
1955   "Facts on national minorities," <u>China</u> <u>Reconstructs</u> 4,2: 9-12.

    Lisu number fewer than 200,000 (p. 10).

Wyss, Peter
1969   "Thai orthography for Akha, Part 2," in Peter Hinton,

ed., *Tribesmen and Peasants in North Thailand*, Chiang Mai, Tribal Research Centre: 113-16.

Xià, Tíng-yù
1928 "Luǒ-lo shū lüè (A brief account of the Lolo)," <u>Zhōng-shān da-xué yǔ yán lì shǐ yán jiū suǒ zhōu-kān</u> (Sun Yat-sen University Language and History Research Institute) <u>3</u>, <u>35-36</u>.

Xin, Wen: see Hsin, Wen.

Xīn-huà News Agency: see New China News Agency.

Xú, Yi-táng: see Hsú, Ítáng.

Yang, Bin-zhuan, and Wang, Ji-shen
n.d. <u>Notes on the investigation of northern Yunnan</u>, n.p. Lisu "cultivate by sword and plant by fire" (slash and burn). They love wine.

Yang, Ch'êng-chih (also Young, Ching-chi or Ching-che) (Pinyin: Yáng Chéng-zhī)

1929 "Yún-nán luǒ-lo diào chá jìn xìn (Recent report on the Yunnan Lolo)," <u>Mín-sú</u> (Minority Customs) <u>57-59</u>.

1930a "Lolo shuō lüè (Introduction to the Lolo)," <u>Líng-nán Xué-bào</u> (Lingnan Bulletin) <u>1,3</u>.

1930b "Lólo wén de qǐ yuán jí qí nèi yǒng yì bān (The origin and general content of the Lolo language)," <u>Lì shǐ yǔ yán yán jiū suǒ, Zhōng yāng yán jiū yuàn</u> (Bulletin of the Institute of History and Philology, Academia Sinica) <u>11</u>.

1931a "Yún-nán lolo zú wū shī jí qí jīng diǎn (Yunnan Lolo shamans and their script)," <u>Zhōng-shān da-xué wén-shǐ xué yán jiū suǒ jí</u> (Sun Yat-Sen University, Cultural and Historical Research Institute)<u>1,1</u>.

1931b	"Yún-nán lólo de wén zi (The written language of the Yunnan Lolo)," Xīn-yǎ Xī-yǎ (New Asia) 2,2.
1931c	"Yun-nan lolo jing ba (Yunnan Lolo sutras)," Xīn-yǎ Xī-yǎ (New Asia) 2,1.
1932	"Cóng xī nán mín zú shuō dào dú lì lólo (Comments on the southwestern minorities including the independent Lolo)," Xīn-yǎ Xī-yǎ (New Asia) 4,3.
1933	"Lólo tài shàng chīng jīng xīao zāi jīng dùi yì (A Lolo transliteration of T'ai-Shang-Ch'ing-Ching-Hsiao-Tsai-Ching)," Lì shǐ yǔ yán yán jīu suǒ, Zhōng yāng yán jiū yuàn (Bulletin of the Institute of History and Philology, Academia Sinica) 4,2: 175-98.
	Lolo sutra on tranquility and evading calamity, in Lolo, and Chinese translation.
1934a	"La langue, l'écriture et les manuscrits lolos," London, Premier Congres des Sciences Anthropologiques et Ethnologiques: 313-16.
1934b	"Zhōng guó zī nán mín zú zhōng de lólo zú (The Lolo among the southwestern minorities of China)," Dì-xué zá-zhì (Geographical Magazine) 22,1.
1934c	"Wǒ duì yǔ yún-nán lólo zú yán jiū de jì huà (My plan for research on the Yunnan Lolo)," Yǔ-gōng 1,4.
1935	L'Ecriture et les manuscrits lolos, Thèse, Université de Paris, Genève (Publications de la Bibliothèque Sino-Internationale 4).
	Lolo divided into Ts'ouan white or west (Pei-Man) and black or east (Wou-man) in sixth century. The name "Lolo" first appears in the Yuan Annals. In the History of the T'ang dynasty, it is mentioned that the Wou-man,

including the Man Lou-lou, entered into marriage relations with the Nan-tchao. During the Three Kingdoms (221-264), General Tchou Ko-leang made one of his followers King of the Lo-tien (kingdom of the Lolo). Names by which the Lolo are referred to in Chinese documents and histories. Meanings of various names. Five legends regarding the origin of Lolo writing. The P'i-Mo is a specialist in sacred written formulas, not to be confused with a magician with curative powers, Cho-Ngi-Ngi or Hsi-Ma (d'Ollone confuses these). The former is hereditary, while the magician is inspired. Nan-Tchao-Yé-Che mentions 1,100 characters in Ts'ouan-tseu. The oldest Lolo writing was found on two funerary stele at Kin-Tsingfou (405 A.D.) and Lou-Leang-Tcheou (458 A.D.). Other stele. Difficulties of translation due to, among other things, the secret nature of the books, which sorcerers recite without full understanding. Texts in Lolo, phonetic transcription, Chinese and French translations. D'Ollone's classification of manuscripts into 23 categories.

1936a "Hypothese sur les origines des Lolos," Zhōng-shān dà-xué wén kē yán jiū suǒ shi xué zhūan (Sun Yat-sen University, Arts Research Institute Special Publication) 1,2.

1936b "Remarques inédites sur la civilisation Lolo," Anthropos 31: 672-78.

Lolo first mentioned in Se-Ma Ts'ien's "Biographie des étrangers du sud-ouest." Yang claims to have three manuscripts even older than d'Ollone's, written by a

	Lolo sorcerer in 1566-69. Lolo are not descended from the "Ts'ouan." The stele of Tche-Tcheng (971), the most ancient Lolo inscription, does not mention the Ts'ouan.
1936c	"Sommaire de la grammaire lolo," Zhōng-shān dà-xúe wén kē yán jiū suǒ yǔ yán wén xúe zhuān (Sun Yat-sen University, Arts Research Institute, Special Linguistics Publication) <u>1,1</u>.
Yang, Cang	
1956	"A short sketch of the Ningland Yi autonomous xian," Yúnnán rì-bào, Oct. 5. (English translation: <u>Survey of China Mainland Press</u> <u>1438</u>: 28-29.)
	Yi number 75,000 of the xian's 110,000 inhabitants.
Yang, Gladys, translator	
1955a	"'Ashma,' The oldest Shani ballad," <u>Chinese Literature</u> <u>1</u>: 181-85.
	See 1955b, below.
1955b	"Ashma (A Shani ballad)," <u>Chinese Literature</u> <u>3</u>: 3-51.
	Shani are a Lolo people in Kueishan district, Lunan county, Yunnan. This narrative poem of 4,000 lines is about Ashma and her brother, Ahay. Ashma is kidnapped by a wicked rich man, and eventually she is changed into an echo. Previously published in Chinese in <u>Southwest Literature</u> and <u>People's Literature</u>. See Huang, Yang, and Liu, eds., 1954.
Yang, Han-kuang: see Wen, Yu, and Yang, Han-kuang.	
Yang, Te-fan	
1955	"Rehabilitation of the Nu Kiang Lisu nationality autonomous area," Gūang-míng rì-bào, May 31. (English

translation: <u>Survey</u> <u>of</u> <u>China</u> <u>Mainland</u> <u>Press</u> <u>1076</u>; 15-16.)

 Lisu (the English translation gives the ethnic group as Lolo, apparently an error) make up 75% of the 110,000 inhabitants of the Nukiang area, which includes four xian: Kungshan, Fuking, Pikiang, and Lushui. They grow maize, rice, wheat, buckwheat, kaoliang, millet, olives, potatoes, soya beans, broadbeans, cotton, varnish, bitter bark (huanglien), and China root, and they collect bear's gall and musk, and hides. Kanpeng village of Pikiang paid 11 different taxes in 1948, amounting to 3 picul of maize per household; in 1953, 8 of the 24 households paid no tax, and the others paid 5 or 6 sheng of grain. State aid. Early spring planting was begun in 1951, production work teams in 1953. Improvements in agriculture, marketing, medical and educational facilities, and transport have resulted in a higher standard of living. Song gives thanks to Chairman Mao and the Communist Party.

Yang, Zheng-shi (or Shr-dwo or Cheng-shr)
1963a "The pearl of the frontier shines again," <u>Guang-ming</u> <u>ri-bao</u>, May 12.

 Lahu make up 42% of the 220,000 inhabitants west of Lan Tsang River in Yu Mai region of southern Lu Shan. "La-gu" means "hunt the tiger, divide and eat." One hundred years ago, Meng Lang Ba, capital of the autonomous county, flourished like a pearl, but under oppression the pearl lost its luster, and rebellions flared. In 1950, the People's Liberation Army found only five families left. In 1953, a hospital was established, malaria controlled, and tea cultivation encouraged. Today, there are 10,000 inhabitants.

1963b   "Reed pipe music filled the air of Meng Lang Ba," Mínzú Huàbào (Nationalities Pictorial) 3: 18.

Lahu: Meng Lang Ba, capital of Lan Tsang Lahu autonomous zhou, had only ten households, and was known as an "area of pestilence." Now, it is a city of 10,000, with a hospital, stores, and factories. On market days, five local trading centers set up stalls where Lahu youths buy books and reed pipes. Photographs of paddies, high school students, and youths buying reed pipes.

Yáng, Zhǐ-yǒng: see Huáng, Tǐe, Yáng Zhǐ-yǒng, and Liú Yǐ, eds.

Yaoshan Commune Party Committee

1972   "Socialism brings new life to minority peoples in Southwest China commune," New China News Agency, Peking, Oct. 27. (English translation: Survey of China Mainland Press 72-45: 74-77.) Excerpted from: "Chairman Mao shows us the way to happiness," Hóng-qí (Red Flag) 10.

Yi are included in the commune, which is in Hokou Yao autonomous xian, Yunnan. 80% of the inbabitants are Yao, the rest include Yi, Miao, Chuang, and Han.

Yǐ, Fēi

1935   "Dían xī shēn shān zhōng de luǒ-ló pó (The Lolo within the mountainous regions of western Yunnan)," Shēng bào yùe-kān (Shin Pao Monthly) 4,10.

Yì, Mèng-yì
n.d. "Yún-nán lolo zú shǐ lüè (A short history of the Yunnan Lolo)," Zhí biān yuè-kān (Shi Bian Monthly) 1,3.

Yí, Míng-dé
1933 "Diàn biān yě-rén shān jǐ eng-méi-kāi jiāng mài-lì-kāi jiāng liú yù rén zhǒng (The peoples of the valleys of the Engmeikai and Mailikai rivers in Lisu Shan on the Yunnan border)," Dì-lǐ xué-jí (Geographical Quarterly) 1,2.

Lisu women are fond of the Chinese character for "land" on their dresses; they also wear kerchiefs with flower designs.

You, Guo-en
1942 "Discussions on the torch festival," Xī-nán biān-jiāng wèn-tí yán-jiū bào-gào (Study-report on problems of the southwest border) (Hua-chung College) 1: 2-9.

Lolo torch festival and its origin. In Chinese. See Chao 1950.

You, Jing-yuan
n.d. Wei-xi jian wen lu (Wei-hsi diary), n.p.

Lisu use almost all their grain to make wine. Their clothes are made of black cotton or hemp; the men wear straw hair nets, and copper belts on their foreheads. Bear trap, monkey trap, tiger trap (using goat as bait). Hunting.

Young, Ching-chi: see Yang, Ch'eng-chih.

Young, E. C.
1907 "A journey from Yun-nan to Assam," Geographical

Journal 30: 152-80.
Lissu (or Liso) sell herbs to the Chinese. Photos.

Young, Gordon: see Young, Oliver Gordon.

Young, Harold Mason

n.d. To the mountain tops, A sojourn among the Lahu of Asia, Ms. (A copy is located in the Library of Congress.) 250 pp.

Lahu legend says that they came from Peking and Nanking to Central China, and by 1830 to the southwest. Mong Myen is said to have been taken by the Chinese when they tricked Lahu women into exchanging staghorn triggers of their bows for Jew's harps. Quarrel with Karen over sharing of meat spurred southern migration. God had given Lahu writing on a rice cake, but it was eaten; and had given them a sacred seal, but this was given to the Shans as a fine for touching a Shan girl. Lahu subgroups include Na, Shi, Na Mwe, Ku Lao, Kai Shin, and A Do A Ga. Distribution. Their villages are located above 3,000 feet, with a hill or ridge above the village, and a rising hill above that ("the pillow and the foot-rest" of the village, ensuring prosperity and security). The Kai Shin and many Na build their houses on the ground, but others build them on posts. A village usually has a chief (Kha Sheh), second chief (Hka Leh), and a caller (Pu Lan). Settling of disputes. Proverbs. Food. Temperament, morals, vices (opium, betel, clay eating), outlook on life and death. A Wa massacre of a Lahu village of 36.

Dress. Names. Bride service lasts at least three
years. Agriculture, livestock, blacksmiths, and silver-
smiths. Courting and marriage, love charms, translation
of the "song of the Lahu love-meet" (pp. 96-123).
Animism, theism. Shamans usually male. Lahu used to
have temples (fu) with priests; three remain in Yunnan
(Nam Wai, Hka Lang, Mong Hka). Now, each village has
an altar in a hut in a spirit grove; offerings and
prayers are made there during the full and end of each
moon by the chief, any shaman or dreamer (Paw Hku).
Famous religious leaders include A Sha of Mong Hka
(died 1895) and Pu Kyan Long (a Wa who opposed the
Chinese). Three of the latter's disciples met William
Marcus Young in Kengtung in 1905, and were convinced
that Christianity was what Pu Kyan had prophesied.
He died shortly after learning of this. Songs of the
bards show similarities with Christianity. Dreamers
are mid-way between old-time religious leaders and
today's witch-doctors. They are responsible for a
diversity of sects; they build templelike bamboo
structures, miniature sand pagodas, engage in gay
dancing. Some teach that devotion alone will fill the
granaries (thus causing poverty). Leather extractors
(She Pa) extract leather and other foreign objects
that evil spirits place in humans to cause disease.
Man-gods are fanatics; story of the one on Awng Lawng
mountain 1930-32. Driving out evil spirits and calling
back spirits. Revenge. Funerals. Invocations. Where
spirits dwell. Ghosts. Werewolves. Signs, omens,

auspicious days. Sickness, herb doctors. Holy days. Games. Folk stories: "The flying rocks," "The lost bride," "The dog and the pig," "The simpleton and the bear," "The frog child," "The ghost and the goiter," etc. (pp. 180-210). Hunting, fishing, traps, hunting stories (pp. 231-45). Changes include more contact with state administration and other ethnic groups, military service, missions, and schools. This may lead to a split between the educated Lahu, who will merge with non-Lahu, and others, who will remain Lahu.

    Young was a missionary who spoke fluent Lahu. This manuscript has excellent information on religion, folklore and hunting, but in other areas suffers from an attempt to generalize for all Lahu.

Young, Harold Nelson
1962   <u>Translation</u> <u>of</u> <u>leaflet</u> <u>symbols</u> (<u>Musers</u> <u>tribe</u>), Bangkok, United States Operations Mission. 4 pp.

    Muser (Lahu) interpretations of symbols used in propaganda.

Young, Oliver Gordon
1961   <u>The</u> <u>hill</u> <u>tribes</u> <u>of</u> <u>nothern</u> <u>Thailand</u>, Bangkok, United States Operations Mission. (Reprinted in 1962, 1969, and 1975 by the Siam Society.) 120 pp.

    Akha, Lahu, Lisu cultural summaries. Young, the son of a missionary, grew up among the Lahu, about whom he is a recognized expert. His information on the Akha and Lisu suffers a bit because of this "Lahu bias." Among the errors in his survey of the Lisu: his population estimates are much too high; "maw-hpi" is Thai, not Lisu; defense is no longer a consideration in choosing village sites nowadays (in fact, water supply makes most of them very vulnerable); the power of the headman varies greatly from village to village; the ritual center is not mentioned. Map, photos.

Review: Walker, 1975, Siam Society, Journal 58,2: 355-70.

1962 "Thailand's Mussuh Daeng," Explorer's Journal 40,2: 58-65.

Mussuh Daeng (Lahu Nyi) hunters are ranked according to performance of 10 kills (elephant, saladang, tiger, leopard, bear, wild boar, etc.). Religious leaders (Paw Khu) may promulgate doctrinal changes as a result of their dreams or imagination. Map, photos.

1965 "A light in the jungle," Sawaddi 3,4: 10-11, 26. Photos.

1967 Tracks of an intruder, London, Souvenir Press. 191 pp.

Akha, Lahu, Lisu mentioned, especially in connection with hunting in Thailand. Photos.

Young, Vincent, translator

n.d. G'ui sha ve li hpu aw suh (New Testament in Lahu), Taipei, privately published (ca. 1955).

Yú, De-jun: see Cháng Lúng-chìng, Shī Huāi-ren, and Yú Dé-jùn.

Yu, Ying-shih (Pinyin: You, Ying-shi)

1967 Trade and expansion in Han China, Berkeley and Los Angeles, University of California Press. 251 pp.

Southwest barbarians (pp. 111-17). Trade tied to tributary system.

Yuán, Jiā-húa (or Chia-hua or Chih-hua)

1946 "The A-si love songs and the A-si language," Frontier Politics (Nan-k'ai State University) 3: 5-6.

  A-si are a people of Lu-nan district, Yunnan, perhaps the same as Liétard's Ahi Lolo. See 1953, below, and Guang 1954.

1947 "Er-shan Wō-ní Yǔ Chu-tan (Preliminary investigation of the Woni language of Erh-shan)," Tientsin, Publication of the Frontier Peoples' Culture Department, Literary and Scientific Institute, Nan-k'ai State University, vol. 4.

1948 "Wō-ní yù yīn xi (Woni pronunciation system)," Xué-yūan (Source of Knowledge) 1,12.

1953 "A-xī shī jiā jí chí yǔ-yán (A-hsi mín-tsú-ko chí ch'i yù-yén) (Ahsi folksongs and their language)," Yǔ-yán xúe chūan kān 5 (Peking, Chinese Scientific Institute, Linguistic Research Department Special Publication 5). 245 pp.

  A-si Yi. See 1946, above, and Guang 1954.

Yule, Sir Henry

1903 The book of Sir Marco Polo the Venetian concerning the kingdom and marvels of the East, 2 vols., London, John Murray. Additional notes by Henri Cordier. First ed. 1871, 2d ed. 1875, 3d ed. numerous reprints including 1926 and 1971 by AMS Press, New York.) 462 and 662 pp.

  Lissu or Lisau are wild hill-robbers and great musk hunters (2: 60-64, 90). Lolo are equated with Polo's Coloman or Toloman; quotes from Richthofen, Baber, Hosie, Vial, Anderson, and Owen (2: 60-64,

69-70, 90, 123). Henri Cordier notes that we can only assume that the Coloman are mountain peoples of Yunnan. Sketches.

Review: Pelliot, 1904, Ecole française d'Extrême-Orient, Bulletin 4,3: 768-72. Disagrees with Yule's statement that Lo-lo is a late form of Ko-lo, since the former are mentioned in T'ang dynasty writings (cf. Pelliot 1904).

Yúnnán rì bào, Kunming

1956a   "Over 40,000 minority nationals recruited into Chinese Communist Party membership in Yunnan province," Sep. 21.

Yi have 20,351 Party members (1.26% of their population), Hani 3,163 (0.7%), Nasi 1,981 (1.4%), Lisu and Lahu not listed.

1956b   "Ninglang Yi Autonomous xian established," Oct. 5. (English translation: Survey of China Mainland Press 1438: 27-28.)

Yi, Lisu, Nahsi, Mosuo, and eight other nationalities live in Ninglang xian.

Zaborowski-Moindron, Sigismond

1900   "La Chine et les chinois," Société d'Anthropologie de Paris, Bulletins et Mémoires série 5,1: 544-60.

Lolo have Caucasian element. Thorel of the Garnier mission claimed that there were Gypsies among Lolo. Leclère (in La Géographie (1900): 276) says Lolo are Mongols from Kou-Kou-Nor.

1901   "Photographies de femmes Lolo, Miao-tsé et de natives de la ville de Yunnan, Collection de chaussures du sud de la Chine," Société d'Anthropologie de Paris, Bulletins et Mémoires série 5, 2: 140-43.

Lolo resemble Tibetans. Photographs (by Beauvais).

1902 "Le Yun-nân: sa population," Revue Universelle 66: 360-63.

Lolo is most ancient population of southwestern China. Some seem Chinese, others resemble peoples of Tibet-Assam-Burma, but none seem Mongol.

1904 "Notes sur les Lo-lo du Kien-tchang," Société d'Anthropologie de Paris, Bulletins et Mémoires série 5,4: 642-43.

Lolo photographs (by François). Extracts from Chinese works by Beauvais.

1905 "Les Lolos et les populations du sud de la Chine d'aprés les ouvrages chinois," Revue de l'Ecole d'Anthropologie de Paris 15,3: 86-95.

Lolo have Caucasian element, but with Chinese intermixture. Beauvais' translation of "Atlas des tributaires de la dynastie imperiale actuelle."

Zēng, Zhāo-lún (or Tseng, Chao-lun)

1947 Dà liang shān yi gōu kǎo chá jì (Tà liang shān i ch'ü k'ǎo ch'á chì) (A travelogue of the Yi area of Ta Liang Shan), Chungking, Zhōng Chīng qiu zhēn chū bǎn shè (Chiu Ching Publication Company). (Second edition, 1948, Shanghai, Chin Chin Press.) 316 pp.

Yi seen in market in Lichiang, also drinking on streets. Ninglang has problems administering the Yi, and suppressing opium cultivation among them.

Estimates of Yi population range from 100,000 to 2 million in the Liang Shan area. Chinese expeditions into the area include the West China Science College expedition in 1934, a team from the Central Military Academy in Chengtu in 1935, an expedition of the Military Affairs Commission in 1936, the Szechwan-Sikang Scientific Research Group, including Ma Chang-shou, in 1939, a group from the Szechwan Education Department, including Hsü I-táng, in 1940, and the writer's Szechwan-Sikang Scientific Research Group of the Southwestern Amalgamated Universities in the summer of 1941. The Han call them Lo Yi, the Republican government has decreed that they should be called "border people," but they call themselves Nosu. They claim that the gods gave birth to three humans: the eldest was Yi, the next Tibetan, and the youngest Han. The youngest was most loved, and he was given the plains, the next was given the hills, the Yi was left with the poor lands of the high mountains. The Yi of Yunnan have been sinicized to a great degree, where the division between Black and White Yi is not as strict. The Black Yi of Liang Shan call themselves "Shi po," and the White Yi call themselves "Wa tse." It is not true that the White Yi are former Han who were kidnapped and enslaved. The least sinicized Yi are in the Ning and Da Liang Shan areas. This area is divided into branches, which in turn are subdivided. They identify themselves as members of such-and-such a clan.

Zhang, Cui (or Chang, Ts'ui)
1964   "Zài Nù shān Nù shuǐ zhī jiān (Between the Nu Mountains and the Nu River)," <u>Mínzú Tuánjié</u> nos. 11-12: 22-25.
        Lisu: Review of economic and cultural progress among Salween Lisu since 1950.

Zhang, Guang-nian (or Chang, Kuang-nien)
1944   <u>A-xī</u> <u>di</u> <u>xuǎn jí</u> (A-hsi ti hsien chi) (A-hsi Lolo folk songs), n.p. 170 pp.

Zhāng, Lián-máo
1929   "Yún-nán zhāo tōng xian zhī yì biē (A glimpse of chao-tung county of Yunnan)," <u>Zhōng-shān dà-xué yǔ yán lì shǐ yán jiū suǒ zhōu-kān</u> (Sun Yat-sen University, Language and History Research Institute, Weekly) <u>76</u>.
        Lolo mentioned.

Zhang, Xu (or Chang, Hsu)
1958   "The Lisu of Nukiang leap over several centuries," <u>Guāng-míng rì-bào</u> (Peking), Nov. 19.
        Lisu: Changes since 1950 include increases in grain yields due to increased irrigation, use of manure, agricultural cooperatives, changes in old class and clan concepts, new factories, schools, and mines. Zhang was vice-secretary of the Communist Party Nukiang Frontier Working Committee.

Zhāo, Huà-ēng
1928   "Diān shěng xī nán de yí zú (The Yi tribes of south-western Yunnan)," <u>Zhōng-shān dà-xué yǔ yán lì shǐ yán jiū suǒ zhōu-kān</u> (Sun Yat-sen University Language and History Research Institute Weekly) <u>3,35-36</u>.

Zhōng-gúo Qīng-nían-bào (Chūng-kúo ch'īng-níen pào) (Peking)
    1956a   "600 youths in Lantsang, Yunnan, Lahu nationality Autonomous Zhou admitted to Youth League," Zhōng-gúo Qīng-nían-bào (English translation: Survey of the China Mainland Press 1310: 17).
              Lahu and Hani: A third of the youths were girls.
    1956b   "What are China's minorities?" Zhōng-gúo Qīng-nían-bào 4 Nov. (English translation: Survey of the China Mainland Press 1418: 6.)
              1953 census figures.

Zhōng-gúo yín-háng diao chá zǔ, Chúng ching (Bank of China Investigation Group, Chungking)
    1935   "Mǎ bian yí-rén diao chá (An investigation of the Yi people of the Ma border area)," Chūan bian jì-kān (Szechuan Border Quarterly) 1,3.
              See Wú 1935.

Zhōng-gúo zuo jia xie hui (Chūng-kúo tso chia hsieh hui)
    1962   Kūn míng fen hui Yún-nán gǒ zǔ mín jian gu shi xuǎn (Anthology of the folklore of the diverse peoples of Yunnan), Peking.
              Lisu stories: three, including one from Zui et al. 1959.

Zhūang, Xúe-běn (Chuang, Hsueh-pen)
    1941   Sī-gāng yì-zǔ diao-chá bào-gào (Sikāng i-tsu tiao-ch'á pào-kào (Ethnological report on the Lolo of Sikang), n.p., Provincial Government of Sikang.
    1942   "Lǒ-lo wen zi de yán jiu (A study of the written language of the Lolo)," Shūo-wén yùe (Shuowen Monthly) 32.

Zui, Lin, et al.
1959 Lì-sù yǔ yǔ-fǎ gāng-yào (Outline of Lisu grammar), Peking, Academy of Sciences.

  Lisu dialect of Yunnan: phonology, morphology, and texts. Discribes a recently-devised native writing system.

INDEXES

INDEX BY ETHNIC GROUP

The name (and alternate names) of each ethnic group is followed by references to authors and the last two digits of the publication date. Items followed by an asterisk are detailed ethnographies.

ACHANG (MAINGTHA, MÖNGHSA, NGACHANG)
    Anderson 71 Bernatzik 54 Bruk 59b Coggin Brown 13
    Davies 09 Enriquez 23 Leach 54 Metford 35 Scott &
    Hardiman 00 Shabad 72 Shafer 55 U.S. Army 61 Whitaker &
    Shinn 72
A-CHE: A-SI
A-CHI: A-SI
A-CHO: A-CH'O
A-CH'O (A-CHO) (A YI subgroup)
    Henry 03 Lin 47
A-DJAY: YI
AH-CHANG: ACHANG
AH-HSI: A-SI
A-HI: A-SI
AI-SI: WONI
AJA (A YI subgroup)
    Henry 03
AKA: AKHA or WONI
AKHA (AKHÖ, EKAW, HANI, IKHO, KAW, KHA KO, KHO, KO, WONI)
    Abadie 24 Adams 74 Antisdel 11a Arritola 72 Ba Te 26 Bangkok
    Post 73a Baumann 70 Beauclair 56b Benedict 47 Bernatzik 47[*],54

Bernot 71, 72 Bhruksasri 70 Brandt 65 Bruk 59b Brun 73
Bunnaakh 63 Chang, C. 56 Chariwan 70 Charusathira 65
Chaturaphun 70 Cochrane 15 Coolidge & Roosevelt 33 Dauffes 06
Dellinger 67, 69 Dept. Public Welfare 62 Deydier 54 Dussault 24
Eink 68 Embree & Thomas 50ab <u>Encyclopedia Britannica</u> 73
Enriquez 18 Feingold 68-74 Flatz, Pik, & Sringham 65 Flatz &
Sringham 64 Franjola 1972 Gaide 03 Garnier 73 Gau 60 Geddes 65
Grierson 03-28 Halpern 61 Hammerton 22-24 Hanks, J. 64abc
Hanks, Hanks, & Sharp 64, 65 Hanks, Hanks, Sharp, & Sharp 64
Henderson 71ab Henry 03 Hill Tribe Welfare 67ab, 68b Huang 58b
Huard 39 Hudspith 69 Izikowitz 39, 43, 51 Jacobs 70 JUSMAG Psy.
67 JUSMAG Seventh 68 Kacha-ananda 71 Kandre 67 Kanthathatbamrung
65, 67 Katsura 65ab, 66ab, 68c, 70 Kauffman 34 Kerr & Seidenfaden
50 Kickert 66, 67, 69 Kunstadter 67 Lamjuan 69 Larnlue 70 Lasher
63 Layton 68 LeBar & Suddard 60 LeBar, Hickey, & Musgrave 64
Lefèvre-Pontalis 02 Leroi-Gourhan 53 Lewis, E. 69 Lewis, P. 68abc,
69, 69-70*, 70abc, 73, 74 Li, H. 58 Lin, Y. 44c Lindgren 67
Linguistic Survey 17 Lo 45a Macey 07 Madrolle 08, 25 Manndorff 62,
62-63, 63, 65, 66 Manndorff, Scholz, & Volprecht 64-65 Maung Shwe
Wa 63 Menguy 60 Meyer 30 Military RDC 68 Mitsumori 45 Morrock 72
Moseley 67ab, 73 Murchie 69 Nabangxang 64 National Geog. 71 New
China News Agency (NCNA) Kunming 56ac, 59b, 64be, 72b Ngoenyuang
69 Nishida 65-66, 66-67, 67b Nyunt 69 Orléans 98 Oughton 69
Palangtirasin 70 Puttawatana 63 Rajan 70 <u>Rén-mín rì-bào</u> 73
Robinson 75 Roux, H. 24, 52 Ruenyote 67 Saihoo 63ab Saw Aung Din
& Sowards 63 Sayamnotr 66 Scholz 67 Schrock 70 Scott & Hardiman
00 Schweinfurth 69 Seidenfaden 58 Shabad 72 Shafer 38a, 55
Smalley 64 Soulié & Tchang 08 Srisawat 52, 54, 63 Stevenson, H.
44 Story & Story 69 Suo 62 Tatu & Montgomery 69 Telford 17 Temple

10 Teston 32 Thatnaasuwan 68 Tinker 56 Tirrell 72 Tribal Data 71-72 Tribal Research 67-73 United Nations 67 Urbani 71, 74 U.S. Army 61 USOM 63 Walker (ed.) 75 Wang, T. 56 Wen, H. 70 Whitaker 72 White 67 White & Garrett 61 Wiin-tham 73 Wissmann 43 Wood 65 Woods 69 Woodthorpe 97 Wyss 69 Young, O. 61, 67 Yüan 47 Yúnnàn rí-bào 56a

AKHÖ: AKHA
A-LI: YI
ALLO: YI of Indochina
ANU: LUTZU
ANUNG: LISU
A-SI (A-CHE, A-CHI, A-HI, A-HSI, A-XI) (A YI subgroup)
    Gūang 54 Liétard 04, 09ab, 11-12, 13 U.S. Army 61 Yuán 46, 53 Zhāng G 44
A-SU: YI
A-XI: A-SI

BISU
    Nishida 66, 66-67, 67
BOLOTSZE
    Torrance 32
BULI AKHA: AKHA

CHE-NUNG: LISU
COSUNG: YI of INDOCHINA
CUAN (TS'UAN): YI

EKAW: AKHA
EN-CHA: YI of Szechwan

FOU-LA: YI of Indochina

GNI: YI of Yunnan
GU-ZONG (A YI subgroup?)
    Fan 31

HANG-I: WONI
HANI: AKHA or WONI
HAONI: WONI
HEI-I: YI
HEI KUT'OU: YI
HE LOU JEN: YI
HO: YI of Indochina
HONI: WONI
HOUEI-HOUEI: YI
HOUNI: WONI
HOUTSANG: YI
HPON (PHON)
    Leach 54 LeBar, Hickey, & Musgrave 64 Scott & Hardiman 00
    Shafer 55
HUNI: WONI

I: YI
I-BIEN: YI
I-CHIA: YI
I-PIEN: YI

IKHO: AKHA

KADO: WONI
KADU (KUDO, MAWTEIK, PUTEIK, SAK)
    Embree & Thomas 50 Leach 54 LeBar, Hickey & Musgrave 64
    Scott & Hardiman 00 Suo 62
KAKO: AKHA
KAW: AKHA
KELAO: YI of Indochina
KHADO: WONI
KHA KO: AKHA
KHA-TO: YI subgroup of Indochina
KHAE LISAW: LISU
KHAE LISO: LISU
KHO: AKHA
KHUSUNG: YI of Indochina
K'I-LAO: YI subgroup of Indochina
KO: AKHA
KOLO: YI
KONI: WONI
KO-PU: YI
KOUO-LO: YI
K'OU-TS'ONG-JEN: KUTSUNG
KUDO: KADU
KUTSUNG (K'ou-TS'ONG-JEN, K'UTS'UNG) (See also WONI)
    Cordier 15-16 Henry 03 U.S. Army 61

LAGU: LAHU
LAHU (LAGU, LAKU, LOHEI, MUHSO, MUSO, MUSSO, MÛSSÖ, MUSSUH, MUSSUR)

(See also LAHU NA, LAHU NYI)

Adams 74 Anonymous 55, 59, 70ab Anthony & Moorman 64
Antisdel 11abc Arritola 72 Audretch & Chaffee 69 Ba Te 12
Bangkok Tech. 68 Bangkok World 67 Baumann 70 Beauclair 56b
Benedict 48 Bernatzik 40, 47, 54 Bernot 71, 72 Bhruksasri 70
Boon-Itt 6-[?] Bradshaw 52 Brandt 65 Bruk 59b Bunnaag 63
Burling 66, 67 Chang, C. 56 Chao, Y. 43 Chariwan 70
Charusathira 65 Chaturaphun 71 Chen, Y. 64 Cochrane 15
Davies 09 Dept. Public Welfare 62 Diao 67 Embree & Thomas 50ab
Flatz, Pik, & Sringham 65 Flatz & Sringham 64 Franjola 72
Geddes 65 Graham W 24 Grierson 03-28 Gūang-Míng ri-bào 57, 63
Hammerton 22-24 Hanks, J. 64ab Hanks, Hanks, & Sharp 64, 65
Hanks, Hanks, Sharp, & Sharp 64 Henderson 71ab Hill Tribe Welfare
67ab, 68ab, 70 Hinton, P. 68, 69 Huang, C. 58a Hudspith 69
Jamieson, E. 09 Jones, D. 66, 67, 68 JUSMAG Psy. 67 Kandre 67
Kanthathatbamrung 65, 67 Kasemsri 73 Katsura 68ab Kauffmann 34
Keen 73 Kerr 23 Kerr & Seidenfaden 50 Kickert 66 Kunstadter 67
Lamjuan 69 Larnlue 70 Lasher 63 Layton 68 BeBar, Hickey, &
Musgrave 64 Lefèvre-Pontalis 02 Lewis, E. 74 Lewis, P. 70abc
Lewis, P. (ed.) 69-, 70 Lewis, Yohan, & Ca Ui 66 Lin, Y. 44c
Lindgren 67 Linguistic Survey 17 Lyall 65 Madrolle 25 Manndorff
62, 62-63, 63, 65, 66, 70 Manndorff, Scholz, & Volprecht 64-65
Matisoff 66, 67*, 69abc, 70, 72ab, 73ab* Maung Shwe Wa 63 McCarthy
02 McCoy 72 McGilvary 12 Menguy 60 Mieyaa 72, 73 Military RDC 68
Mínzú Huàbào 58 Missions Catholiques 38 Mitsumori 45 Mitton 36
Monpeyrat 05 Moore 34 Morrock 72 Moseley 67ab, 73 Murchie 69
Nabangxang 64 NCNA, Kunming 59d, 63ab, 64be NCNA Peking 59a
Nishida 67b, 69 Oughton 69 Oxibar 59 Palangtirasin 70 Peet 61
Puttawatana 63 Rajan 70 Raquez 02 Rén-mín rì-bào 73 Rorak 69

Ruenyote 67 Ruey 48b Saihoo 63ab Saint-Guily 64 Saw Aung Din & Sowards 63 Sayamnotr 66 Schrock 70 Scott & Hardiman 00 Seidenfaden 30, 58 Shabad 72 Shafer 55 Smythe 64 Spielmann 67, 68ab, 69 Srisawat 52, 54, 63 Stevenson, H. 44 Stevenson, W. 59 Story & Story 69 Tatu & Montgomery 69 Taylor, L. 56 Telford 37, 38*, 49, 53 Telford & Saya Ai Pun 39 Temple 10 Thailand Info. 70 Thamsukati 73 Thavisin 73 Thomson 68 Tinker 56 Tirrell 72 Toa Kenkyujo 40 Tribal Data Project 71-72 Tribal Research 67-73 Trumbull 63 Tung, T. 53 United Nations 67 Urbani 68, 70 U.S. Army 61 United SOM 63 Van Roy 71 Walker 66-69, 69, 70ab*, 72abc*, 73ab 74abcde, 74/75, 75ab Walker (ed.) 75 Webb 12 Weed 69 Wehrli 04 Whitaker 72 Whitaker & Shinn 72 White 67 Wissmann 43 Wood 65 Woods 69 Woodthorpe 97 Wu 55 Yang, C. 63ab Young, H. M. n.d.* Young, H. N. 62 Young, O. 61, 62, 65, 67 Young, V. n.d. Yúnnán rì-bào 56a Zhōng-guó Qīng-nián-bào 56ab

LAHU NA (BLACK LAHU) (See also LAHU)
Bernot 71, 72 Bruk 59b Chaturaphun 71 Jamieson, E. 09 Jones, D. 66, 67* Kerr 23 LeBar, Hickey, & Musgrave 64 Manndorff, Scholz, & Volprecht 64-65 Matisoff 67*, 69abc, 70ab, 73b* Scott & Hardiman 00 Spielmann 68, 69 Telford 37, 38* Walker (ed.) 75 Young, O. 61

LAHU NYI (RED LAHU) (See also LAHU)
Chaturaphun 71 Jamieson, E. 09 Jones, D. 67*, 68 LeBar, Hickey, & Musgrave 64 Walker 66-69, 69, 70ab*, 72abc*, 73ab, 74abcdef, 75ab Walker (ed.) 75 Young, O. 61, 62

LAKA: YI
LAKU: LAHU
LAO-PA: YI of Indochina
LASAW: LISU
LASHI: LISU

LASI: LISU
LAULAU: YI
LEISU: LISU or YI
LEMO (A YI subgroup?)
    NCNA, Kunming 58g
LESHU O-OP'A: LISU
LESOU: LISU
LESUO: LISU
LEUR SEUR: LISU
LI: LISU
LI-HSAW: LISU
LIP'A: LISU
LIP'O: LISU
LISAW: LISU
LI-SHAW: LISU
LISHU: LISU
LISO: LISU
LISSAU: LISU
LISSO: LISU
LISSOU: LISU
LISU (ANUNG, CHE-NUNG, KHAE LISAW, KHAE LISO, LASAW, LASHI, LASI, LEUR SEUR, LESUO, LE SHU O-OP'A, LI, LI-HSAW, LI-SHAW, LISAW, LISO, LISHU, LIP'A, LIP'O, LOISU, LU-TZU, SHISHAM, YAOYEN, YAWYIN, YEH-JEN)
    Aàdsăalii 63 Adams 74 Anderson 71, 76 Anthony & Moorman 64 Arritola 72 Baber 82 Bacot 09, 12, 13 <u>Bangkok Post</u> 73b <u>Bangkok World</u> 73 Barnard 25, 30 Baumann 70 Beauclair 56b Benedict 48 Bernatzik 38, 47, 54 Bernot 71, 72 Bhruksasri 70 Biet & Croizier 77 Boh 67 Bradshaw 52 Brandt 65 Broomhall M 17 Brown 10 Bruk 59ab

Bruk & Apenchenko 64 Bunnaag 63 Burling 67 Carrapiett 29 Chang,
C. 56 Chang, S. 59 Chao, Y. 43 Chariwan 70 Chaturaphun, 71b
Chén 47, 47-48 China News 43 China Pictorial 63 China Reconstructs
60, 69, 75 Chou 63 Clarke 11 Collis 1938 Colquhoun 83, 84 Cooper
71 Cordier 15-16 Cramer 70 Credner 30, 35ab Crider 63 Davies 09
Dawson 12 Dept. Public Welfare 62 Desgodins 72, 73 Dessaint, A.
71ab, 72a*bc Dessaint, W. 63 Dessaint W. & A. 75 Devéria 86
D'Mazure 61 Dǒng & Xúe 59 Dubernard 73, 75 Du Halde 35 Durrenberger
69-70*, 70, 71*, 73, 75abcd Eberhard 42 Eickstedt 44 Embree &
Thomas 50ab Enriquez 21, 23, 24 Fitzgerald 41 Flatz, Pik, &
Sringham 65 Flatz & Sringham 64 Fletcher 27 Forrest 08, 10 Fraser
22*, 38 Fürer-Haimendorf 68 Garnier 73 Geddes 65 Geis 12 George
15 Gill 80 Goré 39 Goullart 55, 57 Graham, W. 24 Gregory &
Gregory 24 Grierson 03-28 Guāng-míng rì-bào 71, 73ab Guebriant
99 Guíbaut 37, 38ab, 40, 47, 67 Guibaut & Liotard 41, 45 Hanks,
J. 64a Hanks, Hanks, & Sharp 64, 65 Hanks, Hanks, Sharp, & Sharp
64 Hansen 60 Henderson 71 Hertz 12 Hill Tribe Welfare 65, 67ab,
68ab, 70 Hope 68, 69, 72, 73 Hsu, H. 65 Hu 60 Huang 58, 59ab, 65
Hudspith 69 Hutton 62 Intharaksa 70 Johnston 08 Jones, P. 66
JUSMAG Psy. 67 Kanthathatbamrung 65, 67 Kauffmann 34, 66 Keen 73
Kerr 23 Kerr & Seidenfaden 50 Kickert 66 Ku n.d. Kuhn 47, 56, 57,
59, 60 Kunstadter 67 Lamjuan 69 Larnlue 70 Lasher 63 Leach 54
LeBar, Hickey, & Musgrave 64 Lee 41 Legendre 13ab Lewis P 70 Lî C
37 Lichiang RCCP 73 Liétard 09, 12, 13 Lin, Y. 44c Lindgren 67
Ling 61 Linguistic Survey 17 Litton 04ab, 06 Lowis 19 Luce 68
Lyall 65 Ma, Y. 58 Madrolle 08 Manndorff 62, 62-63, 63, 65, 66
Manndorff, Scholz, & Volprecht 64-65 Menguy 60 Metford 35 Military
RDC 68 Mínzú Huàbào 63, 66 Mínzú Tuánjié 61, 65 Moore 34, 63
Morrock 72 Morse 62, 74 Moseley 67ab, 73 Murchie 69 Nabangxang 64

National Geog. 71 NCNA, Kunming 55abc, 56b, 58abefghi, 59ace, 64acdfgh, 65ac, 68, 69ab, 70b, 72ade, 73 NCNA, Peking 56a, 58a, 59ac Ng 71 Nishida 66b, 67ab, 68a Ollone 11 Orléans 96, 98 Oughton 69 Palangtirasin 70 Paw, U. 61 Peking Review 75 Playfair 76 Pritchard 14 Puttawatana 63 Rachanee 72 Rajan 70 Rén-mín ri-bào 59a, 62, 63, 70, 72b Rocher 79-80 Rock 47 Rockhill 91 Roop 69, 70* Rose 09, 12 Rose & Coggin Grown 11* Roux, E. 97 Ruenyote 67 Ruey 48a* Saihoo 63ab Sayamnotr 66 Scherman 15 Schrock 70 Scott 21, 32 Scott & Hardiman 00 Seidenfaden 58 Shabad 72 Shafer 55 Shǐ-lào xún-kān 30 Shǐ-shi shou-oe 56ab Siguret 37 Simonnet 49 Smythe 64 Soulié & Tchang 08 Srisawat 52*, 54, 63 Stevenson, H. 44 Stevenson, W. 59 Story & Story 69 Takemura 57-58 Tao 45, 48* Tatu & Montgomery 69 Taw & Eastes 15 Taylor, L. 56 Taylor, M. 44 Telford 37 Temple 10 Terrien 94 Teston 32 Thailand Info. 70 Thomas 65 Thompson, H. 26 Thompson, P. 56 Tinker 56 Tirrell 72 Tong 36 Tribal Data 71-72 Tribal Research 67-73 Tung, T. 53 United Nations 67 U.S. Army 61 USOM 63 Vacca 34 Voegelin & Voegelin 65 Walker 75c Walker (ed.) Wang, L. 59 Wang, S. 55 Wang, T. 56 Ward 12, 13, 18, 20, 21, 23ab, 24, 49, 56 Webb 12 Weed 69 Wehrli 04 Whitaker & Shinn 72 White 67 Wiens 54 Wiin-tham 72 Wilcox 65 Wood 65 Woods 69 Wu 55 Yang T 55 Yang & Wang n.d. Yi 1933 Young, E. 07 Young, O. 61, 67 Yu n.d. Yúnnán ri-bào 56 Zhang, C. 64 Zhang, H. 58 Zhōng-guó Qīng-nián-bào 56b Zhong-guo zuo jia 62 Zui 59

LISUO: LISU
LOHE: YI
LOHEI: LAHU
LOISU: LISU
LO-KUEI: YI

LOLO: YI
LÔ-MI (BLACK HOUNI): WONI
LO-SOU: YI
LOU-LOU: YI
LOUTSE: LUTZU
LU: YI
LULU: YI
LU-MA: AKHA subgroup
LUSU: LISU
LUTZE: LUTZU
LUTZU (ANU, LOUTSE, LUTZE, NOUTZE, NOUTZU, NU, NUSU, NUTSU, NUTZU)
    (See also LISU)
    Beauclair 56b Bruk 59b Chang, C. 56 China News 43 China
    Reconstructs 75 Cooper 71 D'Mazure 61 Dubernard 73 Guāng-míng
    rì-bào 73ac Huang, C. 59 Jones, P. 56 LeBar, Hickey, & Musgrave
    64 Lichiang RCCP 73 Lo, C. 45b Robinson 75 Rose 09 Shabad 72
    U.S. Army 61 Ward 13 Whitaker & Shinn 72
LYSSOU: LISU

MÂBÈ: MÂHÈ
MÂHÈ (MÂBÈ) (A WONI subgroup)
    Gaide 03 Henry 03
MA-KHO: YI of Indochina
MAN-CHIA: YI
MAN-TSE: YI
MAN-TZU: YI
MAU-TSE: YI
MAWTEIK: KADU
MESSU: LAHU

MIMO: NAKHI
MOSO: NAKHI
MOSSO: NAKHI
MOSU: YI
MO XIE: NAKHI
MUC-CHI: AKHA subgroup
MUJI (A YI subgroup?)
    Henry 03
MU-SO: LAHU
MUSSO: LAHU
MÛSSÖ̈: LAHU
MUSSUR: LAHU
MUSSUR: LAHU
NAHSI: NAKHI
NASHI: NAKHI
NEISU: YI
NESU: YI
NGOSU: YI
NISSOU: YI
NO: YI
NORSU: YI
NOSOU: YI
NOSU: YI
NOUTZE: LUTZU
NOUTZU: LUTZU
NU: LUTZU
NU-JEN: LUTZU
NUNG: LUTZU
NU-QUAY: AKHA subgroup
NUSU: LUTZU

NUTSU: LUTZU
NUTZU: LUTZU

O-MA: AKHA subgroup
O'PA: AKHA subgroup
OUANG LOLO: YI

PANGLUNG: PENGLUNG
PEI-I: YI
PEI KU T'OU: YI
PENGLUNG (PANGLUNG)
    Huang 58a NCNA, Peking 59c
PEUNN-JEN: WONI or YI
PEU-PA: YI of Indochina
PHON: HPON
PHU-SANG: AKHA subgroup
PI-YO (WHITE HOUNI): WONI
PIZA: WONI
POULA: YI of Indochina
POUTOU: WONI
PUDU: WONI
PULA (A YI subgroup)
    Henry 03 NCNA, Kunming 60 b Orléans 98
PULANG (BULANG)
    Huang 58a NCNA, Kunming 63a
PULI: AKHA
PUPIAO: YI of Indochina
PUTEIK: KADU

SAK: KADU
SANI: A YI subgroup
    Ma, X. 40, 51 U.S. Army 61
SANSU (A YI subgroup?)
    Henry 03
SHANI (A YI subgroup)
    Huang, Yang, and Liu 54 Yang, G. 55ab
SHISHAM: LISU
SHU-CHING: YI
SIANG-TAN: YI
SI-MOU-LOU: WONI
SU-KO: YI

T'OU-JEN: YI
TOULAO: YI
T'OU-MIN: YI
TRUNG
    Lo 45d
TSI-CHO: YI
TS'UAN: YI
TSUAN-MAN: YI
TULI
    Lyall 65
TULUNG
    China Reconstructs 75 NCNA, Peking 68 NCNA, Kunming 58g, 72e
    Peking Review 75
UNI: WONI

WOLI: WONI

WONI (HANI, HAONI, HONI, HUNI, KONI, KUTSUNG, WUNI) (See also AKHA)
 Beauclair 56 Central Census 60 Davies 09 Ha, B. 64 Henry 03
 Hu & Dai 64 Huang 58b Jiang 58 Kao 55, 58 LeBar, Hickey, &
 Musgrave 64 Lefèvre-Pontalis 02 Li, H. 38 Lo 45a Madrolle 25
 Mong 57 Orléans 98 Teston 32 U.S. Army 61 Wissmann 43 Yuan 47, 48
WU-MAN: YI
WU-NI: WONI

XA: YI of Indochina
XA-PHO: YI of Indochina

YA LOHE: YI
YAOYEN: LISU
YAW-YEN: LISU
YAWYIN: LISU
YE-REN: LISU
YEH-JEN: LISU
YELANG: NAKHI
YI (A-HSI, ASI, HEI-I, HEI KU T'OU, I, I-BIEN, I-CHIA, KOLO, KO-PU,
 KOUO-LO, LAKA, LAULAU, LEISU, LOHĒ, LO-KUEI, LOLO, LOU-LOU,
 MAN-CHIA, MAN-TZU, MAU-TSE, MOSU, NEISU, NESU, NGOSU, NISSOU,
 NO, NORSU, NOSU, PEI-I, PEI KU T'OU, PULA, SHANI, T'OU-JEN,
 TSUAN-MAN, WU-MAN, Y-JIN) (See also YI of Indochina, YI of
 Kweichow, YI of Szechwan, YI of Yunnan) Abadie 24 Ainscough 15
 Asian Analyst 69 Baber 82 Bastian 66-71 Beauclair 56ab Beauvais
 07 Benedict 41, 47, 48, 72 Bernatzik 54 Bernot 71, 72 Bertreux
 22 Bishop 99 Boell 99 Boiteux 35 Bonifacy 05, 06, 08, 19, 24
 Bonin 99, 03, 07, 11 Bons 04ab Boucher 35 Bourne 88 Boutmy 89
 Bridgman 59 Broomhall, A. 47, 53 Broomhall, M. 07, 17 Bruk 59ab

Bruk & Apenchenko 64 Buchanan 70 Carey 99 Carriquiry 39 Chang, C.
56 Chang, J. 52 Chang, S. 59 Chao, W. 50 Chao, Y. 43 Charria 05
Chavannes 06, 09ab, 12 Chazarain-Wetzel 10 Chen, Z. 48ab, 72
Cheng & Liang 45 Chevalier 99 Chieri 43 China at War 41 China
Journal 31 China News 43 China Reconstructs 53, 73, 75 Clarke, H.82,
83 S. 11 Colquhoun 83, 84, 85 Cook 36 Cordier 07 Crabouillet 73
Cultural & Ed. Sect. 58 Cunningham 33 Davies 09 De Francis 51
Dessirier 23 Devéria 86, 91 Diao 67 Ding 35, 36 Diringer 62
Dŏng 40 Dreyer 70 Eberhard 42, 43, 68 Edgar 34 Edkins 71 Eickstedt
44 Fang 45abc Farjenel 10 Fei 51-52, 52 Fei & Lin 56 Feng &
Shryock 38 Fenouil 62 Fergusson 10, 11 Février 48 Fides 42
Fitzgerald 41 Fleurelle 10 Franck 25 François 04 Fu 44ab, 45ab,
51, 57 Gaide 03 Garnier 73 Gjessing 57 Gould 85 Goullart, 55, 59
Gourdin 79 Graham, D. 26-29, 30, 31, 54, 55 Graham, S. 61
Grillières 05 Guāng-míng rì-bào 59, 72ab Guébriant 99, 08
Haberlandt 22-23 Hammerton 22-24 Hart 88 Haudricourt 57-58
Henry 02, 03 Hestermann 15 Hicks 10 Hinton, H. 55 Hsin 73 Hsu,
H. 38, 42 Hsú, Ĭ. 32, 42, 44 Hsu, K. 75 Huang 58b Investigation
Gp. 71 Its 68 Jack 04 Jamieson C 23 Jensen 35 Ji 58 Jiang, D. 38,
48ab Ji-niu-bu 71 Johnston 08 Jones, P. 66 Kao 58 Kauffmann 34
Ko 38, 49 Kunstadter 67 Lasker 50 Laufer 16 LeBar, Hickey, &
Musgrave 64 Lê 55 Leclère 00 Lefèvre-Pontalis 92, 02 Legendre
05, 09ab, 10abcd, 13ab Lei, B. 21 Leparoux 05 Le Roux 35 Lévi-
Strauss 49 Li, Fei, & Chang 43 Liao 40 Lichiang RCCP 73 Liétard
04, 09ab, 11-2, 12, 13*, 47 Lǐn, H. 31 Lǐn, Y. 44abcd, 46, 47*
Lǐng, C. 38 Lǐng, G. 48, 50 Liu, C. 54 Liu, C.H. 32, 37 Lǐu, Y.
54 Lo, C. 44ab, 45ac, 50 Lowy 47 Luce 68 Lunet 06 Mǎ, C. 42-44
Mǎ, X. 31, 40, 44, 47, 48ab, 49, 51, 55, 62 Ma, T. 76-83 Madrolle
98, 08 Maire 82 Matsuzaki 47 Meares 09ab Meillet & Cohen 52

Menguy 60 Měngzàng xún-kān 35 Mesny 84 Mínzú Huàbào 65 Mínzú
Túanjie 59 Missions Catholiques 81-82, Morrock 72 Moseley 67c,
73 Mueller 13 Nature 88 NCNA, Chaochueh 56ab NCNA, Chengtu
56abcde, 58ab, 59abcd, 63abc, 64ab, 65abcdefg, 66,
71, 73 NCNA, Kunming 56bcd, 58cd, 59be, 60ab, 61, 63a, 64be, 65bc
70a, 71, 72abce NCNA, Kwieyang 59, 73 NCNA, Peking 56b, 58b, 59b,
72 Newsweek 46 Ollone 07abcd, 11, 12ab Orléans 98 Parker 95
Parsons 31 Pelliot 04 People's Republic 54 Playfair 76 Pollard
11, 21 Pua 58 Qŭ 34 Ratzel 88 Reclus 02 Reinhard 55, 56 Rén-mín
rì-bào 59bc, 72a, 73 Richthofen 03 Rocher 79-80 Rock 47 Rockhill
91, 95 Roy 53 Sainson 04 Savina 30 Shabad 65, 72 Shafer 38b, 52,
55 Shiratori 57 Shirokogoroff 30 Snow 37, 62 Soulié & Tchang 08
Starr 11 Start & Wright 36 Stevenson, P. 27, 32 Stevenson, W. 59
Stübel 52 Studia Serica 40-41 Sun 42 Szèchwan rì-bào 56 Takemura
57-58 Taw & Eastes 15 Taylor, L. 56 Terrien 82abc, 94ab Thompson,
V. 37 Tie 59 Tian 59 Tiessen 07 Tilke 45 Torrance 32 Tsung 54
Tung, T. 53 Upcraft 92 Valtat 15 Vannicelli 44 Vaulserre 07 Vial
88, 90ab, 93-94, 98*, 09, 17 Vissière 14 Wa-cha-mu-chi & Wang 59
Wang, C. 51 Wang, H. 59 Wang, L. 59 Wang, M. 46 Wang, S. 55
Wang, T. 56 Wang, W. 59 Wén, B. 24 Wén, C. 36 Wén, X. 70 Wén, Y.
36ab, 40ab, 45, 47, 48, 50 Whitaker & Shinn 72 Wiens 54, 62, 73
Wilson 71 Winnington 59* Wissmann 43 Xia 28 Yang, C. 30, 32, 33,
34ab, 35, 36ab Yang, G. 55ab Yang, K. 56 Yaoshan CPC 72 Yu, K. 42
Yu, Y. 67 Yúan 46, 53 Yúnnán rì-bào 56ab Zaborowski-Moindron 00,
01, 02, 04, 05 Zēng 47 Zhang G 44 Zhuang 41

YI of Indochina (COSUNG, FOU-LA, HO, KHUSUNG, LAO-PA, PEU-PA, POULA,
PUPIAO, SILA, XA, XA-PHO) (See also YI)
Abadie 24 Bonifacy 05, 06, 08, 19, 24 Bruk 59a Central Census 60
Coolidge & Roosevelt 33 Diguet 08 Dussault 24 Ecole Francaise 21

　　　　Gourou 51 Ha, V. 56 Lê 55 LeBar, Hickey, & Musgrave 64 LeBar &
　　　　Suddard 60 Leroi-Gourhan 53 Lunet 04, 06 Madrolle 25 Nguyen 34
　　　　Nhom Nghien 59 Schrock 72 Smith H 67 Teston 32 Tuyen 73, 75
YI of Kweichow (See also YI)
　　　　Beauclair 56b Bourne 88 Clarke 11 Fei 51-52 LeBar, Hickey, &
　　　　Musgrave 64 NCNA, Kwieyang 59, 73 Winnington 59*
YI of Szechwan (BLACK LOLO, INDEPENDENT LOLO, NOSU, YI of TA LIANG
　　　SHAN) (See also YI)
　　　　Beauclair 56b Broomhall, A. 47, 53 Chang, Shi, & Yu 35 Chi 58
　　　　Chieri 43 <u>China Reconstructs</u> 53 Clarke 11* Cook 36 Crabouillet
　　　　73 Cultural & Ed. Sect. 58 Cunningham 33 Dèng 30 <u>Dì-xué zá-zhì</u>
　　　　13, 22 Du 59 Fei & Lin 56 Feng & Shryock 38 Fergusson 10, 11
　　　　Franck 25 Fu 44ab, 45ab, 51 Goullart 55 <u>Guāng-míng rì-bào</u> 59
　　　　Hammerton 22-24 Hicks 10 Hu 57 Investigation Gp. 71 Jǔn 35 Ko 49
　　　　LeBar, Hickey, & Musgrave 64 Legendre 10d Lǐ X 35-36 Lín, Y. 44b,
　　　　46, 47 Lo, C. 44-45 Mǎ, C. 42-44 Ma, X. 44 <u>Mínzú Huàbào</u> 65 <u>Mínzú
　　　　Tuánjié</u> 59 Missions Catholiques 81-82 NCNA, Chaochueh 56ab NCNA,
　　　　Chengtu 56a, 58ab, 59abd, 63bc, 64ab, 65abcefg, 66, 71, 73 Ollone
　　　　07abcd, 11 Parsons 31 Pollard 11, 21 <u>Rén-mín rì-bào</u> 59bc, 72a
　　　　Sun 42 Tian 10 Tie 59 Valtat 15 Wa-cha-mu-chi & Wang 59 Wang, C.
　　　　51 Wang, H. 59 Wang, W. 59 Wén, J. 53 Winnington 59* Wú, S. 22, 35
　　　　Zēng 45, 47 <u>Zhōng-guó yín-háng</u> 35
YI of Yunnan
　　　　Boutmy 89 Buchanan 70 Carey 99 Chang, C. 56 Chazarain-Wetzel 10
　　　　Chiang 48 China News 43 Colquhoun 84 Cordier 15-16 Davies 09
　　　　Henry 03 LeBar, Hickey, & Musgrave 64 Leclère 00 Legendre 13ab,
　　　　Lei, J. 44 Lǐ, C. 37 Lín, Y. 44c MacFarquhar 59 Madrolle 25 NCNA,
　　　　Kunming 56bcd, 58cd, 59be, 60ab, 61, 63a, 64be, 65bc, 70a, 71,
　　　　72abce Orléans 98 Pu 58 Rocher 79-80 Snow 62 <u>Studia Serica</u> 40-41

-336-

Tian 59 Vial 88, 90ab, 93-94, 98, 09, 17 Wén, Y. 40a, 45 Wissmann 43 Yang, C. 29, 31abc, 34c Yang, C. 56 Yǐ, F. 35 Yǐ, M. n.d. Yúnnán rì-bào 56ab Zaborowski-Moindron 01, 02 Zhang 29 Zhāo 28

YI-CHIA: YI
YI-KIA: YI
Y-JEN: YI
Y-JIN: YI
Y-KIA: YI
YOLO: YI

INDEX BY PERIODICAL

This index lists the periodical source, followed by references to the authors published therein and the last two digits of the publication date. Reviews are indexed under the author being reviewed. Place of publication is indicated only when the periodical is not well known and the title is not descriptive.

Academia Sinica: Lì shǐ yǔ yán yán jiū suǒ, and Shè huì kē xué yán jiū suǒ
Acta Linguistica Hafniensia (Copenhagen), Matisoff 69bc, n.d. (a)
Acta Orientalia, Brun 73 Walker 74b
Acta Sociologica, Gjessing 57
Agricultural Credit Newsletter (Bangkok), Hinton, P. 68
American Academy of Political and Social Science, Annals, De Francis 51
American Anthropological Association, Annual Meeting Papers, Durrenberger 70, 73 Feingold 69a, 70, 73b, 74
American Anthropologist, Ch'en, T. 34 Graham, D. 30 Van Roy 71
American Journal of Sociology, Ko 49
American Oriental Society, Journal, Benedict 48 Matisoff 70
Annales de Géographie, Guibaut & Liotard 41, 45
Annales de la Propagation de la Foi, Fenouil 62
Annales d'Hygiene et de Medicine Coloniales, Gaide 03
Annals of Human Genetics, Flatz, Pik, & Sringham 65 Flatz & Sringham 64
Anthropological Institute: Royal Anthropological Institute
Anthropological Linguistics, Lewis, P. 68b, 73 Voegelin & Voegelin 65
Anthropological Quarterly, Durrenberger 75c

Anthropologie, L', Guibaut 40
Anthropos, Liétard 12 Vannicelli 44 Yang, C. 36b
Archiv für Anthropologie, Scherman 15
Archiv für Völkerkunde, Manndorff 62-63
Asia, Sun 42
Asia Major, Fu 51
Asian Folklore Studies, Durrenberger 75d
Asiatic Review, Ollone 12b
Asiatic Society of Bengal, Journal, Brown 10 D'Mazure 61
    Rose & Coggin Brown 11
Asie du Sud-est et Monde Insulindien, Bernot 71, 72 Scherman 15
Asie Française, Ollone 12b
Asie Française, Comité: Comité Asie Francaise
Athenaeum, The, Clarke, H. 82 Terrien 82a
Atlantis, Bernatzik 40
A Travers le Monde, Chazarain-Wetzel 10 Fleurelle 10

Baessler Archiv, Mueller 13 Reinhard 55, 56
Bangkok Post, Bangkok Post 73ab Kasemsri 73 Palangtirasin 70
    Thamsukati 73 Thavisin 73
Bangkok Post Magazine: Standard Bangkok Magazine

Bangkok World Bangkok World 67, 73 Chariwan 70 Larnlue 70
Behavior Science Notes, Benedict 75 Dessaint 71a Jones, D. 68 Lewis,
    P. 68c
Bian-jiang ren-wen (Border Culture and Humanities), Lo, C. 44a, 45c
Bian-jiang yen-jiu lun-cong (Pien-chiang yen-chiu lun-tsung)
    (Frontier Studies), Ma, C. 42-44 Tao 45
Bian-zheng gong-lun (Pien-cheng kung-lun) (Frontier Affairs)

-339-

Chén, Z. 47-48, 48ab Fang 45abc Hsú, I. 42 Jǐ 44 Léi, J. 44
Lǐn, Y. 44bd Lǐng, G. 48 Lo, C. 44b, 45b Mǎ, X. 44, 47, 48b Wēn &
Yáng 42

Bijdragen tot de Taal-, Land-en Volkenkunde, Durrenberger 75a

Bollettino della Reale Società Geografica Italiana: Reale Società

Border Political Commentary: Biān-zhēng gōng lùn

British Association for the Advancement of Science, Report,
    Henry 02

Bulletin de l'Université l'Aurore: Université l'Aurore

Bulletin du Museum, Legendre & Lemoine 10

Bulletin on Narcotics, Saihoo 63a United Nations 67

Burma Gazetteer, George 15 Hertz 12

Burma Research Society, Journal, Antisdel 11abc Ba Te 12, 26
    Barnard 25 Enriquez 21, 23b Luce 68 Taw & Eastes 15
    Taylor, L. 56 Telford 37

Catholic Life,   Rorak 69

Census of India, Geis 12

Central Asian Society, Journal, Barnard 30

Chéng-dū dà-xúe shǐ xúe zá-zhì (Chengtu University Historical Magazine),
    Dèng 30

Chiang Mai, Intharaksa 70

China at War, China at War 41 China News 43

China Journal, The, China Journal 31 Stevenson, P. 27

China Journal of Science and Arts, Jamieson, C. 23

China Magazine, The, Wang M 46

China Monthly Review, Chang, J. 52 Fei 51-52

China News Agency, China News 43

China Pictorial, China Pictorial 63 Chou 63
China Reconstructs, China Reconstructs 53, 60, 69, 73, 75
    Hsin 73 Hsu, H. 65 Hsu, K. 75 Ma, H. 55, 62 Wu 55
China Review, Kingsmill 00-01 Playfair 76
China Weekly Review, Lee 41
Chinese Culture (Taipei), Tung, T. 53
Chinese Literature, Yang, G. 55ab
Chinese Recorder, Upcraft 92
Chinese Recorder and Educational Review (Shanghai), Ts'ai 41
Chinese Recorder and Missionary Journal (Shanghai), Edkins 71
    Hicks 10
Chuān biān ji-kān (Szechuan Border Quarterly), Wú, S. 35 Zhōng-guó yín-háng 35
Chūng-kuó Ch'ing-nien pao: See Zhōng-guó Qīng-nián-bào
Chūng-kuó wen-hua yen-chiu hui-k'an: Zhōng-guó wén-huà yán-jiū huì-kān
Chūng-kuó yu-wen: See Zhōng-guó yǔ-wén
Chūng yāng yen chiu yuan: Lì shǐ yǔ yán yán jiū suǒ
Comité Asie-Française, Bulletin, Cordier 07 Davies 09 Legendre 09b
Congres des Sciences Anthropologiques et Ethnologiques,
    Spielmann 68a Yang, C. 34a Feingold 68, 73c
Cultural Reconstruction: Wén-huà jiàn-shè
Current Affairs: Shí-shì shǒu-cè
Current Background (Hong Kong), Fei & Lin 56 Shí-shì shǒu-cè 56ab

Dà-lù zá-zhì (Continental Magazine), Ling 53
Dì-lǐ xué-bào (Geographical Bulletin), Ding 35
Dì-lǐ xué-jí (Geographical Quarterly), Yi 33
Dì-lǐ zá-zhì (Geographical Magazine), Lei, B. 21
Dì-xué zá-zhì (Geographical Magazine), Wú, S. 13, 22 Yang, C. 34b

Documentation Française, La, Menguy 60
Dú-lì pǐng-lùn (Independent Critic), Wén, J. 53

Eastern Horizon (Hong Kong), Robinson 75
Eastern World, Smythe 64
Ecole Française d'Extrême-Orient, Bulletin, Beauvais 07
 Bonifacy 05, 08 Charria 05 Dauffès 06 Davies 10
 Ecole Française 21 Liètard 09ab Lunet 04, 06 Maitre 08
 Maitre & d'Ollone 09 Meillier 18 Ollone 07c Pelliot 04ab
 Roux, H. 24 Soulié & Tchang 08 Vissière 14 Wen, Y. 40b
Enciclopedia Italiana, Vacca 34
Encyclopedia Britannica, Encyclopedia Britannica 73 Fürer-Haimendorf
 68 Hutton 62 Shabad 65 Wiens 73
Ethnology, Dessaint 71b
Ethnos, Izikowitz 39, 43
Eveil Economique de l'Indochine, L' (Hanoi), Bonifacy 23
Extracts from China Mainland Magazines (superseded by Selections
 from China Mainland Magazines) (Hong Kong), Du 59
 Wa-cha-mu-chi & Wang 59 Wang, W. 59
Explorer's Journal, Young, O. 62

Fāng-zhǐ yùe-kān (Fang-zhi Monthly), Qǔ 34
Far Eastern Economic Review, Fei 52 Franjola 72 Hinton, H. 55
 Jones, P. 66 Moseley 67ab Thomson 68 Walker 73ab
Far Eastern Quarterly (superseded by Journal of Asian Studies),
 Benedict 47
Far Eastern Survey, Hu, H. 42
Feuilles Missionnaires, Mieyaa 72, 73 Oxibar 59 Saint-Guily 64
 Urbani 68, 70, 71, 74

Folk, Dessaint, W. & A. 75 Walker 74-75
Forward (Rangoon), Boh 67
Foundations of Language, Hope 73
France-Asie, Roux 52
Freedomways, Graham, S. 61
Frontier Affairs: Biān-zhèng gōng-lùn
Frontier Politics (Nan-k'ai State University), Yüan 46
Frontier Studies: Biān-jiāng yén-jiù lùn-cóng

Geographical Journal, The, Carey 99 Chao, Y. 43 Davies 09
    Fergusson 10 Forrest 08 Geographical Journal 09
    Ward 12, 18, 20, 23a Meares 09ab Orléans 96 Pollard 21
    Pritchard 14 Rose 09, 12 Thompson, H. 26 Young, E. 07
Geographical Magazine, The, Ng 71
Geographical Magazine: Dì-xúe zá-zhì or Dì-lì zá-zhì or Dì-lì xúe-bào
Geographical Review, Stevenson P 32
Géographie, La., Bonin 07 Bons 04a Cordier 07 Grillières 05
    Guibaut 38b Leclère 00 Ollone 07cd Vaulserre 07 Zaborowski-
    Moindron 00
Guāng-míng rì-bào (Guang-ming Daily) (Peking), Cultural & Ed.
    Sect. 58 Guāng-míng rì-bào 57, 59, 63, 71, 72ab, 73abc Jiang 58
    Li, H. 58 Ma, Y. 58 Pu 58 Wen, X. 70 Yang, Z. 63a Yang, T. 55
    Zhang, X. 58
Guardian, The: Burma's National Magazine, Nyunt 69
Gúo-jì wén-hùa (Kúo-chì wén-hùa) (International Culture)
    (Peking), Ruey 48b

Harvard Journal of Asiatic Studies, Feng & Shryock 38

Guibaut 38a Lin, Y. 46 Lo, C. 45ad
Hé běi dì yī bó wù yuàn huà bào (First Museum of Hopei Pictorial), Lǐ, X. 35-36
Historical Material Quarterly: Shǐ-liào xún-kān
Hóng-qí (Red Flag) (Peking), Chi-niu-pu 71 Lichiang RCCP 73
    Yaoshan Commune 72
Hsīn-huá shè: New China News Agency
Hsin-nan pien-chiang wen-t'i yen-chiu pao-kao (Hua-chung College):
    see Xī-nán biān-jiāng wèn-tí yán-jiū bào-gào
Hsin ning-yuan: see Xin ning-yuan
Huá xī xié hé dà xué zhōng guó wén huà yán jiū suǒ: Studia Serica
Human Relations Area Files, Bernatzik 47 Davies 09 Fitzgerald 41
    Graham, W. 24 Lǐn, Y. 47 Tao 45 Clarke 11
Hūng-ch'i: Hóng-qí

Indian Antiquary, Parker 95
Institut Indochinois pour l'Etude de l'Homme, Bulletin (Hanoi),
    Huard 39
Internationales Archiv für Ethnographie, Wehrli 04
International Culture: Guó-jì wén-huà
International Journal of American Linguistics, Burling 67
International Review of Missions, Broomhall, M. 17

Jén-min Jih-pào: Rén-mín rì-bào
Jiào-yù zá-zhì (Educational Magazine), Tian 10
Jīn-líng Xué-bào (Nanking Journal), Ko 38
Joint Publications Research Service (Washington, D.C.), Ha, B. 64,
    Ha, V. 56 Tie 59
Journal Asiatique, Chavannes 09ab Davies 09 Devéria 91

Farjenel 10 Lefévre-Pontalis 92 Vissière 14
Journal of American Folklore, Graham, D. 55
Journal of Asian Studies, Benedict 72 Matisoff 69a, 71
Journal of Social Science Research (Bangkok), Puttawatana 63
Journal of Sociology and Anthropology (Chiang Mai University),
 Bhruksasri 70 Lewis, P. 69
Journal of Southeast Asian Studies (Singapore), Van Roy 71
Journal of the Indian Archipelago and Eastern Asia, Logan 58
Kāng-zàng qián-bàng (Sikang-Tibet Pioneer), Jūn 35
Kúang-míng Jih-pào: Gūang-míng rì-bào
Kúo-chī wén hùa: see Gúo-jì wén-hùa

Language, Burling 67
Lì shǐ yǔ yán yán jiū sǔo, Zhōng yāng yán jiū yuàn (Lì shǐh yǔ
 yén yén chiù sǒ, Chūng yāng yén chiù yùan) (Bulletin of the
 Institute of History and Philology, Academia Sinica), Líng, C. 38
Mǎ, X. 48a, 49 Ruey 48a Shirokogoroff 30 Tao 48 Yang, C. 30b, 33
Líng-nán Xúe-bào (lingnan Bulletin), Yang, C. 30
Lotus, Le, Vial 90b

Man, Liu, C. 32, 37
Manchester Memoirs, Start & Wright 36
Méng-zàng xún-kān (Mongolian-Tibetan Quarterly), Méng-zàng xún-kān 35
Mín-sú (Minority Customs), Yang, C. 29
Mínzú Huàbào (Nationalities Pictorial), Gau 60 Mínzú Huàbào 58, 63,
 65, 66 Suo 62 Yang, C. 63b
Mínzú Túanjie (Nationalities Unity), Chen, Y. 64 Du 59 Huang 59a
 Mínzú Túanjie 59, 65 Tie 59 Wa-cha-mu-chi & Wang 59 Zhang, C. 64
Mín-zú Xúe-yùan (Nationalities Research), Dǒng 40 Ma, C. 46

Missionary Review of the World, Parsons 31

Missions Catholiques, Les, Boiteux 35 Boucher 35 Boutmy 89 Carriquiry 39 Chauveau 73 Crabouillet 73 Dubernard 73 Fides 42 Gourdin 79 Guébriant 99, 08 Leparoux 05 Le Roux 35 Lesserteur 78 Liétard 04, 09a Maire 82 Missions Catholiques 81-82, 38 Ollone 12b Valtat 15 Vial 88, 93-94, 17

Mitteilungen der Anthropologischen Gesellschaft in Wien, Manndorff 62, 65, 70

Mitteilungen Deutsche Gesellschaft für Natur- und Völkerkunde Ostasiens (Tokyo), Rheinwald 42

Mitteilungen k. k. Geographisch und Geologisch Wien, Davies 09

Moniteur d'Indochine, Bonifacy 24

Monumenta Serica, Ch'en, T. 47 Eberhard 43

Nanking Journal: Jīn-líng Xué-bào

Nation, The (Bangkok), Rachanee 72

National Geographic, Forrest 10 Lowy 47 Moore 34, 63 National Geographic 71 Perazic 60 Smith, A. 30 White 61, 67

Nationalities Pictorial: Mínzú Huàbào

Nationalities Unity: Mínzú Tuánjié

National Research Council (Bangkok), Katsura 65ab Matisoff 66 Nishida 67b Spielmann 67

Natural History, Dessaint 72c

Nature, Cummingham 33 Nature 88

New Asia: Xīn-yǎ Xī-yǎ

New China News Agency (Hsin-hua she), Investigation Gp. 71

New China News Agency (Chaochueh), 56ab

New China News Agency (Chengtu), 56abcde, 58ab, 59abcd, 63abc, 64ab, 65abcdefg, 66, 71, 73
New China News Agency (Kunming), 55abc, 56abcd, 58abcdefghi, 59abcde, 60ab, 61,63ab, 64abcdefgh, 65abc, 68, 69ab, 70ab, 71, 72abcde, 73 Huang 59b Wang, T. 56
New China News Agency (Kweiyang), 59, 73
New China News Agency (Peking), 56ab, 58ab, 59abc, 68, 72 Ji-niu-bu 71 Yaoshan Commune 72
New Leader, The, MacFarquhar 59
New York Times, Trumbull 63
Newsweek, Newsweek 46
Nhan Dan (The people) (Hanoi), Central Census 60 Ha, B. 64, Ha, V. 56, Mong 57
North China Herald, Richthofen 03 Starr 11
Onso Kagaku Kenkyū: Studia Phonologica
O.S.T. (Bangkok), Thatnaasuwan 68
Pacific Affairs, Dreyer 70 Tinker 56
Peking Review, Chang, S. 59 Huang 58a, 65 Peking Review 75 Wang, L. 59
People's China (superseded by Peking Review), Fu 57 Liu, C. 54 Tsung 54 Wang, C. 51
People's Literature, Yang, G. 55ab
Pien-cheng kung-lun: Bian-zheng gong-lun
Pien-chiang yen-chiu lun-tsung: Bian-jiang yen-jiu lun-cong
Public Museum of the City of Milwaukee, Bulletin, Starr 11

Quarterly Bulletin of Chinese Bibliography, Liu, H. 40-41

Reale Società Geografica Italiana, Bollettino, Chieri 43
Reconstruction Weekly, Ren n.d.

Record, The (Board of Commercial Development, Siam), Kerr 23
Rén-mín rì-bào (People's Daily) (Peking), Dǒng & Xué 59
    Fei & Lin 56 Huang 58b Rén-mín rì-bào 59abc, 62, 63, 70,
    72ab, 73 Tian 59 Wang, H. 59
Revue de l'Ecole d'Anthropologie, Legendre 10d Zaborowski-Moindron 05
Revue de l'Extrême-Orient, Mesny 84
Revue des Troupes Coloniales (Hanoi), Bonifacy 06b
Revue d'Ethnographie et de Sociologie, Bacot 12
Revue Indochinoise, Cordier 15-16 Fleurelle 10 Macey 07 Monpeyrat 05
Revue Universelle, Zaborowski-Moindron 02
Royal Anthropological Institute of Great Britain and Ireland, Journal,
    Colquhoun 84 Henry 03 Hsiao 46 Woodthorpe 97
Royal Asiatic Society, Journal, Terrien 82b Walker 72b, 74c
Royal Asiatic Society of Bengal: Asiatic Society of Bengal
Royal Asiatic Society, Hong Kong Branch, Journal, Wiens 62
Royal Asiatic Society, North China Branch, Journal, Bridgman 59
    Clarke 11 Davies 09
Royal Asiatic Society, West China Branch, Journal, Cunningham 33
    Graham, D. 26-29
Royal Geographic Society, Supplementary Papers, Baber 82 Terrien 82c
Royal Siam Society: Siam Society
Royal Society of Arts, Journal, Temple 10

Sawaddi (American Women's Club of Thailand) (Bangkok),
    Arritola 72 Layton 68 Lewis, E. 69, 74 Lewis, P. 74
    Morse 74 Young, O. 65
Schriften zur Geopolitik, Wissmann 43
SEATO Record, Geddes 65
Selections from China Mainland Magazines (Hong Kong),

Ji-niu-bu 71 Lichiang Regional 73

Shakai Jinruigaku (Social Anthropologist) (Tōkyō), Takemura 57-58

Shàng-yóu (Upstream) (Chengtu), Wang, W. 59

Shè huì kē xué yán jiū suǒ, Zhōng yāng yán jiū yuàn (Bulletin of the Social Science Research Institute, Academia Sinica), Lin, H. 31

Shēng bào yuè-kān (Shēn Pào Monthly), Yì, F. 35

Shí-shì shǒu-cè (Shih-shih shǒu-tsè) (Current Affairs), 56ab

Shǐ-liào xún-kān (Historical Material Quarterly) 30

Shuō-wén yuè (Shūowén Monthly), Zhūang, X. 42

Siam Society, Journal, Dessaint 72b Durrenberger 75b Kacha-ananda 71 Metford 35 Roux 52 Seidenfaden 30 Spielmann 69 Walker 70a, 72a, 74af, 75a Wongprasert 75

Sinologica, Beauclair 56a

Sino-tibetica, Shafer 38ab

Sino-Tibetan Language and Linguistic Studies, International Conference, Matisoff 73c

Smithsonian Institution, Annual Report, Legendre 10d

Société Academique Indochinoise, Mémoires, Biet & Crozier 77

Société d'Anthropologie de Paris, Bulletin et Mémoires, Bonifacy 06 Francois 04 Legendre 10ab, 13b Zaborowski-Moindron 00, 01, 04

Société de Géographie de Hanoi, Cahiers, Bonifacy 24 Dussault 24

Société de Géographie de l'Est, Bulletin, Fleurelle 10 Legendre 10a

Société de Géographie de Lyon et de la region lyonnaise, Bulletin, Ollone 07ab

Société de Géographie de Paris, Bulletin (superseded by La Géographie), Desgodins 75

Société de Geographie de Paris, Compte Rendu, Bonin 99
Société Linguistique de Paris, Bulletin, Haudricourt 57-58
   Shafer 38b
Sociologus, Manndorff 63, 66 Stübel 52
Southeast Asia, Durrenberger 74 Walker 74d
Southeast Asian Studies: Tōnan Ajia Kenkyū
Southern California Occasional Papers in Linguistics,
   Matisoff 73a
Southwest Literature, Yang, G. 55b
Sovetskaia Etnografiia, Bruk 58
Standard Bangkok Magazine (Sunday Supplement to Bangkok World),
   Chaturaphun 70, 71ab Eink 68
Studia Phonologica (Kyoto), Nishida 65-66
Studia Serica (Huá xī xié hé da xué zhōng guó wén huà yán jiu suǒ)
   Bernatzik 47 Chao 50 Studia Serica 40-41 Wen, Y. 40ab, 50
Sun Yat-sen University: Zhōng-shān da-xué
Survey of China Mainland Press (Hong Kong), Cultural & Ed.
   Sect. 58 Dǒng & Xué 59 Huang 59b Investigation Gp. 71
   Jiang 58 Ji-niu-bu 71 Li, H. 58 NCNA, Chaochueh 56ab
   NCNA, Chengtu 56abcde, 58ab, 59abcd, 63abc, 64ab,
   65abcdefg, 66, 71, 73 NCNA, Kunming 55abc, 56abcd, 58abcdefghi,
   59abcde, 60ab, 61, 63ab, 64abcdefgh, 65abc, 68, 69ab, 70ab, 71,
   72abcde, 73 NCNA, Kweiyang 59, 73 NCNA, Peking 56ab, 58ab, 59abc,
   68, 72 Pu 58 Szēchwān ri-bao 56 Tian 59 Wang, H. 59 Wang, T. 56
   Wen, X. 70 Yang, C. 56 Yang, T. 55 Yaoshan Commune 72 Yúnnán
   ri-bāo 56b Zhōng-guó Qīng-nián-bào 56a
Szechuan Border Quarterly: Chuān biān ji-kān
Szēchwān ri-bao (Chengtu), 56
Tái-wān wén-huà (Taiwan Culture) (Taipei), Ruey 50

-350-

Textile Museum Journal (Washington, D.C.), Adams 74
Tien-jīng dà gōng bào (Tientsin News), Wen, Y. 36ab
Tōnan Ajia Kenkyū (Southeast Asian Studies) (Kyoto), Katsura 66ab, 68abc, 70 Nishida 66ab, 66-67, 67a, 68ab, 69
T'oung Pao, Bonin 03 Chavannes 06, 12 Chen, T. 05 Cordier 07 Davies 09 Eberhard 42, 43 Guibaut 37 Laufer 16 Legendre 09a Liètard 11-12 Madrolle 08 Shafer 52 Shirokogoroff 30
Tour du Monde, Le, Roux, E. 97
Tribal Research Centre, Bulletin (Chiang Mai), 67-73

United Asia, Charusathira 65
Université l'Aurore, Bulletin (Shanghai), Liètard 47
United States National Museum, Report, Rockhill 95
Upstream: Shàng-yóu

Wén-huà jiàn-shè (Cultural Reconstruction), Lǐ, C. 37 Wáng, J. 37
West China Border Research Society, Journal, Cook 36 Edgar 34 Lin, Y. 44ac Torrance 32 Wēn, Y. 45
Wiener Völkerkundliche Mitteilungen, Kauffmann 66
Wiener Zeitschrift für die Kunde des Morgenlandes, Hestermann 15
Wiin-tham (Bangkok), 72, 73
Wolfenden Society on Tibeto-Burman Linguistics, Occasional Papers, Matisoff 69a, 71
Word, Shafer 55

Xīn-huá shè: New China News Agency
Xī-nán biān-jiāng wèn-tí yán-jiū bào-gào (Hua-chung College), You, G. 42
Xīn ning-yùan (Hsin ning-yüan) (Xi-chang), Liao 40

Xīn-yǎ Xī-yǎ (New Asia) Yang, C. 31bc, 32
Yǔ-gòng, Tong 36 Yang, C. 34c
Yún-nán bàn-yùe-kān (Yunnan Bimonthly), Fàn 31
Yúnnán rì-bào (Kunming), Yang, C. 56 Yúnnán rì-bào 56ab
Zeitschrift für Ethnologie, Kauffmann 34
Zhí biān yùe-kān (Zhi Bian Monthly), Yì, M. n.d.
Zhōng-gúo Qīng-nían-bào (Chinese Youth) (Peking), Wen, B. 24
    Zhōng-gúo Qīng-nían-bào 56ab
Zhōng-gúo wén-hùa yán-jiù huì-kān (sǔo) (Institute of Chinese
    Cultural Studies, Bulletin) Mǎ, X. 40 Wēn, Y. 47, 48
Zhōng-gúo xī bù kē xúe yùan (West China Union University, Bulletin)
    (Chengtu), Cháng, Shī & Yǔ 35
Zhōng-gúo yǔ-wén (Chūng-kúo yǔ-wén) (Chinese Linguistics),
    Hu & Dai 64
Zhōng-shān dà-xúe wén kē yán jiù sǔo (Sun Yat-sen University,
    Arts Research Institute), Yang, C. 36ac
Zhōng-shān dà-xúe wén-shǐ xúe-yán jiù sǔo jí (Sun Yat-sen
    University, Cultural and Historical Research Institute),
    Yang, C. 31a
Zhōng-shān dà-xúe yǔ yán lì shǐ yán jiù sǔo zhōu-kān (Sun Yat-sen
    University Language and History Research Institute, Weekly),
    Xià 28 Zhāng 29 Zhào 28

INDEX BY SUBJECT MATTER

This index follows the subject categories presented in Outline of Cultural Materials, 4th rev. ed., by George P. Murdock et al. (New Haven, Human Relations Area Files, 1971). Reference should be made to this work for details on the definition of the categories, and for cross-references between categories. Each reference is listed under the subjects that it covers best; the index is therefore not exhaustive, but is a point of departure for the study of any given subject. If a researcher is interested in a specific subject among only one or two ethnic groups, he should use both the index by ethnic group and this index simultaneously. The following detailed ethnographies have not been fully indexed, because they cover a great many subject categories:

Bernatzik 1947 (Akha)
Dessaint 1972a (Lisu)
Hsu, I. 1944 (Yi)
Lewis 1969-70 (Akha)
LeBar et al. 1964 (all groups)
Liétard 1913 (Yi)

Lin 1947 (Yi)
Tao 1948 (Lisu)
Walker 1970b, 1972c (Lahu)
Winnington 1959 (Yi)
Young, O. 1961 (Akha, Lahu, Lisu)
Young, H. n.d. (Lahu)

10. ORIENTATION
101. IDENTIFICATION

Beauclair 56a Blakiston 62 Bonifacy 06, 19
Bridgman 59 Broomhall, M. 17 Brown 13 Bruk 58, 59ab
Chang, C. 56 Cheng & Liang 45 Clarke 11 Cook 36 Cordier 07
DeFrancis 51 Devéria 86 Deydier 54 Diguet 08 Eberhard 42
Feng & Shryock 38 Gaide 03 Gūang-mīng rì-bào 57 Johnston 08
Lesserteur 78 Lunet 06 Morse 74 Mueller 13 Nature 88
Pelliot 04 Reclus 02 Scott 21 Siguret 37 Spielmann 69
Toa Kenkyujo 40 Vissière 14 Wehrli 04 Woods 69 Yang, C. 35
Yule 03

102. MAPS

Anderson 71, 76 Baber 82 Bacot 09 Barnard 30 Bernatzik 47, 54 Bernot 72 Bertreux 22 Blakiston 62 Bonin 99 Bons 04b Broomhall, A. 47, 53 Bruk 58, 59ab Bruk & Apenchenko 64 Cheng & Liang 45 Davies 09 Dessaint 71b, 72ab Devéria 86 Deydier 54 D'Mazure 61 Eickstedt 44 Embree & Thomas 50a Enriquez 23a Fergusson 11 Fletcher 27 Forest 08, 10 Gaide 03 Gjessing 57 Guibaut 38a Guibaut & Liotard 41, 45 Hanks, Hanks, & Sharp 64 Hsǔ, I. 44 Jack 04 JUSMAG 68 Kauffmann 34 Kerr 23 Kickert 67 Lasher 63 Leclère 00 Legendre 05, 10c Liétard 04 Lin, Y. 44a LeBar, Hickey, & Musgrave 64 Lunet 06 Meares 09b Menguy 60 Military RDC 68 Mueller 13 National Geographic 71 Ng 71 Ollone 11, 12b Orléans 96, 98 Pollard 21 Rocher 79-80 Rock 47 Rose 09 Roux, E. 97 Roux, H. 24 Schrock 70 Srisawat 63 Stevenson, H. 44 Tảo 48 Temple 10 Thatnaasuwan 68 Thompson, H. 26 Toa Kenkyujo 40 Tribal Data Project 71-72 Valtat 15 Vannicelli 44 Walker 70b Ward 12, 20, 21, 23a, 24 Wehrli 04 Wiens 62 Wissmann 43

                Young, O. 61, 62
11. BIBLIOGRAPHY
                Bernath 64 Boon-Itt 6-[?] Cordier 07 Cramer 70 Dessaint
                71a Jacobs 70 LeBar, Hickey, & Musgrave 64 Embree &
                Thomas 50ab Liu 40-41 Shafer 57, 63 Takemura 57-58
                Tribal Research 67
13. GEOGRAPHY
    131. LOCATION
                Abadie 24 Anderson 71 Asian Analyst 69 Bernatzik 47
                Bons 04 Bonifacy 06, 19 Bridgman 59 Broomhall, M. 07
                Bruk 58, 59ab Bruk & Apenchenko 64 Chang, J. 52
                Chaturaphand 71 Chauveau 73 Chen, Y. 64 Cheng & Liang 45
                Chieri 43 Cooper 71 Davies 09 DeFrancis 51 Deydier 54
                D'Mazure 61 Dubernard 73 Eickstedt 44 Fei 51 Fergusson
                10 Forrest 08 Gūang-míng rì-bào 57 Hanks, Hanks, &
                Sharp 64 Hanks, Hanks, Sharp, Sharp 64 Jamieson, E. 09
                JUSMAG 67 Kerr 23 Lê 55 Lefèvre-Pontalis 02 Madrolle 25
                Military RDC 68 Mueller 13 Rock 47 Rose & Coggin Brown
                11 Shabad 72 Stevenson, P. 32 Súo 62 Temple 10 Thailand
                Info. 70 Thatnaasuwan 68 Tribal Data Project 71-72
                U.S. Army 61 Ward 13 Wissmann 43 Woodthorpe 97
    133. TOPOGRAPHY AND GEOLOGY
                Legendre & Lemoine 10
14. HUMAN BIOLOGY
                Cunningham 33 Eickstedt 44
    141. ANTHROPOMETRY
                Legendre 10ab Rose & Coggin Brown 11
    142. DESCRIPTIVE SOMATOLOGY
                Lín, Y. 44b Lunet 06 Nature 88 Stevenson, P. 27, 32

Guibaut 40 Zaborowski-Moindron 01, 04, 05
143. GENETICS
Hsiao 46
144. RACIAL AFFINITIES
Hutton 62 Zaborowski-Moindron 00, 02
15. BEHAVIOR PROCESSES AND PERSONALITY
Grillières 05 Legendre 09a, 13 Stevenson, P. 27, 32
157. PERSONALITY TRAITS
Barnard 30 Fides 42
16. DEMOGRAPHY
Ng 71
161. POPULATION
Beauclair 56b Bruk 58, 59ab Bruk & Apenchenko 64
Central Census 60 Chen, Y. 64 Dessaint 72b Halpern 61
Ji 58 Ko 49 NCNA, Kweiyang 59 Shabad 72 Tribal
Data Project 71-72 Yang, C. 63a Zhōng-gúo Qīng-nían 56b
166. INTERNAL MIGRATION
Dessaint 71 b Kickert 66
17. HISTORY AND CULTURE CHANGE
Asian Analyst 69 Chen, Y. 64 China Reconstructs 53
Clarke 11 Colquhoun 83 Cook 36 Davies 09 Dubernard 73
Eberhard 42 Enriquez 21 Fei 51-52, 52 Feng & Shryock 38
Franck 25 Gau 60 Goullart 55 Gūang-míng rì-bào 57, 59
Hicks 10 Hsu, I. 32 Huang, C. 58a, 65 Investigation
Gp. 71 Ji 58 Jiang 48 Ji-niu-bu 71 Johnston 08 Jones,
P. 66 JUSMAG 67 Lefèvre-Pontalis 02 Legendre 05 Li, H.
58 Li, Fei, & Chang 43 Mǎ, C. 42-44 Manndorff 65
Menguy 60 Mínzú Húabào 58, 65 NCNA, Kunming 58 Ollone
11 Pu 58 Rén-mín rì-bào 59a, 72ab Rocher 79-80

-356-

Seidenfaden 30 Suo 62 Telford 37 Tian 59 Tie 59
Vial 98 Wachamuchi & Wang 59 Ward 13 Wiens 54, 62
Yang, C. 63ab

171. DISTRIBUTIONAL EVIDENCE

Ward 12, 21, 23b, 24

173. TRADITIONAL HISTORY

Chavannes 06, 09ab, 12 Ch'en 48a Clarke 11
Colquhoun 85 Ding 36 Dŏng 40 Fang 45ab Lo, C. 44ab,
45ac Mǎ, C. 42-44, 46 Shiratori 57

174. HISTORICAL RECONSTRUCTION

Bacot 12, 13 Barnard 25 Beauclair 56b Chang, C. 56
Cochrane 15 Enriquez 23 Graham 54 Hertz 12 Líu, Y. 54
Luce 68 Shiratori 62 Stevenson, P. 32 Yang, C. 36a

175. RECORDED HISTORY

Bonin 11 Broomhall, A. 47 Chêng & Liang 45 Farjenel 10
Jamieson, C. 23 Kingsmill 00-01 Líng 38 Ma, T. 76-83
Playfair 76 Rock 47 Sainson 04 Yang, C. 36b

177. ACCULTURATION AND CULTURE CONTACT

Bangkok Tech. 68 Baumann 70 Bertreux 22 Bhruksasri 70
Birnbaum 70 Bonifacy 08 Bons 04 Bourne 88 Brandt 65
Broomhall, A. 53 Broomhall, M. 17 Carey 99 Chang, C. 56
Chariwan 70 Charusathira 65 Chauveau 73
Chen, C. 72 Chevalier 99 <u>China at War</u> 41 Cochrane 15
Coolidge & Roosevelt 33 Cooper 71 Cultural & Ed. 58
Dassé 74 Dessirier 23 Devéria 86, 91 Dŏng & Xúe 59
Durrenberger 75c Fergusson 11 Fides 42 Gjessing 57
Goullart 59 Graham 54 Guébriant 08 <u>Gūang-mǐng rì-bào</u> 63
Ha 64 Hanks, J. 64 Hanks, Hanks, & Sharp 64, 65 Hill
Tribe Welfare 65, 67 Hinton, H. 55 Hsu, K. 75 Hu, H. 42

Huang, C. 58b, 59ab Jack 04 Kanthathatbamrung 65, 67 Kickert 66 Ko 49 Lamjuan 69 Larnlue 70 Lasher 63 Layton 68 Lefèvre-Pontalis 92 Legendre 10c Lewis, P. (ed.) 70 Lichiang Reg. 73 Liétard 04 Lin, Y. 44ac Lindgren 67 Lunet 04, 06 Ma, Y. 58 Manndorff 63, 66 Mínzú Huàbào 63, 66 Mínzú Tuánjie 61 Morse 62 Moseley, G. 67abc, 73 Murchie 69 NCNA, Chaochueh 56a NCNA, Chengtu 56abcde NCNA, Kunming 56bd, 58e, 59ce, 63a, 64de, 65c, 68, 69ab NCNA, Peking 68 Orléans 96 Palangtirasin 70 Parsons 31 Pollard 21 Pritchard 14 Rajan 70 Reclus 02 Rén-mín rì-bào 59b, 62 Richthofen 03 Rock 47 Rose 09 Ruenyote 67 Sayamnotr 66 Schrock 70 Smythe 64 Snow 37 Stevenson, W. 59 Stübel 52 Sun 42 Szěchwān rì-bào 56 Tatu & Montgomery 69 Tirrell 72 Torrance 32 Trumbull 63 USOM 63 Walker (ed.) 75 Wang, C. 51 Wang, L. 59 Wang, T. 56 Weed 69 Wén, C. 36 White 67 Wilson 71 Yang, T. 55 Young, H. 62 Zeng 47 Zhang, X. 58

178. SOCIO-CULTURAL TRENDS

Chang, H. 58 Chang, T. 64 Collis 38 Dǒng & Xué 59 Hu, C. 60 NCNA, Chengtu 59cd, 65abc NCNA, Kunming 58fg, 64g, 70a, 72bc NCNA, Peking 58b, 59b Tirrell 72 Walker 73ab Wang, W. 59 Ward 18, 23b, 24 Wen, X. 70 Yang, T. 55

18. TOTAL CULTURE

Investigation Gp. 71 Lewis, P. 74 Morse 74

185. CULTURAL GOALS

Ji-niu-bu 71

19. LANGUAGE

Anonymous 70ab Bonifacy 05 Dellinger 69 Diringer 51

Fraser 22 Fu 44ab Hope 72, 73 Kao 55, 58 Katsura 65ab, 66a, 68ac, 70 Lewis, E. 69 Liétard 09ab Linguistic Survey 17 Lo, C. 45bd Ma̒, X. 40, 51, 54 Matisoff 67, 69abc, 73bc Nishida 65-66, 66ab, 66-67, 67ab, 68ab, 69 Peet 61 Roop 70 Telford 38 Telford & Saya Ai Pun 39 Vial 90a, 98 Yang, C. 30b, 34a Yuan 46, 47, 53 Zui 59

192. VOCABULARY

Anderson 71 Antisdel 11a Baber 86 Bernot 71, 72 Biet & Croizier 77 Boell 99 Bonifacy 08 Bonin 03 Bourne 88 Brun 73 Clarke 11 Davies 09 Desgodins 73 Edgar 34 Edkins 71 Garnier 73 Grierson 03-28 Hope Ms. Lefèvre-Pontalis 92 Lewis, P. 68a Liétard 09, 11-12, 12 Lunet 06 Ma̒, X. 51 Macey 07 Madrolle 98, 08 Matisoff, n.d. (b) Monpeyrat 05 Nature 88 Ollone 11, 12a Orléans 98 Roux 24 Scott & Hardiman 00 Studia Serica 40-41 Taw & Eastes 15 Vial 09 Wên, Y. 40

193. GRAMMAR

Hope 68 Matisoff 69b, 72b, 73b Roop 70 Yang, C. 36c

194. PHONOLOGY

Benedict 48, 72 Burling 66 Dellinger 67 Haudricourt 57-58 Hu & Dai 64 Katsura 66b, 68b, 70 Lewis, P. 68b, 73 Matisoff 66, 69a, 70, 71, 72a, 73a, n.d. (a) Meillet & Cohen 52 Ruey 48a Shafer 38a, 52 Shirokogoroff 30 Smalley 64 Voegelin & Voegelin 65 Wên, Y. 48 Yuan 48

197. LINGUISTIC IDENTIFICATION

Benedict 47 Bernot 71, 72 Boell 99 Burling 67 Chao, Y. 43 Colquhoun 84 Devéria 91 Ecole Française 21 Garnier 73 Goré 39 Loufer 16 Luce 68 Matisoff 69a, 71, 72a, 73ac Meillet & Cohen 52 Nishida 66-67, 68b Roop 69

Shafer 38b, 55 Taw & Eastes 15 Taylor, L. 56 Tung, T. 53 Wĕn, Y. 50

20. COMMUNICATION

China Reconstructs 69 Schrock 70 Story & Story 69 Young, H. 62

202. TRANSMISSION OF MESSAGES

Sun 42

204. PRESS

Gjessing 57 Lewis 69 NCNA, Kunming 73

207. RADIO AND TELEVISION

Story & Story 69

21. RECORDS

212. WRITING

Baber 82 Bangkok Post 73b Brun 73 Charria 05 Chavannes 06, 09ab, 12 Clarke, H. 82, 83 Cultural & Ed. 58 Dellinger 69 Devéria 91 Ding 35, 36 Eickstedt 44 Février 48 Fu 57 Hestermann 15 Jensen 35 Jiang, D. 48a Ko 38 Li̦, L. n.d. Liu, C. H. 32, 37 Ma, X. 48ab, 49, 51, 55, 62 Mesny 84 Mueller 13 NCNA, Kunming 58d, 59a Ollone 07e, 12b Parker, E. 95 Pollard 21 Studia Serica 40-41 Terrien 82ab, 86, 94 Vial 90ab, 98 Wĕn, Y. 36ab, 40, 45, 47 Wyss 69 Yang, C. 31abc, 33, 34, 35a, 36

22. FOOD QUEST

224. HUNTING AND TRAPPING

Izikowitz 39 Ruey 48 Young, O. 62, 67

23. ANIMAL HUSBANDRY

Kauffmann 34

24. AGRICULTURE

Anthony & Moorman 64 Buchanan 70 Chang, S. 59 Credner

35a Dawson 12 Dept. Public Welfare 62 Dessaint, W. & A. 75 George 15 Goullart 55 Gourou 51 Gūang-mǐng rì-bào 59, 71 Hinton, P. 68 Hsin 73 Hsu, H. 65 Kauffmann 34 Kerr 23 Legendre 10c, 13 Li, Fei, & Chang 43 Manndorff, Scholz, & Volprecht 64-65 Metford 35 NCNA, Chengtu 58ab, 59a, 63c, 65deg, 66 NCNA, Kunming 55b, 58bcgh, 59d, 64ef NCNA, Peking 58a Oughton 69 Rose & Coggin Brown 11 Schweinfurth 69 Spielmann 68a Srisawat 52 Van Roy 71 Vial 17 Walker 66-69 Wang, H. 59 Ward 13, 23b Yang, T. 55

241. TILLAGE
Huang, C. 58b

249. SPECIAL CROPS
Chang, J. 52 Colquhoun 83 Davies 09 Dessaint 72c Manndorff 62 Richthofen 03 Saihoo 63a United Nations 67

26. FOOD CONSUMPTION
Legendre 09a NCNA, Chengtu 59b NCNA, Kunming 58h

261. GRATIFICATION AND CONTROL OF HUNGER
Cordier 15-16 Teston & Percheron 32

262. DIET
Chaturaphand 70

266. CANNIBALISM
Stevenson, W. 59

27. DRINK, DRUGS AND INDULGENCE

276. NARCOTICS AND STIMULANTS
Guibaut 38a

278. PHARMACEUTICALS
China Journal 31

28. LEATHER, TEXTILES AND FABRICS
    286. WOVEN FABRICS
        Start & Wright 36 Woodthorpe 97
    289. PAPER INDUSTRY
        Mínzú Tuánjie 65

29. CLOTHING
        Abadie 24 Adams 74 Anderson 71 Bradshaw 52 Bunnaag 63 Chazarain-Wetzel 10 Cook 36 Coolidge & Roosevelt 33 Crabouillet 73 Diguet 08 Dussault 24 Fides 42 François 04 Gaide 04 Garnier 73 Goullart 55 Hansen 60 Hsū, I. 32 Jack 04 Kauffmann 66 Lefèvre-Pontalis 02 Legendre 09a, 10d, 13 Manndorff, Scholz, & Volprecht 64-65 Meillier 18 Metford 35 Playfair 76 Rockhill 95 Rose & Coggin Brown 11 Soulié & Tchang 08 Srisawat 52 Starr 11 Stevenson, P. 27 Tilke 45 Ward 13, 23b Wilcox 65 Zaborowski-Moindron 01

30. ADORNMENT
        Rockhill 95 Soulié & Tchang 08
    302. TOILET
        Anderson 76 Blakiston 62
    306. JEWELRY MANUFACTURE
        Arritola 72

31. EXPLOITATIVE ACTIVITIES
        NCNA, Chengtu 58b
    311. LAND USE
        Feingold 69 Keen 73 Schweinfurth 69
    312. WATER SUPPLY
        NCNA, Kunming 60b, 70b
    313. LUMBERING

NCNA, Kunming 71
- 314. FOREST PRODUCTS
  Ward 56
- 316. MINING AND QUARRYING
  Barnard 30 Pritchard 14 Ward 56

32. PROCESSING OF BASIC MATERIALS
- 321. WORK IN BONE, HORN, AND SHELL
  China Journal 31

33. BUILDING AND CONSTRUCTION
  Manndorff, Scholz, & Volprecht 64-65

34. STRUCTURES
- 342. DWELLINGS
  Bunnaag 63 Guibaut 38a Jack 04 Kauffmann 66 Legendre 09a, 10d Lin, Y. 44c Metford 35 Morse 74 Rose & Coggin Brown 11 Snow 62 Srisawat 52 Valtat 15 Ward 23b

36. SETTLEMENTS
  Anderson 76 Chiang, Y. 48 Gaide 03 Walker (ed.) 75
- 361. SETTLEMENT PATTERNS
  Dessaint 72b Gourdin 79 Manndorff 65 Ren-min ri-bao 59c Seidenfaden 58 Siguret 37
- 362. HOUSING
  Bertreux 22 Nguyen 34 Scherman 15
- 366. COMMERCIAL FACILITIES
  Beauclair 56b

39. CAPITAL GOODS INDUSTRIES
  Buchanan 70

41. TOOLS AND APPLIANCES
  Kauffmann 34
- 411. WEAPONS
  Starr 11

42. PROPERTY
    423. REAL PROPERTY
        NCNA, Kunming 56c, 59be, 64bh, 72d NCNA, Peking 59c Wang, W. 59 Yaoshan Commune 72
    425. ACQUISITION AND RELINQUISHMENT OF PROPERTY
        Li, Fei, & Chang 43
    428. INHERITANCE
        Ollone 11

43. EXCHANGE
        Rachanee 72 Yu 67 Wongprasert 75
    439. FOREIGN TRADE
        Anderson 76 Guibaut & Liotard 45 Young 07

44. MARKETING
        Chou, T. 63 Durrenberger 74 NCNA, Chengtu 63b NCNA, Kweiyang 73

46. LABOR
        Dessaint 72c Dessaint, W. & A. 75 Walker 66-69, 70b
    462. DIVISION OF LABOR BY SEX
        Bunnaag 63 Kauffmann 34 Srisawat 52

47. BUSINESS AND INDUSTRIAL ORGANIZATION
    474. COOPERATIVE ORGANIZATION
        NCNA, Chengtu 59a, 65eg NCNA, Kunming 58aeg Snow 62

48. TRAVEL AND TRANSPORTATION
    487. ROUTES
        Ainscough 15 Bishop 99 Carey 99

49. LAND TRANSPORT
    491. HIGHWAYS
        <u>China Reconstructs</u> 75 Jiang 58 NCNA, Kunming 55a, 64a

51. LIVING STANDARDS AND ROUTINES

Walker (ed.) 75
- 511. STANDARD OF LIVING
   Li, Fei, & Chang 43
52. RECREATION
- 522. HUMOR
   Matisoff 69c
- 526. ATHLETIC SPORTS
   Vial 88
53. FINE ARTS
   NCNA, Chengtu 64a NCNA, Kunming 56a Vial 93-94
- 532. REPRESENTATIVE ART
   Mínzú Huàbào 65
- 533. MUSIC
   Chang, K. 44 Lewis, P. 73 Liétard 47 Reinhard 55, 56 Yüan 46, 53
- 534. MUSICAL INSTRUMENTS
   Brown 10 Cochrane 15 Starr 11 Valtat 15 Yang, C. 63b
- 538. LITERATURE
   Antisdel 11bc Ba Te 12 NCNA, Kunming 60a, 61 Tsung 54
- 539. LITERARY TEXTS
   Boell 99 Bonin 11 Chang, K. 44 Chao 50 China Reconstructs 60 Durrenberger 75d Fu 45 Graham, D. 31 Gūang 54 Hanks, Hanks & Sharp 65 Henry 03 Húang, Yáng, & Líu 54 Jiang 58 Liétard 47 Líng, G. 50 Mǎ, X. 48ab Ma, Y. 58 NCNA, Kunming 58h Rén-mín rì-bào 63 Rose & Coggin Brown 11 Táo 45 Vial 93-94 Walker 74abc, 75abc Yang, G. 55ab Yúan 46, 53 Zhōng-gúo zuo-jia 62
55. INDIVIDUATION AND MOBILITY
- 551. PERSONAL NAMES
   Bunnaag 63 Líng 53 Lo, C. 44ab, 44-45, 45b Mǎ, C. 42-44

Ruey 50 Srisawat 52 Telford 38 Vial 93-94
56. SOCIAL STRATIFICATION
    Chen, Y. 64 Chieri 43 Clarke 11 Fei & Lin 56 Fei 51-52
    Fides 42 Goullart 55 Guébriant 08 Ko 49 Leach 54 Lin, Y. 44b
    Ollone 11 Siguret 37 Zēng 47
    561. AGE STRATIFICATION
        Zhōng-guó Qīng-nián-bào 56a
    562. SEX STATUS
        Colquhoun 85 Fergusson 11 Jiang 58 Srisawat 52
    567. SLAVERY
        Chang, S. 59 Graham 54 Guébriant 99 Hsu, K. 75
        Lasher 50 MacFarquhar 59 Mínzú Huàbào 65
        NCNA, Chaochueh 56b NCNA, Chengtu 55c NCNA, Peking 56b, 58b
        Newsweek 46 Orléans 96 Pu 58 Rockhill 91
57. INTERPERSONAL RELATIONS
    574. VISITING AND HOSPITALITY
        Bernatzik 40
    575. SODALITIES
        Zhōng-guó Qīng-nían-bào 56a
    577. ETHICS
        NCNA, Peking 72
    578. INGROUP ANTAGONISMS
        Forrest 10 Jack 04
    579. BRAWLS, RIOTS AND BANDITRY
        Bishop 99 Broomhall, A. 53 Chauveau 73 Colquhoun 83
        Fenouil 62 Legendre 10c Gregory & Gregory 24
        Guibaut 38a, 67 Hertz 12 Orléans 96 Rock 47
58. MARRIAGE
    Ba Te 26 Beauvais 07 Chaturaphand 71 Chen, T. 05, 34

        Clarke 11 Chieri 58 Cordier 07 Eink 68 Geis 12 Hicks 10
        Jamieson, E. 09 Ko 49 Leach 54 Lévi-Strauss 49 Lin, Y. 44c
        Metford 35 Ruey 48b Srisawat 52 Telford 38 Temple 10
        Walker 74c Wang, M. 46 Wen & Yang 42
   583. MODE OF MARRIAGE
        Dauffès 06
60. KINSHIP
        Benedict 41 Lévi-Strauss 49 Lin, Y. 46 Scholz 67 Shiratori 57
   601. KINSHIP TERMINOLOGY
        Bernatzik 47 Fu 51 Webb 12
61. KIN GROUPS
        Chen 47 Crabouillet 73 Scholz 67 Telford 37 Tie 59
   613. LINEAGES
        Hanks, J. 64b
   618. CLANS
        Bridgman 59 Enriquez 23, 24 Srisawat 52
62. COMMUNITY
        Fei 51-52 Jones, D. 66, 67, 68 Kickert 69 Scholz 67 Walker 69 Walker (ed.) 75
   621. COMMUNITY STRUCTURE
        Buchanan 70 Roux 24
   622. HEADMEN
        Abadie 24 Goullart 55 Seidenfaden 58 Siguret 37
   625. POLICE
        Baumann 70
   627. INFORMAL INGROUP JUSTICE
        Jamieson, E. 09
   628. INTER-COMMUNITY RELATIONS

Ainscough 15 Anderson 71
63. TERRITORIAL ORGANIZATION
Colquhoun 83 Diao 67 Fei 52 Hinton, H. 55 Hsu, H. 65
Huang, C. 59a Jiang, D. 48ab Jones, D. 67 Liu, C. 54
Menguy 60 NCNA, Kunming 63ab, 64bf, 65c Ollone 07b
Shabad 72 Shi-shí shǒu-cè 56ab Suo 62 Yang, C. 56 Yang,
Z. 63a Yaoshan Commune 72 Yúnnán rì-bào 56
64. STATE
China Reconstructs 53
65. GOVERNMENT ACTIVITIES
Dreyer 70 Moseley, G. 73 NCNA, Kunming 64c Tatu & Montgomery
69 USOM 63 Weed 65 Wiens 54
 651. TAXATION AND PUBLIC INCOME
 Biet & Croizier 77
 652. PUBLIC FINANCE
 NCNA, Kunming 59c
 657. PUBLIC WELFARE
 Rajan 70 Ruenyote 67 Sayamnotr 66
66. POLITICAL BEHAVIOR
Dreyer 70 NCNA, Chengtu 56d NCNA, Peking 56ab, 59a Rén-mín
rì-bào 72ab, 73
 665. POLITICAL PARTIES
 Gūang-míng rì-bào 71, 73a Lichiang Reg. 73 NCNA, Chengtu 64b
 Peking Review 75 Wang, T. 56 Yúnnán rì-bào 56
 668. POLITICAL MOVEMENTS
 Peking Review 75 Ruey 48b
 669. REVOLUTION
 Dubernard 73 Feng & Shryock 38 Fergusson 11 Kasemsri 73
 Rocher 79 Ruey 48b Thamsukati 73 Thavisin 73

68. OFFENSES AND SANCTIONS
> 686. NONFULFILLMENT OF OBLIGATIONS
> Soulié & Tchang 08

70. ARMED FORCES
> China Reconstructs 73 NCNA, Chengtu 73 Qŭ 34 Roy 53 Thomson 68
>> 701. MILITARY ORGANIZATION
>> Audretch & Chaffee 69 Franjola 72

71. MILITARY TECHNOLOGY
> JUSMAG 67
>> 712. MILITARY INSTALLATIONS
>> Beauclair 56a Upcraft 92
>> 714. UNIFORM AND ACCOUTERMENT
>> Chêng & Liang 45

72. WAR
> China at War 41 Dubernard 75 Forrest 08, 10 Legendre 10d Schrock 70
>> 725. TACTICS
>> Guébriant 99 Lowy 47 Missions Catholiques 81-82 Tao 48
>> 726. WARFARE
>> Stevenson, P. 27

73. SOCIAL PROBLEMS
> Rock 47
>> 733. ALCOHOLISM AND DRUG ADDICTION
>> Dessirier 23 Saihoo 63a

74. HEALTH AND WELFARE
> Brandt 65 Chang, J. 52 Chang, S. 59 Cunningham 33 Huard 39

75. SICKNESS
> China Journal 31 Durrenberger 69-70, 71, 73, 75abc Flatz,

Pik, & Sringham 65 Flatz & Sringham 64 Gaide 03 Legendre 13ab Roux 24 Telford 37 Yang, C. 35

754. SORCERY

Mǎ, X. 48ab

755. MAGICAL AND MENTAL THERAPY

Durrenberger 75d Feingold 73 Jamieson, C. 23 Pollard 21

756. PSYCHOTHERAPISTS

Durrenberger 75a Feingold 73

758. MEDICAL CARE

Chou, T. 58 NCNA, Kunming 69a, 72e

759. MEDICAL PERSONNEL

China Pictorial 63 Durrenberger 75a NCNA, Chengtu 65f NCNA, Kunming 72e

76. DEATH

Beauvais 07 Bonifacy 08 Clarke 11 Cook 36 Crabouillet 73 Eink 68 Franck 25 Henry 03 Johnston 08 Metford 35 Ollone 11 Srisawat 52 Vannicelli 44 Walker (ed.) 75 Wang, M. 46

764. FUNERAL

Bertreux 22 Chieri 43 Dauffès 06 Fergusson 11 Ward 23b

769. CULT OF THE DEAD

Abadie 24

77. RELIGIOUS BELIEFS

Bonifacy 08 Chaturaphand 71 Chen, T. 48 Crabouillet 73 Durrenberger 71, 75b Graham, D. 26-29 Henry 03 Hicks 10 Hope 69 Hsú, I. 32 Hudspith 69 Jamieson, E. 09 Johnston 08 Legendre 05, 10cd Parsons, H. 31 Pollard 21 Roux 24 Rose & Coggin Brown 11 Scholz 67 Soulié & Tchang 08 Srisawat 52 Telford 37 Vannicelli 44 Vial 98

772. COSMOLOGY

-370-

Durrenberger 70 Eink 68

773. MYTHOLOGY

Antisdell 11bc Bonifacy 06 Fleurelle 10 Graham, D. 55
Savina 30 Vial 90a, 09

776. SPIRITS AND GODS

Bonifacy 06 Broomhall, M. 17 Gould 85 Graham, D. 30
Raquez 02 Spielmann 68b

78. RELIGIOUS PRACTICES

Boutmy 89 Clarke 11 Durrenberger 71 Lewis, E. 74 Ma, H. 31,
48b Manndorff, Scholz, & Volprecht 64-65 Roux, E. 97
Spielmann 68a Vannicelli 44 Walker (ed.) 75

784. AVOIDANCE AND TABOO

Roux, H. 52

787. REVELATION AND DIVINATION

Broomhall, A. 53 Mǎ, X. 48b Oxibar 59

788. RITUAL

Rockhill 91 Walker 72b, 75b

789. MAGIC

Mǎ, X. 48ab

79. ECCLESIASTICAL ORGANIZATION

Dubernard 73 Manndorff 70 Vannicelli 44 Walker 74d

792. HOLY MEN

Durrenberger 75a Kasemsri 73 Thamsukati 73 Young, O. 62

793. PRIESTHOOD

Lewis, P. 68c

796. ORGANIZED CEREMONIAL

Chao 50 Dauffès 06 Kacha-ananda 71 Lewis, E. 74
Liao 40 Manndorff 71 People's Republic 54 Súo 62
Urbani 74 Walker 70a, 72a Yu 42

-371-

797. MISSIONS

Anonymous 55, 59 Boh 67 Boiteux 35 Boucher 35 Boutmy 89 Broomhall, A. 47, 53 Broomhall, M. 17 Carriquiry 39 Crider 63 Desgodins 72 Fenouil 62 Fraser 38 Goré 39 Gregory & Gregory 24 Hill Tribe Welfare 67, 68 Hudspith 69 Kuhn 47, 56, 59, 60 Leparoux 05 Le Roux 35 Lewis, Yohan, & Ca Ui 66 Liétard 04 Lyall 65 Maire 82 Maung Shwe Wa 63 McGilvary 12 Mieyaa 72, 73 Missions Catholiques 81-82, 38 Pollard 11 Rockhill 91 Rorak 69 Saint-Guily 64 Saw Aung Din & Sowards 63 Seidenfaden 30 Shí-shi shǒu-cè 56b Simonnet 49 Taylor, M. 44 Telford 49, 53 Thompson, P. 56 Ts'ai 41 Urbani 68, 70, 71 Valtat 15 Vial 93-94 Young, V. n.d.

80. NUMBERS AND MEASURES

Fraser 22 Vial 09

805. ORDERING OF TIME

Graham, D. 30

82. IDEAS ABOUT NATURE AND MAN

838. ETHNOPSYCHOLOGY

Henry 03

829. ETHNOSOCIOLOGY

François 04

84. REPRODUCTION

844. CHILDBIRTH

Eink 68

85. INFANCY AND CHILDHOOD

Beauvais 07 Gūang-míng rì-bào 73c Liétard 04

87. EDUCATION

Chang, J. 52 Chang, S. 59 China News 43 Chou, T. 63 Du 59 Investigation Gp. 71 Gūang-míng rì-bào 59, 72ab NCNA,

Chengtu 63a, 71 NCNA, Kunming 55c, 58d, 68, 69b, 72a NCNA, Peking 68 Rén-mín rì-bào 63 Wang, L. 59
871. EDUCATIONAL SYSTEM
Mínzú Túanjíe 59
875. TEACHERS
Gūang-míng rì-bào 73b NCNA, Chengtu 56a
88. ADOLESCENCE, ADULTHOOD AND OLD AGE
883. ADOLESCENT ACTIVITIES
Leclère 00